Timbre

Timbre

Paradox, Materialism, Vibrational Aesthetics

Isabella van Elferen

BLOOMSBURY ACADEMIC
NEW YORK • LONDON • OXFORD • NEW DELHI • SYDNEY

BLOOMSBURY ACADEMIC
Bloomsbury Publishing Inc
1385 Broadway, New York, NY 10018, USA
50 Bedford Square, London, WC1B 3DP, UK
29 Earlsfort Terrace, Dublin 2, Ireland

BLOOMSBURY, BLOOMSBURY ACADEMIC and the Diana logo are trademarks of Bloomsbury Publishing Plc

First published in the United States of America 2021
This paperback edition published in 2022

Copyright © Isabella van Elferen, 2021

Cover design: Louise Dugdale
Cover image © Pobytov / Getty Images

For legal purposes the Acknowledgements on p. ix constitute an extension of this copyright page.

All rights reserved. No part of this publication may be reproduced or transmitted in any form or by any means, electronic or mechanical, including photocopying, recording, or any information storage or retrieval system, without prior permission in writing from the publishers.

Bloomsbury Publishing Inc does not have any control over, or responsibility for, any third-party websites referred to or in this book. All internet addresses given in this book were correct at the time of going to press. The author and publisher regret any inconvenience caused if addresses have changed or sites have ceased to exist, but can accept no responsibility for any such changes.

A catalog record for this book is available from the Library of Congress.

Library of Congress Cataloging-in-Publication Data
Names: Elferen, Isabella van, author.
Title: Timbre : paradox, materialism, vibrational aesthetics / Isabella Van Elferen.
Description: New York : Bloomsbury Academic, 2020. | Includes bibliographical references and index. | Summary: "The first book on timbre (or, tone color), and one that covers both classical and popular music"– Provided by publisher.
Identifiers: LCCN 2020029925 (print) | LCCN 2020029926 (ebook) | ISBN 9781501365812 (hardback) | ISBN 9781501370649 (paperback) | ISBN 9781501365829 (epub) | ISBN 9781501365836 (pdf)
Subjects: LCSH: Tone color (Music) | Psychoacoustics. | Musical perception. | Music–Semiotics. | Music–Philosophy and aesthetics. | Popular music–Philosophy and aesthetics.
Classification: LCC ML3807 .E437 2020 (print) | LCC ML3807 (ebook) | DDC 781.2/34–dc23
LC record available at https://lccn.loc.gov/2020029925
LC ebook record available at https://lccn.loc.gov/2020029926

ISBN:		
	HB:	978-1-5013-6581-2
	PB:	978-1-5013-7064-9
	ePDF:	978-1-5013-6583-6
	eBook:	978-1-5013-6582-9

Typeset by Integra Software Services Pvt. Ltd.

Series: Alternate Takes: Critical Responses to Popular Music

To find out more about our authors and books visit www.bloomsbury.com and sign up for our newsletters.

*To Peter Gambie and the Renaissance Choir,
for singing like a thunderstorm over the Yorkshire Moors.*

Contents

List of illustrations	viii
Acknowledgements	ix
Introduction	1
1 Ecologies of sonorous difference	17
2 Index, icon, grain	51
3 Excess, sublime, lure	91
4 Vibration and vitality	133
5 Aesthetics of vibration	175
Threshold	209
References	218
Index	230

Illustrations

3.1	Arnold Schoenberg, chord group from *Erwartung* (1909)	109
3.2	Anton Webern, excerpt from *Ricercar a 6* (1935)	111
4.1	Vincenzo Bellini, *Norma* (1831), excerpt from 'Casta Diva'	169
4.2	Roberta Flack, excerpt from 'The First Time Ever I Saw Your Face' (1972)	170
4.3	Barbra Streisand, excerpt from 'Woman in Love' (Barry and Robin Gibb 1980)	171

Acknowledgements

Parts of this book have been published elsewhere and I am grateful to be able to include them here. Sections of Chapter 3 have appeared in Isabella van Elferen, 'Drastic Allure: Timbre between the Sublime and the Grain' in *Contemporary Music Review* Volume 36 Part 6, 2017 (copyright Routledge, Taylor & Francis Group). Sections of Chapter 4 have appeared in Isabella van Elferen, 'Timbrality: The Vibrant Aesthetics of Tone Color' in Emily Dolan and Alexander Rehding (eds), *The Oxford Handbook of Timbre*, 2018 (copyright Oxford University Press). All translations from French, German and Dutch in this work are mine.

Large sections of this book were written during a research leave granted by Kingston University London and a Visiting Research Professorship at Aalborg University, and I am grateful to both universities for their generosity. I am grateful, also, to Leah Babb-Rosenfeld and Amy Martin at Bloomsbury; to the peer reviewers who provided thoughtful feedback on my manuscript; to Greg Bechtel, Peter Buse, Steen Christiansen and Helen Palmer for reading drafts; to George Reid for processing the musical scores in this work; to Melanie Tipples, more than I can say; and to F and T, always.

Introduction

It's about timbre

When I tell people what I've recently been working on I typically get one of two answers. Those without a musical background ask, 'What's that?' and music scholars or practitioners simply laugh and exclaim, 'Well, good luck!' Both responses are spot on, of course. How do you explain what timbre is, and what it does for musical experience?

As a music listener I have always suspected that timbre is much more decisive for musical aesthetics than we are consciously aware. Switch on the radio, press play on an audio device, enter the concert hall, and listen: before rhythm, harmony or melody, before lyrics or libretto, what you hear first is timbre. The very first encounter with any kind of music takes the shape of hearing familiar or unfamiliar sonorities that instantly evoke an almost primitive affective response. Sometimes these get translated into half-conscious reflections – I like this sound, this is horrible, oh this sends shivers down my spine – but mostly the timbral encounter happens on an unconscious level, morphing into the overall music-aesthetic experience (cf. Fales 2002: 59–61). But if we try to listen for timbre, we notice that a remarkably large part of our initial musical appreciation involves precisely the immediacy of our timbral encounter. The immediacy of this encounter translates to a directness of response: at the first tones of her 'Casta Diva', Maria Callas's divine sonorities make me cry, and I am filled with skyrocketing elation as soon as Diana Damrau's amber timbres utter the first syllables of the Queen of the Night aria. There is nothing I can do about it; these responses are not even tied to my conscious assessment of the qualities of their voices, and they are certainly not objective or universal. But those are my immediate responses, and this is how my musical experience is shaped, or rather coloured. A wealth of empirical research proves that I am not the only one with such immediate and intense responses. Timbre is a determining factor for our musical experience, and it shapes our musical taste. It is timbre that makes us love certain music, and timbre that makes us dislike other types of music.

As a musician, moreover (I am a choral singer, so I speak of choral singing here), I have often experienced that my aim in performance is first and foremost timbral. Of course I try to be precise in my pitch, and I try to be musically expressive, but more often than not I find that producing a tone of voice that suits the music I perform is at the heart of my musicking. In the same way that one listens to timbre, this reaching for a timbrally delineated goal in performance is not always, or perhaps not at all, a conscious process. Trying too hard to sing 'beautifully' will inevitably result in an overly self-conscious performance, which is a certain road to musical misery. But sometimes, when I'm in the flow of music, and performing in a church whose acoustics enhance timbral resonance, I forget my worries and I just get carried away by *singing*: and in these moments I can hear that my voice blends perfectly with the other voices in the choir, that our sonorities reverberate through the space, and I can enjoy my own singing as much as I do Callas's or Damrau's even if I know I am but a lowly amateur. When a whole choir – or, for that matter, an orchestra or a band – is led by music's agency in this way, timbral magic happens, the singers sing their hearts out, and audiences are swept off their feet. In these cases, timbre is not necessarily 'beautiful'. (What is a beautiful timbre anyway, and why would beauty be relevant for timbre?) It is simply *there*, and it is simply *right*, and it is the quality whose immediacy touches musicians and listeners alike.

The question of timbre has always nagged me as a music researcher. Timbre is an important part of the music I have studied, but I have never been quite satisfied with the ways in which I, and others, have described it. Sometimes we simply list orchestrational facts as an indication of the timbral make-up of a composition. Alternatively, we study the conventions around timbral connotations and 'meanings': Johann Sebastian Bach scores the aria 'Aus Liebe will mein Heiland sterben' in the *Matthew Passion* for soprano, traverso flute and two oboes d'amore to represent the faithful soul, eschatological bliss and love respectively; horror film scores often use organs and harpsichords, which is a long-standing timbral convention aimed to evoke the Gothic uncanny. It is possible to verify such timbral signifying conventions through the study of historical music treatises, musical discourses and musical cultures, and so these assessments definitely have their validity. But that approach leaves out the performativity of timbre which is at the heart of those conventions: how is timbre able to evoke such strong connotations, and moreover how is it able, simultaneously, to be vague enough to evade those connotations? A flute timbre does not *equal* eschatology, but timbre's evasiveness somehow makes it exactly the appropriate musical expression of something as unquantifiable as eschatological bliss. Approaching the problem from another angle, we sometimes refer to Roland Barthes's 'grain of the voice' to indicate the materiality inherent in timbre that exceeds any form of language or signification. This is a legitimate, straightforward approach: the oboe d'amore is a woodwind instrument with a double reed and keys, and we can definitely identify these elements in its sound along with the player's corporeality. But that approach is not entirely satisfying either, as it leaves out timbre's ephemerality and its strangely sublime agency. So to negotiate the problems of timbral signifying conventions, materiality and sublimity, we quote philosophers like Jean-Luc Nancy, who asserts that timbre is 'the communication of the incommunicable' to indicate the ineffability of which timbre is capable (Nancy 2007: 41). Such philosophical considerations can embed the surplus of musical expression in Bach's 'Aus Liebe' aria – those aspects of timbre that affect us because they are in excess of orchestrational signification and corporeal identity – in wider aesthetic considerations. Combining all those approaches, I have gone so far as to write somewhere that Goth music is 'obsessed' with timbre (Van Elferen 2012: 168): and even though I still think that that is the case, I am not at all sure how to describe that obsession in any detail.

It's about timbre. In fact, it's *all* about timbre. 'Actually, I never stop talking about timbre', says Nancy, 'and as a philosopher I seek to give timbre to my discourse' (2007: 39). But what does that tell us?

What's that?

Timbre puzzles music researchers to the point of frustration. Despite continued efforts, researchers from the areas of organology, acoustics, psychoacoustics, neuroscience, (ethno)musicology and music philosophy have not been able to find a satisfying definition for it. Neither have composers, performers, instrument builders, acoustic engineers, studio engineers and producers, even though these musicians spend most of their time creating and working with timbre. As a result, timbre has become simultaneously one of the most interdisciplinary and one of the least understood areas of music and sound research.

One of the reasons for this musicianly and academic confusion (and frustration) is precisely that timbre *can* be studied and defined from all those different perspectives. Timbre was held by Carl Seashore to be 'the most important basic attribute of all music' and more recently by Daniel Levitin to be 'the most important and ecologically relevant feature of auditory experience' (Seashore 1936: 24; Levitin 2006: 45). They are each right. Timbre is the most basic attribute not just of music, but of sound: there is no sound without timbre, and a sound does not even need to be heard for it to have a timbre. The sound of a tree falling in a wood still has a timbre even if there are no ears around to hear it. And yet, we can access this not-necessarily-cochlear aspect of sound, create any shade of tone colour we like with meticulous precision: we can influence the materials we use, the acoustic design in which we perform and record, the articulation, sustain and decay of our tone, and even the sound waves and spectrum frequencies we produce. So, timbre is both inherent to sound *qua* sound and manipulable in its sonic genesis.

When timbre *is* heard, when we move from timbral ontology to timbral phenomenology and timbral aesthetics, timbre is crucial for many aspects of the listening experience. It contains information about a sound's source and its production, and it conveys information about the size, shape and materials of a sound's acoustic surroundings. It may also give us ideas about the sound's possible meanings or emotional content (in the examples above: eschatological bliss, or the uncanny) and it helps us identify the space and time of the genre and era from which it originated (German baroque sacred music, horror cinema of the twentieth century, the Goth subculture). But timbral perception also involves other things, things that are not so easily described without reverting to such intangible concepts as the sublime and ineffability. Timbre, once perceived, has the rare capacity to detach itself from the material quantities that identify its ontology and that determine its phenomenology, and to evoke the impression of being absolutely exterior to the known world. This aspect of timbre is responsible for my rapture when listening to sopranos whose voices I love, and for audiences describing an amateur choral timbre as 'angelic'.

Timbral ontology, timbral phenomenology and timbral aesthetics are entangled in many intricate ways, and it is this entanglement that engenders the widespread epistemological confusion around timbre. How can we know timbre? Can we know it at all? Does disentangling the timbral knot lead to anything but partial insights that will inevitably obscure our understanding of the whole domain?

'Perhaps it is better to drop the term', Albert Bregman suggests in a notorious passage from his *Auditory Scene Analysis*: '[t]he problem with timbre is that it is the name for an ill-defined wastebasket category' (1990: 92, 94; cf. Siedenburg and McAdams 2017; cf. Hajda et al. 1997: 255–6). Bregman is not alone in his timbral defeatism. Roger Scruton wants to set timbre aside as a 'secondary' characteristic of music aesthetics for the sole reason that 'we find ourselves baffled' when trying to describe it (1997: 77–8); Michel Chion has argued repeatedly that the causal notion of timbre as we know it is not tenable and should therefore be discontinued as a part of musical discourse (2011; Chion 2016: 174). In a slightly more constructive mode of criticism, Dennis Smalley has often questioned, defined and redefined timbre, both in his compositions and in his writing. In 1994, he braved the question to which composers, theorists and philosophers cannot find an answer:

> What is timbre? When is it meaningful to use the term? How useful is a concept of timbre in the context of electroacoustic music? Defining timbre is a hazardous operation. 'Talking about timbre', says Philippe Manoury 'is as delicate as talking about taste' (1991). Moreover, timbre cannot easily be pinned down. Claude Cadoz (1991) goes so far as to state that any discussion of timbre provokes debate on the very nature of music, while Jean-Baptiste Barrière (1991) finds in timbre 'the inevitable breaking-point of every musical discussion and every compositional confrontation. It represents opposed notions of music, opposed aesthetic positions.' Indeed, the book which includes these writers is called *Timbre, métaphore pour la composition*. You cannot get more all-embracing than that ...
> [Timbre] is one of those subjects where the more you read and the more you have hands-on compositional experience the more you know, but in the process you become less able to grasp its essence.
> (Smalley 1994: 35)

The more you know about timbre, the more you are aware that it is ungraspable. This is not only because its ontology, phenomenology and aesthetics are entwined in a complex epistemological puzzle. It is also, quite simply, because it is so hard to separate timbre from other musical factors: one reason why we do not necessarily hear timbre consciously is it is always mingled with so many other musical events occurring at the same time. When we listen to, say, Eric Clapton playing a guitar solo, we hear a great number of musical factors contributing to the overall timbre. In terms of set-up, there is a vintage Gibson Les Paul or Fender Stratocaster guitar, Marshall tube amps or Fender Tweed Twins, often a Vox Clyde McCoy wah-wah pedal, volume and tone settings, and a 3-coil bridge pickup. On top of these equipment specs, there is an extensive range of playing and articulation mannerisms that are personal to Clapton, such as his use of Blues-breaker style, his indebtedness to B.B. King and Buddy Holly, his playing with pentatonic scales, the 'Slowhand' articulation that gave him his nickname, his gut-wrenching glissandos. Produced by such a staggering list of contributing factors – which is far from complete here – is it really possible to pinpoint *what is timbre?* Timbre, whether in Clapton's solos, in Mahler's symphonies or in Gregorian plainchant, cannot be pinned down, reduced to one cause or one effect. It is a musical quality more than a quantity, and one that emerges from a heterogeneous assemblage of musical or non-musical agents. And yet we recognize that particular indeterminable quality, and identify it as Clapton's timbre, and Clapton's inimitable timbre is one reason why he is considered one of the greatest guitarists of all time.

Reflecting on timbre's indeterminacy, Anthony Gritten observes that '[t]he event of timbre is forever on the brink of not quite happening, not quite arising into consciousness; or (the flipside) it is forever at risk of a sudden cover-up by sound-objects and their attendant listening regimes' (2017: 537). He considers this predicament to be an inherent part of timbre's entwined ontology and phenomenology, and argues that it is precisely why timbre plays such a key role in music aesthetics:

> the encounter with the 'unprepared materials', with the essential surprise at the heart of timbre, is both the most important job played by music – raising awareness of just how profoundly we depend on timbre – and the lasting transferable skill that the ears and their listening subject take away from listening.
>
> (Gritten 2017: 541)

The encounter with timbre, as Gritten says, is one that is always marked by surprise. Timbre is unpredictable. No two cellists will ever produce the same tone, and neither will one cellist ever produce the same tone twice; by the same token, no two listeners will hear the same cello tone, and neither will one listener ever hear the same cello tone twice, even if it is a recording of a cello tone that she plays over and over again. Even if we accept, thus, that timbre is the unpredictable outcome of an indeterminable jumble of factors, we face the next problem: the fact that timbral perception and interpretation are just as unpredictable, and that, moreover, it is that very unpredictability that is crucial for timbral aesthetics.

Surprise and wonder guide my aesthetic experience as I listen to Clapton's guitar solo on 'Old Love' in the recording made in Madison Square Garden,

New York, on 30 June 1999. I went to Madison Square Garden, years after the fact, just to be in the physical space where this miracle happened. But standing there, although it was thrilling, had no relation to my musical experience of the solo recorded there. That performance is a miracle that has nothing to do with the physical location in which it occurred. It is a miracle for me, at least: but that very personal angle is precisely the core of timbre's aesthetic surprise. Every music lover has such intense listening experiences, and knows that no degree of physicality can possibly approach the sublime heights that her musical sensitivity allows her to reach. And every music lover knows that this experience is highly personal. Musical miracles may start off in the physical domain, but they take you – *you*, in *your* own way, *your* most intimate experience – somewhere else, into the realm of the infinite. And very often it is timbre that triggers the most profound experiences: it is the sound of a certain voice as it curves into the farthest ends of a dreamy melody, the sound of an oboe as its exuberant darkness pierces an orchestral texture, or the colour of a particular Fender Stratocaster while it bends towards a top G and back, that sends me, you, personally and intimately, reeling.

As the unpredictable musical outcome of the indeterminable interaction between heterogeneous sonic factors which evoke surprise and wonder, timbre is not just hard to define but also hard to capture in musical notation, to describe and to assess. Musical notation is a fairly precise system of visualization for a sonic phenomenon, but it favours pitch and rhythm over other musical parameters. When we say a melody rises or falls we can see that the notes in the score go up or down, and we can pinpoint the intervals and the pitch of melodies. Rhythmic elements such as note values, punctuation and metres can be notated with a great deal of concision and precision in a musical score. Combining our hearing of music with our viewing of a score and a specific idiom, we can tailor our assessment of harmony: consonance, dissonance, cadencing and modulation are as easy to see in a score and to discuss in language as they are to hear. But timbre is not notated: timbral indicators exist only in orchestration and in verbal instructions of articulation such as *sforzando* or *pizzicato*. For more extensive timbral instructions, composers and musicians must revert to metaphoric descriptors that are written into the score. These can become very vague, as there is no descriptive or analytical language for timbre: Alexander Scriabin's synaesthetic timbral indicators such as 'très parfumé' (very perfumed, in the *Poem of Ecstasy*) are famous examples of this practice.

The timbral indicators we find in musical scores illustrate just how difficult it is to find words for timbre's sonic manifestation. Lacking a specified timbral discourse, we revert to metaphor. Timbre is known in musicianly, academic and popular Western musical discourses by its visual synonym 'tone colour'; acousticians and recording engineers use the tactile metaphors of 'wet' and 'dry' sound; psychoacoustics employs sets of non-sonic adjectives such as 'warm' and 'bright' for its empirical research; and vocal pedagogy actively endorses the use of timbral metaphors to steer the learning process. How are we to know what anyone really means when they talk about these things?

The linguistic confusion around tone colour runs even deeper than the level of colourful descriptive imagery, as the term 'timbre' itself is not consistently used. In popular music, for instance, the term 'sound' prevails over 'timbre', while many electroacoustic composers prefer the word 'tone'. There is the added difficulty of translation, as different languages have different words: English uses 'timbre', 'sound' and 'tone'; in French the word 'timbre' is used but also replaced, in many contexts, by 'son' and 'sonorité'; German uses the words 'Ton', 'Klang' and 'Klangfarbe'; my native language, Dutch, borrows the French 'timbre' and the English 'sound' next to the Dutch words 'klank', 'toon' and 'klankleur'.

And the final blow: no one without knowledge of the French language even knows how to *pronounce* the word timbre.

The paradoxes of timbre

Cornelia Fales's 2002 article 'The Paradox of Timbre' marked a milestone in timbre research. For the first time, timbre was questioned from an aesthetic angle as well as the empirical perspectives used in sound physics or music psychology. Based on extensive psychoacoustic and ethnomusicological research, Fales argues that a fundamental paradox governs timbral perception: the fact that the perceived timbre concept in the listener's mind differs from the actual sound-object in the physical world (2002: 57–8, 91).

After the publication of Fales's essay, musicology returned to silence on the topic of timbre for over a decade. The 2010s, however, saw a sudden rise in the study of the subject. Emily Dolan's music-historical study *The Orchestral Revolution: Haydn and the Technologies of Timbre* (2013) traces the origins of timbral aesthetics in mid-eighteenth-century music philosophy, as well as the ramifications of this development for later orchestrational practices. Dolan's groundbreaking work is currently being followed up across the various subfields of musicology. The special issue on timbre of *Contemporary Music Review*, which I guest-edited in 2017, received a large number of strong contributions on topics including the use of timbre as a structuring device in the work of individual composers, on timbre's visual and tactile implications, on timbral metaphor in vocal pedagogy, and on timbral aesthetics and philosophy. In 2018, Emily Dolan and Alexander Rehding edited the *Oxford Handbook of Timbre*, which features contributions from the areas of, among others, musicology, ethnomusicology, music theory, anthropology, the history of science, and psychoacoustics. Finally, a collection on timbre in popular music edited by Robert Fink, Melinda Latour and Zachary Wallmark, *The Relentless Pursuit of Tone: Timbre in Popular Music*, was published in 2018. The burgeoning field of musicological timbre research promises insights into the area of music that we least understand and are most frustrated by.

Timbre: Paradox, Materialism, Vibrational Aesthetics explores the aesthetics of tone colour in Western classical and popular music. It specifically addresses the epistemological confusion evoked by the strange overlaps between materiality and ephemerality in timbral aesthetics: the ways in which such thoroughly material phenomena as Maria Callas's vocal timbre or Eric Clapton's guitar sound can make listeners soar high above the mundane. How is it that timbre enchants us when it is, in its sonic origin, such a physical thing, generated by vocal folds and diaphragms, manipulated by guitar pickups and amplifiers? Fales suggested that timbre perception is fundamentally paradoxical. This book introduces a number of other timbral paradoxes: it argues that every aspect of timbre – from its production to its perception, from its indexical relation to sound sources to its iconic relation to metaphor, and to its poised aesthetic position between the material and the sublime – appears to be characterized by insurmountable paradoxes. Because of these pervasive paradoxes, existing theorizations of timbre are divided into two schools of thinking: a number of theorists take a materialist approach studying the circumstances of sound production and the carnal phenomenology of perception, while others assume an idealist approach studying the effects that timbre has on the listening experience and on musical aesthetics while leaving timbre 'in-itself' at a distance. Each of these approaches has yielded valuable results, but their practical and intellectual exclusivity has led to an undesirable musicological dead end. Timbral theory, or rather timbral theories, have separated the two elements that form the paradoxically entwined basis of the timbral event: the material dimension of timbral aesthetics has become bifurcated from its immaterial dimension, and with that, the two schools of timbral materialism and timbral idealism have undergone a seemingly irreconcilable epistemological separation.

This separation of materialist and idealist approaches in the specialized area of timbral theory is in many ways symptomatic for musicological thought more generally (cf. Cox 2011: 156–7; cf. Dodd 2007). Music epistemology has long been divided between work-orientated and performance-orientated ontologies, with the more traditional, idealistically informed view of music-as-work gradually making space for a phenomenologically informed material view of music as performance. While close readings of musical scores and recordings are still widespread, performative and carnal approaches to music 'beyond the score' (Cook 2013) have been proliferating since the turn of the twenty-first century. Carolyn Abbate has famously characterized the former as a 'gnostic' and the latter as a 'drastic' approach to music, and argued for the infusion of the hermeneutic methodology of gnostic musicology with the drastic eventness of music as performance (2004). The two approaches have, however, remained remarkably separate. With the earliest calls to include musical performance in musical ontology dating back to the 'New Musicology' of the 1990s, this strand of musical scholarship still largely distances itself from more traditional work- and score-orientated musicology. The other way around, musicological explorations of the lives and works of the great composers very seldom engage with the performative aspects of their subject matter. More than two decades after the postmodern impulses of New Musicology, the two strands coexist but only rarely integrate (cf. McClary 2008). Nor is this the only rift running through musicology. The work-versus-performance binary is but one of many dichotomies dividing the field: questions of musical materiality and musical meaning, among others, have similarly divided musicologists into schools of thought, and continue to spark intense disagreements.

Instead of privileging either the ontology of the musical work or the phenomenology and aesthetics of musical performance, this book argues, it would be constructive to acknowledge both sides of the musical (and musicological) coin. Binaries often seem to construe the basic mechanics of musicology, and I think that the only way to mobilize them away from static opposition is to acknowledge the fact that these mechanics reflect the paradoxical fabric of the musical event itself and, with that, of music aesthetics. A closer inspection of the dichotomy can help discover a theoretical basis, however paradoxical at first glance, that is able to connect both opposites. Aiming to define and theorize the musical event of tone colour, *Timbre: Paradox, Materialism, Vibrational Aesthetics* seeks to reconnect the two schools of timbral reflection. The book is conceived with the paradoxes of timbre as its theoretical starting point: as the aesthetics of tone colour comprises material as well as immaterial elements, timbral theory should include both materialism and idealism. The consolidation of these traditionally opposite strands of thinking requires a reconsideration of their rootedness in timbral theory and practice as well as music philosophy. Renegotiating preconceptions around timbral – and with and through that, sonic and musical – materiality, the book ultimately aims to discover a music epistemology that can harbour the kaleidoscope of musical materialism in its full plurality and multidimensionality.

The first three chapters of the book address the various existing debates around timbre. Chapter 1, 'Ecologies of Sonorous Difference', charts the definitions of timbre used in organology and orchestration, acoustics and psychoacoustics, physiology and neuroscience. As each of these disciplines occupies itself with the physics of sound and music, their definitions of timbre tend to be based on a functional type of timbral materiality. There are good grounds for that: the materiality of sound sources, acoustic environments and frequency spectrums contribute decisively to the concrete manifestation of timbre, and the materiality of the ear and the brain are important aspects of timbral perception. But none of these definitions are entirely satisfying, as sound sources and acoustics are not necessarily timbrally homogeneous, frequency spectrums are not the only physical component of timbre and human physiology is far from reliable. Most importantly, timbre is as much a subjective quality as it is an objective quantity, and therefore empirical science can only offer partially valid methods of assessment. With the help of Eric F. Clarke's musical ecology, the chapter develops a working definition of timbre as an emergent sound quality that is thoroughly contingent: just like the Clapton guitar tone discussed earlier, all timbre emerges from an assemblage of heterogeneous actors, and is therefore undetermined, unpredictable and to a significant extent unquantifiable.

Chapter 2, 'Index, Icon, Grain', investigates the ways in which timbral discourse is able to complement and qualify the empirical facts charted in Chapter 1. The chapter opens with a discussion of the indexicality of timbre, and argues that timbral causality and identity are far less straightforward than they seem. The vocal timbre emerging from the musical ecology of the Queen of the Night aria, for instance, points indexically to a soprano; but although this is indeed, orchestrationally speaking, a soprano aria, 'soprano' alone does not suffice to describe the timbre of each possible performance of the piece. A further problem arises when we take timbral sources, in this case the singer, into account. A soprano timbre – like any vocal timbre – seems to point to the person of the singer, who in the example I mentioned earlier was the German opera diva Diana Damrau. To what extent does Damrau's timbre signify the musical identity of the singer, and how does it relate to her personal identity? Does it bear any relation to either at all, and if so, in what way? Although popular conceptions around voice seem keen to assume an equation between a singer and her voice, the relation between the two is based on an untenable form of essentialism that does not take into account the instability, ecology and unpredictability of vocal as well as instrumental and electronic timbres.

Next, the chapter investigates the metaphors comprising the majority of timbral discourse. Metaphors are useful descriptors of timbre as they share on a linguistic level the imprecision that characterizes tone colour on a musical level: for instance, 'Damrau has an amber soprano voice' tells us more than merely 'Damrau has a soprano voice', even though it is absurd to think that voices could literally be amber. Taking the im/precision of timbral metaphor further, the chapter discusses Roland Barthes's poststructuralist 'grain of the voice' and Mladen Dolar's psychoanalytical *objet petit a* of the voice to understand the ways in which timbre exceeds the confines of indexical identity and iconic signification. I argue that this excess is a key ingredient of timbral aesthetics: the aesthetic attraction of timbre lies in the tension it engenders between knowing (physical sound source, acoustic circumstances) and not knowing (metaphor, lack, excess).

Chapter 3, 'Excess, Sublime, Lure' addresses the tension between what we know and what we do not (want to) know of timbre. Starting with the points of desire, lack and excess that ended Chapter 2, this chapter explores the idealism of timbre. Timbral idealism has its historical roots in eighteenth-century philosophy, and the chapter links it specifically to Immanuel Kant's notion of the noumenal and the inapproachable Thing-in-itself as well as to Edmund Burke's notion of sublime delight and terror. The sublime timbral Thing became a focal point in Romanticism and, as the precursor of what became known later as 'absolute music', the guiding principle for nineteenth-century orchestration technique. It also led to what I call the 'timbral imperative' of twentieth-century composers including Arnold Schoenberg, Pierre Schaeffer, Karlheinz Stockhausen and Pierre Boulez. The timbral idealism that inspired these composers to formulate their dreams of tone coloured music was partially disenchanted by the renewed emphasis on timbral materialism through the invention of sound technology. Closing with a discussion of Jean-François Lyotard's theory of timbre as sublime 'sound-feeling' (1991: 176) and Vladimir Jankélévitch's physical and mental 'ineffable' (2003), the chapter argues that timbral aesthetics engenders the sublime aporia of being physically and mentally touched by an 'immaterial materiality' that strikes us as impossible.

Each of the first three chapters culminates in a list of paradoxes, which are summarized in Chapter 4 as 'paradox 0': timbre is material *and* immaterial. This ur-paradox of timbre, which is at the core of timbral as well as musical epistemology, can be instrumentalized through what Lydia Goehr calls 'doubleness', a philosophical theory that 'respects its own systematic limits' and 'supports a theory of open and critical practice' (2004: 5). Similar to traditional dialectics, doubleness explores both sides of any philosophical conundrum, but it is not bound to a teleological development towards one unambiguous conclusion: rather, doubleness serves to 'preserve both in theory and in practice the two or more sides of conflicts' (ibid.: 5). While Goehr employs doubleness to overcome the dichotomy between formalism and metaphysics in nineteenth-century music philosophy, it is also very suitable to bridge the philosophical divide between timbral materialism and timbral idealism (which, as Chapter 3 argues, is adjacent to the dichotomy studied by Goehr).

Chapters 4 and 5 develop a theory of timbre based on an acknowledgement of the importance of the material/immaterial and materialist/idealist paradoxes in timbral aesthetics. Through an application of the radical equivocation inherent to philosophical doubleness, these chapters do not choose either side of any binary, but rather take into account all aspects of timbral aesthetics, even and especially when they appear to be paradoxical. In order to achieve such an inclusive theory of timbre, a fundamental philosophical shift is required. The transcendentalism at the root of existing timbral theories must be replaced by a form of immanence that is able to accommodate timbre's unpredictable movements between both realms. The immanence proposed as a timbral mode of analysis in Chapter 4, 'Vibration and Vitality', is derived from a combination of Michel Chion's acoulogy and Jane Bennett's vital materialism. Music, this chapter suggests, is vibrant matter moving between what Chion calls the 'verberation' of material sonic origin and the much less material 'auditum' of sonic perception (2016: 16, 192). In musical vital materialism, these two realms are no longer separated by an unbridgeable divide but rather represent two connected aspects of a vibrational continuum. Musical sound waves vibrate across this meta-acoustic continuum: the motion from instruments to listening bodies to minds and sublime imagination is not one that is stopped by the limits of philosophy. The vitality inherent to musical vibrant matter is the sonic energy carried by sound waves as they move across the continuum: it is the energy through which this particular form of vibrant matter 'affects and is affected' (Bennett 2015: 95–6). Timbre occupies a specific place in the vibrant im/materiality of music. With its sonic energy distributed across the two domains, timbre has the potential to exert its vital agency across the entire vibrational continuum. More than other musical agents such as melody, rhythm and harmony, timbre's vitality is particularly affective both in the most intense materialities (of bodies, instruments and sound technology) on the one hand, and the most intense immaterialities (of excess and lack, the sublime and the ineffable) on the other. While bridging the dichotomies that constitute timbral binarism, thus, a musical vital materialist approach to timbre also affords an engagement with the larger epistemological question of the materiality and immateriality of music.

Chapter 5, 'Aesthetics of Vibration', offers a timbral aesthetics on the basis of the musical vital materialist outlined in Chapter 4. The chapter argues that the very fact of timbre's inherent paradoxes is at the core of timbre's aesthetic allure. Timbre's vibrational aesthetics invites listeners to participate in the boundary-crossing flow of timbral energy. The sonic energy carried by timbre's vibrating sound waves is an affectively powerful vitality interacting with musical assemblages of humans and non-humans. Starting from Rancière's 'distribution of the sensible', the chapter diverges sharply from the former in its acknowledgement of the timbral sublime in aesthetic experience. A comparative rereading of Lyotard's poststructuralist theory of the sublime and Herder's *empfindsam* philosophy of timbre leads to an understanding of the ways in which timbral aesthetics may appear to be paradoxical, but, in its vibrant entanglement of the material and the less material, can be considered an 'en-chanting' (Bennett 2001: 6, 34, 153) circulation of musical vitality. In aesthetic experience, timbre's vibrant vitality engenders 'tone-pleasure' (Herder 2006: 113) in a 'sound-feeling' (Lyotard 1991: 176) that includes material practice, identity and politics as well as affective lines of flight and sublime aporia. Timbral aesthetics, thus, is a 'distribution of the sensible' affecting the material and the less material at the same time.

Timbral aesthetics tangibly and ineffably presents listeners with the bewildering fact that the vibrant aesthetics of tone-pleasure bridges the gap between verberation and auditum, body and thought, material origins and immaterial effects. Superseding binarism, timbre *is* the very fact of paradox in musical aesthetics. Participating in timbral aesthetics is the lively interaction with music epistemology itself, with confusion at its core. And that confusion, that aporia, I argue, is precisely what we desire from musical experience.

The timbral contemplations in this book are illustrated by examples from Western art music and popular music, which are the musical worlds I inhabit. These examples should not be read as objective descriptions of timbre or as delineations of its musical scope, but rather as illustrations of the subjective potential of timbral aesthetics. If these brief musings approximate anything concrete, it is only language's inadequacy to describe the aesthetic experience of timbre. These sections, which I have set off from the general narrative of the book, are invitations to similar readerly experiments. How do *you* experience timbre?

1

Ecologies of sonorous difference

The date is 20 May. I attend a performance of the vocal ensemble VocaMe in the Schauspielhaus in Leipzig, Germany. It takes place in the context of the annual Gothic festival Wave-Gotik-Treffen, *and – as an Early Music researcher and singer as well as a Gothic researcher and subcultural participant – I cannot believe my luck that this concert is programmed at the event I visit every year. I've looked up VocaMe's website beforehand. The ensemble performs late Medieval and early Renaissance music in innovative arrangements for two sopranos, two mezzo-sopranos, and a multi-instrumentalist doubling as tenor. The singers are each renowned in the Early Music world, and two of the performers are part of the Goth electro-medieval band Qntal. VocaMe's musical aim is explicitly timbre-orientated: they wish to create a 'homogenous unison' through a blend of four very different, highly expressive voices (VocaMe).*

The programme contains excerpts from the twelfth-century Codex Calixtinus, *compositions by the Notre Dame School of Léonin and Pérotin, and the fourteenth-century* Messe de Tournai. *Sung by four female voices with the occasional male addition, and accompanied by instruments from the domain of secular music such as lute, theorbo, hurdy-gurdy, and hammered dulcimer, this is certainly a wholly new timbral approach to late Medieval sacred music. But it works. From plainchant to early polyphony, the voices blend into a mesmerizing mixed timbre, and the instrumental colours add hushed, warm tones to their sonorities.*

One sublime moment stands out for its dazzling timbral brilliance. The ensemble changes positions, and one of the mezzo sopranos sings a top line over a falsobordone *vocal setting accompanied by a hurdy-gurdy. If I was impressed by the timbral richness of the ensemble before, a sudden energy now vibrates through the room and utterly blows me away. This singer's timbre, her phrasing and legato, her portamentos and dynamic changes hit me like a violent bolt of lightning that cracks my skull open and reaches into the darkest heart of my being, exposing the deepest desire I had never known: to simply be in this place at this time and* dissolve *as this voice sings. I am struck by the force of my own reaction. Tears roll down my cheeks, uncontrollably, and doubtlessly creating black eyeliner traces on my Gothed-up face. I don't care if they do. People next to me turn in their plush red seats, their elaborate costumes rustling, to ask if I'm okay. Yes, I am, I'm very much okay, thank you – I'm just completely, devastatingly, deliciously overwhelmed by this timbre. My friends ask why, exactly, but I fail to find the right words.*

Timbre eludes definition in every corner of musicology and philosophy. Organology and acoustics, psychoacoustics and neuroscience, musicology and music philosophy alike have been unable to find firm definitions for timbre, that component of sound production and sound perception that is as ephemeral as it is tangible. Its most concise definition is 'tone colour', timbre's synaesthetic synonym which points both to its grounds in the materiality of sound production and to its capacity to add individuality to tone. But 'tone colour' is a metaphor, not a precise descriptor. The frustrating absence of a clear definition of timbre also obstructs the development of stable research methodologies for timbre (Hajda et al. 1997: 253). In an attempt to chart the variety of possible approaches to and definitions of timbre, this chapter outlines a working definition of timbre that accommodates as many scientifically quantifiable and subjectively ascertainable properties of tone colour as possible. Aiming not to achieve an unambiguous outcome but rather, and explicitly, to highlight the many uncertainties, ambivalences and inherent paradoxes of the sonic phenomenon that is timbre, the accumulative approach in this chapter will set up a flexible, and – to retain, for the moment, the vicarious precision of visual timbral metaphor – kaleidoscopic basis for the considerations of timbral aesthetics that comprise the scope of this book. In order to construct this basis, it is necessary to disentangle the various simultaneously occurring components of timbre that afford its manifold properties.

Sonorous difference

The most often-used and often-dismissed definition of timbre, as cited by psychoacoustician Stephen McAdams in the *Grove Music Online*, is one *ex negativo*. It describes timbre as the quality of sound that remains after pitch, loudness and duration are discounted as tonal differentiators:

> Timbre is the auditory attribute that distinguishes two sounds presented in a similar manner and having identical pitch, loudness and duration.
>
> (McAdams 2001: I; cf. McAdams and Giordano 2016: 113)

This definition identifies timbre as a unique sonic quality that can easily be distinguished by the ear: if the same pitch is produced by a piano and a violin at the same volume, the difference between these two sounds is timbre; by the same token, if the same pitch is sung by soprano A and soprano B at the same volume, then the difference between these two tones is timbre. Because timbre-as-difference is a percept as well as a material fact, McAdams argues, it can be measured by quantifying subjective assessments of the quality and extent of that difference:

> Timbre is now understood to have two broad characteristics that contribute to the perception of music: (*a*) it is a multifarious set of abstract sensory attributes, some of which are continuously varying (for instance, attack sharpness, brilliance, nasality), others of which are discrete or categorical (the 'blatt' at the beginning of a *sforzando* trombone note or the pinched offset of a harpsichord sound), and (*b*) it is one of the primary perceptual vehicles for the recognition, identification and tracking over time of a sound source (a singer's voice, a clarinet, a set of carillon bells) and thus involves the absolute categorization of a sound.
> (McAdams 2001: I)

Timbre's function within individual musical contexts is very different from that of other musical agents. Rhythm and metre organize the temporal dimension of music; harmony and melody create the organic development of tension and resolution that is the basis of any composition. Timbre, while it is a constituent of every possible sound and a crucial aspect of harmony, can only be described as the sonorous agent that adds 'colour' to music. Western music theory does not have a sufficient understanding of timbre's musical functionality, and traditional musical notation lacks timbral indicators beyond orchestrational instructions and articulation marks. As a result, it is impossible to quantify timbre's contribution to music, decisive though it is for musical aesthetics: unlike pitch, duration and loudness, timbre cannot be described in objective relationalities such as 'an A is higher than a C based on a pitch scale measured in Hertz', 'allegro is faster than adagio based on a time scale measured in beats per minute' or 'fortissimo is louder than mezzo piano based on a dynamic scale measured in decibels' (cf. Hajda et al. 1997: 254).

Since the 1960s a wealth of empirical research has attempted to track and categorize the perception of timbral difference through psychoacoustic and physiological methodologies (cf. Howard and Angus 2009: 231–75; Pratt and Doak 1976; Slawson 1985: 91–164; on psychoacoustics and physiology see below). But such mappings of perceived difference, while useful as a documentary tool for the range and scope of timbral perception by human (and sometimes animal, Slawson 1985: 151–2) subjects, do not offer a full picture of timbre as a sonic phenomenon. They do not provide insight, for instance, into timbre's relation to the three factors that contribute to the sounds whose perception is quantified: the factors of pitch, loudness and duration by which timbral difference is aurally distinguishable and upon which such quantitative reviews are implicitly based.

When examined more closely, those factors themselves and their relationships to timbre are far from unequivocal or constant. Because timbre shares a number of variables with pitch, loudness and duration, it is not always easy to distinguish between these elements of sound and sound perception (cf. Bregman 1990: 92–3). If we take harmonic spectrums into account, for instance, pitch can be described not as a separate component of sound that is distinct from timbre, but as a contributing element to perceived timbre: perceived pitch is nothing but a formant within the full spectrum of harmonics that together comprise a specific timbre which is in itself foregrounded by the contingencies of instrumental, vocal, or electroacoustic material circumstances (Howard and Angus 2009: 122–5, 146–50; Parker 2009: 64–7; Smalley 1986: 65–8). Even when there is no clearly identifiable pitch to a sound, that sound still must have a timbre, as harmonic spectrum does not necessarily privilege one formant over other overtones. Loudness's relation to timbre is similarly inconstant: as the human ear is unable to process very quiet or very loud sounds, changes in volume can distort timbral perception (Howard and Angus 2009: 91–100). Dynamic variants, in addition, alter the harmonic spectrum of a sound and thereby its timbre: the louder a sound is, the more high-frequency harmonics will be audible, and this shift in harmonic spectrum inevitably also shifts the perceived timbre of the sound (Parker 2009: 67). The relation between duration and timbre is possibly even more revealing of the instability of the concept of timbre as defined through sonorous difference. There are very few sounds that are absolutely constant over the course of their audible manifestation. Due to the material specificities of sound production, the onset of a sound comes with a different timbre than its steady-state and its offset phase: each of these phases in what is called the 'spectral' or 'note envelope' are marked by different harmonic spectrums and wave forms, and therefore by different timbres (Hajda et al. 1997: 256, 262; Howard and Angus 2009: 233–42; on note envelopes see below). Each sounding tone, moreover, has a different note envelope, even if two tones are produced by the same player on the same instrument in the same environment on the same day, which further complicates an objective quantification of timbral duration (Howard and Angus 2009: 237). If timbre is to be distinguished from duration, as the official definition demands, timbre judgements can only be made either on the most individually distinguished part of the envelope, which is note onset, or on a generalized 'snapshot' of the steady-state phase: the validity of either judgement is necessarily restricted, as they are based on a partial evaluation of the time span of a timbre (Hajda et al. 1997: 263; Howard and Angus 2009: 236). The production and perception of pitch, loudness and duration, thus, significantly interfere with that of timbre, and this interference is always subjective, so that it is very hard (if not impossible) to quantify timbre through cognitive or perception research.

These reservations notwithstanding, timbre can undeniably be defined as sonorous difference: every sound has a unique tone colour, regardless of whether it has an identifiable pitch, independent of loudness, and remaining recognizably constant despite durational development. A timbral definition based solely upon perceived tonal differentiation under identical circumstances pertaining to pitch, loudness and duration, however, is not entirely appropriate. If we wanted to define timbre as sonorous difference, we should amend McAdams's definition: it is a *subjectively identifiable* but *itself undescribed* quality of sound that is not *quite* the same as pitch, volume or duration. Such a caveat-laden definition is hardly satisfying, and – as it is based on negatives – does not even begin to approach the sonic phenomenon that is timbre. How can we describe that evasive quality more positively than as the *relative* absence of *certain* variables?

Sound source

Containing no perceptive caveats and no cognitive uncertainties, organology offers a categorical taxonomy of musical instruments and their timbres based on the materials and practices of sonorous difference (cf. Bregman 1990: 93). A standard work in the field is Curt Sachs's *Handbuch der Musikinstrumentenkunde* (1916), which, with his *Reallexicon der Musikinstrumente* (1913), is still widely used a century after its first publication. Both publications are based on what is known as the Hornbostel-Sachs method of musical instrument classification (Hornbostel and Sachs 1914). Sachs's *Handbuch* offers a systematic overview of each of the instrumental categories, their history and subcategories, instrument design and materials (which he calls the instrument's '*Wesen*', its essence), playing techniques, nomenclature and timbre. The latter descriptions are kept to a minimum, with indications only of which harmonics are audible in the sound ('*Klang*') of the instrument – that is to say, descriptions of timbre are restricted to its objectively verifiable parameters. In rare cases, Sachs describes the ways in which an instrumental timbre is distinguishable from similar timbres. In these passages he uses strikingly subjective discourses rather than his usual scientific language: the sound of the natural horn, for instance, is 'full, but mostly dark, and often lustreless verging on dull' in comparison to other signalling horns, whereas the French hunting horn has a 'soft, dreamy, warm, resounding tone that shines brightly in *forte*' in comparison to other natural horns (1930: 252, 274). These sections stand out in Sachs's otherwise strictly factual, efficiently written handbook, and illustrate the extent to which, on the one hand, the phenomenon of timbre exceeds the boundaries of the material facts that organology adheres to, and, on the other hand, that the description of this excess lacks objective discursive structures. In the Hornbostel-Sachs system, timbre was of secondary importance to instrument categorization into primary classes and subclasses. Tone colour in this system was straightforward and utilitarian, instrumental in both senses of the word: it pointed to the instrument that produced it, which was classified into clear strata, and it could be employed for specific sonorous effects in composition and orchestration. This physiological approach to instruments – in which timbre was conceived of as a subjectively interpreted effect caused by the objective material circumstances of sound production – followed organological traditions that had been in place since Michael Praetorius's 1619 treatise *Syntagma Musicum* (cf. Dolan 2013: 31–6).

Organology was among the first branches of music criticism to adapt the term 'timbre', along with music aesthetics and – as a blend of both – orchestration. The term itself did not appear in music criticism until 1765, when Jean-Jacques Rousseau identified three dimensions of sound in Diderot's *Encyclopédie*: the first two dimensions, so Rousseau argues, are pitch and loudness, and the third is timbre, which he derives from instrumental specificities. 'No one I know has examined this aspect', he comments, and he is only able to describe this third dimension by way of metaphors pertaining to a sound's dullness, brightness, harshness and softness (Dolan 2013: 54–6). Emily Dolan's book *The Orchestral Revolution* provides a wealth of evidence demonstrating a change in musical discourses heralded by the eighteenth-century turn towards timbre. Dolan argues that this turn signals a shift in critical attention towards the immediacy of musical perception (2013: 56–7): music criticism now turned its focus to music aesthetics, besides the building blocks of music practice that had been the main object of music theory in the early Modern age (on timbre in eighteenth-century music aesthetics cf. Chapter 3). Although instrumental and orchestrational treatises appearing after the Enlightenment discuss timbre primarily in relation to their instrumental or vocal sound source just like Rousseau did in the *Encyclopédie* – and therefore follow a fundamentally taxonomic outline – they do include subjective interpretations of the sounds they discuss. Instrumental and orchestrational sources of this period such as, most famously, C.P.E. Bach's *Versuch über die wahre Art das Clavier zu spielen* (1753) and Johann Joachim Quantz's *Versuch einer Anweisung die Flöte trasversiere zu spielen* (1752) include flurries of timbral imagery of the kind that Sachs, too, occasionally dips into: the writers describe not only the material and technical detail required for organological overview but also indications of the expressiveness and aesthetic value of each of the timbres (Dolan 2013: 57–71).

From the Enlightenment turn towards timbre as a music critical concept, then, timbral discourses have been based upon an understanding of timbre as the aural marker of an instrumental sound source: but these discourses have steadily been supplemented, intensified and obscured by the use of non-musical imagery that was meant to sharpen the verbal representation of the quality of tone that was approached, but never entirely captured, through the identification of sound sources. The epitome of such metaphoric qualifications in timbral discourse can be found in Hector Berlioz's 1844 *Grand Traité d'Instrumentation et d'Orchestration Modernes*, which explicitly had as its purpose not just to identify organological aspects of the instruments, but moreover to describe the expressive range and colour that each of the individual timbres could bring to composition, orchestration and performance (Berlioz 2002: 6). In his descriptions of timbre, Berlioz reaches for the most colourful imagery he can find. In the section on the middle register of the flute, for instance, he describes the 'desolate, but also humble and resigned' tone of the instrument, and he waxes lyrical about Gluck's capacity to express the 'thousand-fold sublime wailing of a suffering, despairing shade of the departed' through the flute's timbre (ibid.: 140). We are very far away from organology's factual language here. The synaesthetic timbral metaphor 'tone colour', which still marks timbral discourses today, can be traced back at least to the seventeenth-century Jesuit and *uomo universalis* Athanasius Kircher, who maintained in his 1650 *Musurgia Universalis* that the effects of instrumental tone upon the mind was comparable to that of colour (quoted in Dolan 2013: 26). The term 'tone colour' or *Klangfarbe* started to emerge in German musical theory and aesthetics around the middle of the nineteenth century, having been saliently present in comparisons between tone and colour as early as Johann Leopold Hoffmann's 1786 treatise *Farbenharmonie* (Dolan 2013: 47–9). Dolan argues that the timbral variety and nuance inherent to the term tone colour 'implied the presence of a well-developed orchestral tradition, one that emerged only during the late eighteenth century' (2013: 71). The sonically variegated orchestra in itself however, just like the sonorous richness implied in the concept of *Klangfarbe*, was a result of music-aesthetic interest in the immediacy of music perception that started with Rousseau.

Both traditional organology and Enlightenment music aesthetics based their definition of timbre primarily on the contingencies of its origin, albeit with the help of non-musical imagery to refine this material basis. Timbre, in these contexts, points to such factors as instrument design, material, vocal technique and body physiology. Naturally such factors have a large impact on the specifics of instrumental and orchestral timbral outcomes: the reason, for instance, that the traverso in the baroque orchestra was replaced by the metal flute in the symphonic orchestra was that the wooden traverso's hushed, soft timbre as well as its meantone temperament was no longer sufficiently audible in the expanding orchestra of the eighteenth century, and so it was replaced by its metal, keyed equivalent, the flute with its bright, loud timbre and equal temperament. Loudness and pitch are clearly integral parts of an instrument's tone colour and orchestral value, which demonstrates again that the negative definition of timbre is not always adequate. The positive identification of timbre through instrumental materiality – this timbre is a flute timbre – is both clearer and more helpful in this case. In a similar way, the classification of vocal timbres into four main voice types with their subclasses is an undeniably physical and useful tool to identify singing timbres. An alto voice is distinct from a soprano voice in range as well as timbre, and this difference is based on a singer's physiology; a boy soprano is distinguished from a lyrical soprano, a lyrical soprano is different from a coloratura soprano, and each of these differences is caused by specific corporeal conditions resulting in specific timbres.

With the introduction of sound technology in twentieth-century music, however, such straightforwardly instrumental definitions of timbre encountered at least three serious obstacles. First, recording technology is able to separate a sound from its source so that this source is no longer easily identifiable as the material origin of timbre. Early recorded sound, for this reason, has often been assessed as ghostly, as its recognizable timbre may not come from the expected source (cf. Sterne 2003: 287–333). Second, production technology is able to emulate acoustic sounds and to distort them into unexpected timbral ranges, so that it is no longer clear what material entity is the cause of a sound. Guitar pickups, pedals and effects provide instrument-specific ways of achieving timbral distortion (Gracyk 1996: 118–24). Jimi Hendrix's signature sound, for instance, was achieved by over-amplifying his guitars, which in effect often meant that he distorted his guitar timbre through extremely high volumes: timbre, again, proves itself to be not easily distinguished from loudness, but neither is Hendrix's guitar sound necessarily recognizable as a guitar timbre (cf. Moore 2012: 44–9; Tagg 2013: 309–13). Similarly, production technology is able to enhance the ghostly effect of recorded sound: reverb effects, for instance, are often used in horror cinema as a sonic marker of acousmatic voices emanating from spectral beings (Doyle 2005: 114–17, 169–70; Van Elferen 2012: 41–3, 61–70). Finally, sound technology is able to create entirely new sonorities that have no other material source than the hardware or software that produced it. The electroacoustic experiments of 1950s composers, as well as their popular successor, the timbre machine that was the Moog synthesizer – with its manual control of frequency spectrum, Fourier series and amplitude – revolutionized the soundscape of the twentieth century (cf. Evens 2005: 91–5). Composers such as Stockhausen, Varèse, Xenakis and Ligeti 'liberated timbre and texture as structural elements of musical composition', while pop and rock musicians used feedback, distortion and amplification for the same purpose (Hamilton 2007: 42; cf. Cendo 2010: 1–3). This revolution is ongoing and evolving further in twenty-first century digital experiments. As a result of these technological advances, instrumental origin has lost its relevance in the definition of timbre. Chapter 2 will assess these three dimensions of the technological impact on timbral indexing in more detail; it is noteworthy in the context of the present chapter that instrumental definitions of timbre have been severely complicated by sound technological developments.

In traditional organology and orchestration, timbre was defined primarily as the sonic marker of its instrumental identity. The ambiguities of subjective perception are kept to a minimum in this field. While useful in the context of taxonomies, this restriction is problematic in the light of the many perceptual ambiguities that exist around timbral source recognition: instrumental identification through various registers has proved inconsistent, for instance, and the 'polyphonic' timbral context of several instruments playing at the same time leads to perceptual fusion (cf. McAdams and Goodchild 2017).

The organological definition of timbre becomes unsustainable in the light of technological developments whose ability to obfuscate, alter or even eliminate concrete instrumental sound sources. Perceptual ambiguities around timbre, moreover, are at the core of the twentieth-century fascination with sound technology: composers such as Schaeffer and Stockhausen explicitly aimed to move away from clearly identifiable instrumental timbres, privileging, on the contrary, entirely new and previously unheard sounds as a basis for their compositions (Schaeffer 1952: 12–14; Stockhausen 1963–1984, vol. 1: 142–3; cf. Chapter 3). The persistence of timbral metaphor further hollows out the viability of a purely instrumental definition of timbre. The very fact that even traditional organological discourses consistently include references to non-musical imagery demonstrates that simply stating 'this is a violin timbre' is not a sufficient description of that particular timbre: the addition of a metaphor – 'this is a *warm* violin timbre' – adds something, a '*je ne says quoi*' in Rousseau's words, that is simultaneously not present in sound source identification and crucial for the description of that timbre (Rousseau in Diderot's *Encyclopédie*, quoted in Dolan 2013: 55).

Like the absolutely negative definition of timbre as a sonorous difference that is not pitch, loudness or duration, so the absolutely positive definition of timbre as pointing to a specific sound source fails to capture what timbre is and how it is perceived. Although both definitions are appropriate to a certain extent, and certainly do complement each other, more factors than difference and material origin alone must be taken into account in order to come to an acceptable working definition of timbre.

Physical and virtual acoustics

The first of these factors is acoustics. It is impossible to overstate the interrelatedness of acoustics and timbre – and, with that, the inextricable connection between architectural design, composition and performance in timbre. Aden Evens has noted that

> the sound, the total timbre of an instrument is never just that instrument, but that instrument in concert with all the other vibrations in the room, other instruments, the creaking of chairs, even the constant, barely perceptible motion of the air.
>
> (Evens 2005: 6)

In each sound we hear, the surroundings in which that sound was produced are perceivable to the ear in the shape of timbral elements such as resonance, acoustic reflection, and reverberation (cf. Smalley 1994: 42–3; Zagorski-Thomas 2014: 65). If we listen carefully to the timbre of a sound we will even be able to identify specific physical properties of those surroundings: through timbre we can determine whether a sound is open-air or inside, how large the acoustic space is, whether its walls are made of stone or wood, whether a sound is live or recorded, and, if it is recorded, which production effects were used. In reference to Mikhail Bakhtin's chronotope, Jacob Smith coins the term 'sonotope' for this 'intrinsic connectedness' of space and sound in acoustics (2008: 245). The sonotope is interactive and mutual: a sound source injects sonic energy into the space by way of vibration, and the space may inject its own reverberating energy into the vibrating blend (thus, for instance, enabling the opera diva to sing without amplification) or it may alter the sonic energy already in the room (thereby, for instance, making the diva's voice sound brighter and more legato) (cf. Blesser and Salter 2007: 150–4). The most specific marker of the sonotope, Smith therefore argues, is timbre, which 'indicates the space through which a sound has passed' (2008: 245–6). Acoustics, in short, are as intrinsic a part of timbre as instruments, and acoustic design and material plays a very similar role in timbral nuance as the making of an instrument.

The laws of acoustics are those of vibrating sound waves, sonic energy transmission, and the reflection, refraction and diffraction of waves on surrounding material (Howard and Angus 2009: 28–58; Lewcock and Pirn 2001; Parker 2009: 41–58). Concert venues and recording studios are carefully designed to optimize acoustic conditions, and with attention to the absorption and reflection levels of the materials used for walls, floors and ceilings as well as for diffusion and partition panels (Howard and Angus 2009: 277–363; Lewcock and Pirn 2001; Parker 2009: 244–58). Arguably the most important aspects of acoustic architecture are the distribution and control of reverberation and echo, which, not coincidentally, also have a guiding impact on timbre and timbre perception. Peter Doyle even goes so far as to contend that architectural and acoustic design 'could be seen largely as an attempt to deal with the affective aspects of particular sound properties, especially reverberation and echo' (cf. Doyle 2005: 34). The 'affective aspects' of reverb and echo that Doyle mentions often occur in the realm of timbral aesthetics. Strong reverberation can highlight certain harmonics, making timbres sound brighter; the absence of reverb, on the contrary, dampens overtone reflection, so that timbres sound duller. Because of the temporal delay in reverberation, moreover, a sequence of notes played or sung in a reverberating space will appear to be blending together, that is they will sound more *legato*. The same delay can have a detrimental effect in spaces where reverb time is long in relation to the rhythm of the music, which can make fast notes seem to blur into one another (cf. Blesser and Salter 2007: 122, 139–42). All these affordances of reverb have an impact on the aesthetic and affective perception of timbre: bright timbres have a different emotional impact to dull timbres, and blurred sounds are experienced differently to clearly separated sounds.

On an even more detailed level of the interface between acoustics and timbre, it is possible to analyse and control the vibrating sound waves themselves. Each sound comprises any number of concurrent sound waves, and with the help of Fourier analysis and Fourier transform technology this accumulation of sound waves can be visualized, analysed and manipulated (Evens 2005: 2–5; Howard and Angus 2009: 437–46; Sethares 2005: 13–15). As differently shaped sound waves have different implications for harmonic spectrums, each type of sound wave will produce a different timbre: sine waves have no harmonics, whereas triangle and square waves contain only odd harmonics, and sawtooth waves also contain even harmonics (Evens 2005: 97–9; Howard and Angus 2009: 14–17, 59–62, 437–46). Any alteration – be it an alteration of a complex sound's spectrum, individual wave phase, amplitude or frequency – enables musicians, composers, sound engineers and producers to achieve timbral variation (Evens 2005: 95–106; Howard and Angus 2009: 62–4, cf. 124–7; Sethares 2005: 15–17; Taylor and Campbell 2001: 2, 8.ii). This can be as simple as the difference in wave form between a tone produced by a violin and that generated by a clarinet, and as complex as the detailed manipulation of wave form through sound software.

Because of the decisive influence of acoustics on the distribution of sound waves, architecture is a powerful music-historical agent: the Notre Dame of Paris, the Thomaskirche in Leipzig, and Studio 2 in Abbey Road have had as much input in the development of Léonin and Pérotin's, Johann Sebastian Bach's, and the Beatles' music as the composers did. 'Music and performance spaces', Barry Blesser and Linda-Ruth Salter therefore contend, are 'forever linked' (2007: 79, cf. 92–3, 135–9). The authors of instrumental and orchestrational treatises discussed in the previous paragraph were keenly aware of this connection: Johann Joachim Quantz taught flute players to adjust their performance to the space in which they played (Blesser and Salter 2007: 102), and Hector Berlioz complains about the fashion for open-air performances which create acoustic nightmares – 'open air music *does not exist*' (2002: 319–20, italics in original). In studio recordings, acoustic architecture can be manipulated by placing reverb plates and gobo booths made from sound absorbing or, conversely, highly refractive material in the studio live room in order to create the desired sonic effect. Phil Spector's pioneering 'wall of sound' is doubtlessly the most famous example of this practice. Spector recorded large instrumental and vocal sections (including multiple drum kits and pianos) playing homophonous, often *unisono* lines, and with masses of dubbing and over-dubbing effects; he placed each section in gobo booths which created short reverb times for each individual section, and then ran each track through an echo chamber with speakers and microphones (cf. Moorefield 2010: 9–15). The resulting sound was dense, directly in-your-face and almost claustrophobic. Virgil Moorefield contends that Spector

> was using the studio as his orchestra, arranging the timbres of various voice, instruments, effects, and room tones in much the same way as a more conventional composer would employ the colors of the orchestra ... the point is not just the melody but the overall *sound*, the feel of a recording.
>
> (Moorefield 2010: 14, italics in original)

This 'overall *sound*' and 'feel' has everything to do with the ways in which Spector understood the intricate connectedness between acoustics and timbre, and the possibility, in studio production, to optimize this relation.

Spector's 'wall of sound' illustrates the fact that sound technology has had, and continues to have, vast implications for the field of timbral acoustics. Studio technology is not only able to reproduce existing acoustics but also to simulate acoustics, location and reverberation, engendering a virtual space in which voices and instruments seem to resonate. William Moylan proposes the notion of a 'perceived performance environment' which includes a 'perceived sound stage' (Moylan 2007: 177–9). These virtual acoustic spaces do not necessarily coincide with the actual acoustic circumstances of a recording. In recorded music, instruments can appear to sound from left and right at the same time, or they can even be split in two or more separate components: a drum kit, for instance, may be produced in such a way that the kick drum is placed on one side of the virtual acoustic space and the toms are placed on the other. In an attempt to analyse the recorded acoustic environment in more detail, Allan Moore has introduced the model of the 'soundbox' which describes the temporal and spatial distribution of sounds over the virtual space of a recording (Moore

2012: 29–44). Moore's soundbox differs importantly from Moylan's perceived performance environment in that it offers a more nuanced view of a recording's distribution of texture, timbre and depth. Moore distinguishes four dimensions of location within each soundbox, each of which have a relation to those nuanced levels of sound production and perception: (1) the dimension of time, which is represented by echo and reverberation effects; (2) the relative prominence of instruments, voices and sounds, which is achieved by dynamics and distortion; (3) the gradual scale of pitch registers from high to low; (4) the gradual scale of timbral registers from bright to dull (2012: 31–2). The pervasive presence of timbral aspects in the soundbox model does not just demonstrate the ongoing interrelatedness of timbre and acoustics in the virtual sonic space. It also affords insights into the many ways in which virtual acoustic design is able to privilege timbre, and thereby to foreground its perception, in more ways than is possible in physical acoustics.

Each dimension of Moore's soundbox model illustrates the radical changes that sound technology introduced to the perception of sonic time and space through the manipulation of timbre. Microphones, multitrack recording, reverb effects, equalization and compression are among the most important agents affecting this change. The invention of the microphone in the early twentieth century introduced a new aural relation to proximity. Many writers have commented on the amplification of the human voice in all its timbral detail through sound technology: recordings of crooning, whispering and hissing each artificially place vocalist and listener together in an all too narrow virtual acoustic space, bringing the corporeality of the speaking or singing voice almost too close for comfort – and this is so even if the listener knows that what she hears is a recording, an acousmatic voice emanating from a phantom body (e.g. Connor 2000; Frith 1996: 187–8; Smith 2008: 83–9; Zagorski-Thomas 2014: 57–8). As microphone type, positioning and post-production each have a distinct impact on recorded timbre, this acousmatic sound can have a much wider timbral range than their non-amplified equivalent would have; Simon Zagorski-Thomas has called this effect 'timbral staging' (Zagorski-Thomas 2014: 74, 81–3; cf. Moylan 2007: 268–9, 280–95; Zak 2001: 108–12). Through creative microphone placement and a heterogeneous approach to the use of reverb effects, moreover, it is possible for soundbox environments to contain 'spaces within spaces' or 'soundboxes within soundboxes' (Moylan 2007: 203–6). Some parts of a track may seem to be recorded in a reverberating environment, while other parts of the same track may sound as if they were recorded in a dry, enclosed space (cf. Zak 2001: 100–7). Because they are placed in the same overall soundbox, however, the result is a curious – and physically impossible – spatiotemporal simultaneity that is afforded, effectively, by timbral blend (cf. Van Elferen 2018: 33–5). When a track's sound is finalized through mixing, editing and mastering, timbral modification takes centre stage. As in physical acoustics, echo and reverb are the key timbral agencies in this stage of virtual acoustic design. Effects such as flanging, phasing, double tracking, chorusing and delay effects – as simulated acoustic effects – influence the resonance of harmonics, and determine a track's timbral outline (Doyle 2005: 23–34; Zak 2001: 70–6). Reverb effects can also create something altogether more spectral when the original sound is taken out of the mix and reverb and/or echo are kept in at a louder volume. The process of equalizing shows once more how dependent pitch is on timbre: EQ adjusts the frequency spectrum of the various parts of a track to each other, and is able to highlight certain instruments or vocals by equalizing them into a thundering bass presence or, conversely, a sparkling descant line (cf. Zak 2001: 120–2, 151–5). Dynamic compression, finally, can expand or fuse the overall timbre of a track as well as individual instrumental or vocal colours.

The result of the complex and detailed process of studio production is the timbrally and texturally specific sonic time-space of the soundbox. In its acoustic and timbral precision, a studio production resembles the minutely orchestrated timbre and carefully arranged texture of orchestral music. It is for this reason that studio producers and engineers are now generally understood to fill the complex, multitasking role of composer, aural architect and conductor of the virtual meta-instrument that is the studio (Blesser and Salter 2007: 144, 209–14; Moorefield 2005: 53–8, 71–4; Schmidt Horning 2012: 34–6). Their main job, ultimately, is the shaping of timbre. Through their detailed timbral adjustments of individual instrumental and vocal tracks as well as of the overall timbre of a song, producers and engineers define the 'sound' of rock music that Theodore Gracyk, pointing to timbre as the key ingredient of that sound, identifies as the most central aspect of rock musical aesthetics (1996: 57–67).

William Moylan recognizes the dilemma of having to work with timbre in every aspect of studio recording and production without being able to describe or comprehend precisely this key quality of music. He proposes an empirical approach to tone colour, one that describes the various elements of its physicality:

> Nearly all positions in the entire audio industry need to communicate about the content or quality of sound. Yet a vocabulary for describing sound quality, or a process for objectively evaluating the components of sound quality, do not exist.

Meaningful communication about sound quality can be accomplished through describing the values and activities of the physical states of the components of timbre.

(Moylan 2007: 157)

So far, this chapter has attempted to describe those 'values and activities' pertaining to the material aspects of timbral production. But is that enough to develop a vocabulary that encompasses all aspects of tone colour, and to understand its decisive role in the musical outcome that such material production aims to establish?

I am listening to VocaMe's CD Cathedrals, *which I bought after the Leipzig concert. The piece by which I was so moved during the concert, and which I now know is the 'Benedicamus' from the Codex Calixtinus,*[1] *floods into my ears. It happens again. The singular sonority of the mezzo soprano by whom I was so impressed, and who I now know is called Petra Noskaiová, stirs something powerful inside me, something that exceeds the grasp of words. I have no control over my soaring heart as once again tears begin to run down my cheeks. This has nothing to do with the provenance of the work, or with the details of the performance: I just never want her to stop singing, and I play the track again and again and again.*

Am I overwhelmed because of the uniqueness of Noskaiová's timbre and the ways in which it differs from any other soprano voice I have heard? Is it because it is indistinguishable from pitch and loudness, as her inexplicable timbrality blends staccatos, portamentos, and legatos into a continuum of crescendo and diminuendo? Duration is of no relevance – this timbre continually changes, it occupies and transforms time. Am I overwhelmed because of the physical shape of her vocal instrument, her pharynx, her breathing apparatus, her chest and head resonance? Because of the timbral aims that the ensemble set itself? Because of the sophisticated studio environment in Munich, where this album was recorded, or the mixing desk, or the detailed reverb effects used here? Or because of Michael Popp, Johann Bengen, and Peter Hecker's refined engineering and mixing skills, whose aim it was to create a 'hyperrealistic, more natural than natural' sound? (Popp, personal communication)

All or none of these?

Who can tell?

---

[1] The recording can be found on https://www.k.com/watch?v=-f3-WMPx5fk.

> *The physical aspects of timbral production discussed in this chapter so far certainly shape the tone colours I hear, and they contribute to my immediate – and equally physical – affective response. But they do not explain my feeling of being swept away from space, time, and physicality, and my being guided only by an engulfing desire to hear. Noskaiová's timbre pierces my senses like an impossible beam of dark moonlight. It annihilates my mind as I willingly disappear into a world of sound alone.*
>
> *I know that this is only my affective response, my elation, my glimpse of the sublime and the monstrous. You may not be moved by it at all.*
>
> *That does, however, beg a question.*

As meticulous as the physical and virtual production of timbral acoustics is, its perception shows the same level of subjectivity and individuality as timbral perception. As a result, it is as hard to assess acoustic experience as it is to assess timbre (Howard and Angus 2009: 244; Taylor and Campbell 2001: 4). Acoustics are evaluated in the same type of non-sonic imagery that pervade timbral discourse: room or recording acoustics may be evaluated as wet or dry, warm or cold, bright or dull, intimate or expansive (cf. Blesser and Salter 2007: 218–28). Although these terms are commonly used in the field of acoustic architecture, it is important to bear in mind that even the mathematical and scientific field of acoustic design is still evaluated in such un-mathematical and un-scientific terms: like timbre, acoustics is ultimately assessed by means of metaphor. The acoustic properties of timbre, just like its organological properties, are quantifiable in their material elements, but difficult to qualify in the much less material domain of perception. And yet – as my entirely personal and entirely pathetic superlatives in relation to Noskaiová's 'Benedicamus' aim to demonstrate – it is the latter domain that is vital to the reasons why timbre is such an important part of musical aesthetics. In order to acquire some degree of insight into the subjective area of timbral perception, we must turn to the psychoacoustics of timbre.

Psychoacoustics

Psychoacoustics is a form of cognitive psychology that concerns itself with the perception of sound by (mostly human) subjects. In view of its many physical and perceptive ambiguities, timbre presents a particular challenge to the field. It negotiates the presence of many changeable variables in timbre by focusing on its invariables. The two main physical properties of timbre whose perception has been researched in psychoacoustics are the relatively stable aspects of frequency spectrums and the note envelope.

Spectral analysis

A sound's frequency spectrum is the totality of harmonics that together comprise its specific accumulation of wave forms. The first harmonic concurrent with any sound is the octave above the fundamental frequency which is the lowest and loudest perceived, after which follow the perfect fifth in the higher octave, the perfect fourth (forming the second higher octave), the major third of the second higher octave, the minor third of the second higher octave (forming the fifth of that octave): the list goes on ad infinitum, although the trained human ear is only able to perceive tones at a maximum of 16,000 Hz (Helmholtz 2016: 22–3; Howard and Angus 2009: 122–31, 242–3; Taylor and Campbell 2001: 8.ii). Depending on instrumental, material and acoustic circumstances, certain harmonics may contribute more strongly to the overall sound.

Variations in frequency spectrum, that is, the specific harmonics which resonate with a sounding formant, are a major determining factor not just for perceived pitch but importantly also for timbre (Bregman 1990: 94–103; Helmholtz 2016: 65–9; Howard and Angus 2009: 233–4, 244–52; Sethares 2005: 17–25; Slawson 1985: 22–44; Tagg 2013: 279–80). The material specifics of the channels that generate a sound, for instance the shape and size of a violin's strings and body as well as the manner of bowing, or of a trumpet's cylinder and bowl as well as embouchure and breathing, are key elements determining the spectral particularities of individual instruments (e.g. Helmholtz 2016: 74–88, 99; Howard and Angus 2009: 170–81, 203–7; Parker 2009: 150–2, 171–3). Similarly, in the case of vocal tones, the shape of a singer's larynx, pharynx, head cavities, lip and tongue position determine which frequencies will be generated (Helmholtz 2016: 103–24; Howard and Angus 2009: 219–25; Parker 2009: 195–201; Sundberg 1987). As no two human bodies are the same, each singing voice will carry a slightly different set of harmonics. For this reason, even octaves or *unisono* can appear to be out of tone when played by different instruments or sung by different voices: the spectral dimension of timbre presents one of the especially challenging aspects of a cappella choral singing (cf. Howard and Angus 2009: 225–9; Sethares 2005: 2–7; Sundberg 1987: 134–5).

A great deal of psychoacoustic research has been conducted in the field of frequency spectrums. With spectrographic software it is possible to visualize the frequency spectrums of different instruments and voices: comparisons of these spectrograms provide insight into the spectral differences that constitute different timbres (Howard and Angus 2009: 245–52). As tone spectrums are differently perceived by each human ear and by each individual, these visual analyses of spectrograms have been mapped onto the verbal feedback provided by test listeners. In this type of experiment, listeners will be asked to qualify the timbres they perceive by way of 'timbre descriptors' such as 'pure', 'pleasant', 'sweet', 'dark', 'hollow', 'nasal', 'rough' or 'brilliant' (e.g. Howard and Tyrrell 1997: 71–5; Slawson 1985: 91–164). Certain constant evaluations are notable throughout such experiments: when the fundamental dominates a timbre, evaluations lean towards 'purity' and 'pleasantness' while a prevalence of dominant harmonics is assessed as 'sweet', 'soft' or 'dark', and a dominance of odd harmonics tends to be heard as 'hollow' or 'nasal' (Howard and Tyrrell 1997: 73).

Although frequency spectrums are crucial to the timbral make-up of a tone, they are not decisive. A sine wave – which lacks any harmonics – still has a striking and unique timbre that identifies that particular sound as a sine tone (Dolan 2013: 54; Evens 2005: 4). Moreover, it is hard to obtain solid results from experiments that measure subjective responses, and whose outcomes are evaluated in such imprecise terms as metaphor. An even more quantified spectral definition of timbre can be obtained through the inclusion of the temporal dimension of the frequency spectrum.

Note envelope

No sound offers a stable frequency spectrum, as harmonics resonate more strongly at varying parts in the vibrating event. The frequency spectrum of sound cannot, therefore, on its own be taken to determine timbre or sonorous individuality: it develops over time, and potentially very small measures of time (Hajda et al. 1997: 256, 262). In his pioneering late nineteenth-century work *On the Sensations of Tone*, Hermann Helmholtz argued that the onset and offset of a tone, as they last only a relatively short time, are less relevant to a discussion of timbre than the steady-state middle part of the timbral curve. He proposed to 'disregard these peculiarities of beginning and ending, and confine our attention to the peculiarities of the musical tone which continues uniformly' (2016: 67). Helmholtz's findings have become a standard premise for psychoacoustic research. Carl E. Seashore argued in 1938 that Helmholtz's notion of timbre offered a 'snapshot' of the steady-state portion of the musical signal. He proposed to focus timbral research on the 'successive changes and fusions that take place within a tone from moment to moment', an overall timbral approach to tone that he termed 'sonance' (Seashore 1967: 95, 103; cf. Hajda et al. 1997: 256). As such a median-based approach to timbre offers a conceptual stability that is useful in empirical experimentation, psychoacoustics still employs so-called 'long-term average spectra' (LTAS) as a basis for the frequency analysis of musical notes (Howard and Angus 2009: 233).

Because it focuses on the average frequency spectrum of a tone, LTAS cannot be used to investigate the transient aspects of timbre: the onset and offset of tones (which Helmholtz dismissed) are known to be of importance for the recognition of sound sources (Howard and Angus 2009: 233–4). Since the 1960s a significant amount of psychoacoustic research has been dedicated to the temporal progress of transient aspects of timbral frequency spectrums consisting of the attack, decay, sustain and release of a given sound. Together these transients form the note envelope or ADSR envelope, which determine the individual timbre of that sound to such an extent that taking any of the elements away renders it impossible to identify the sound source (Hajda et al. 1997: 266–78; IRCAM; Schaeffer 1952: 213–25; Schaeffer 2017: 216–31; Sethares 2005: 29–31; Tagg 2013: 277–9). The ADSR envelope can be precisely captured in wave forms and spectrograms, which visualize the spectral differences between various instrumental and vocal timbres as well as elements such as vibrato and vocal formants (Howard and Angus 2009: 234–42; Schaeffer 2017: 423–54). This technology helps map individual timbral difference, thus supporting the traditional difference-based definition of timbre with a database of evidence; it also helps identify the temporal differences between individual instrumental and vocal sounds, thus supporting the organological sound-source definition of timbre. It is also used in vocal pedagogy to help students understand the ways in which their voices shape sound (Yarnall 2017a: 575).

This immensely useful tool does have its shortcomings. Although the note envelope is able to identify the main instruments in the Hornbostel-Sachs classification, it is inadequate for the analysis and description of the blended sounds of electroacoustic composition and spectral music. In his 1994 article 'Defining timbre – Refining timbre', the composer and theorist Dennis Smalley notes the increasing problems that timbral research methodologies in psychoacoustics face in the context of electroacoustic music (Smalley 1994: 37, 43–4). He proposes a timbral definition based on (acoustic or electroacoustic) sound source: 'Timbre is a general, sonic physiognomy through which we identify sounds as emanating from a source, whether that source be actual, inferred or imagined' (Smalley 1994: 36). This appears to be an audacious move for an electroacoustic composer working in an era that has long ceased to privilege traditional timbres based on acoustic sound sources. His aim in doing so, however, is nothing less than saving the concept of timbre from extinction. Smalley's return to sound sources leads to a timbral recognizability that he terms 'source bonding' and without which, he states, the usefulness of timbre as a musical or sonic parameter itself disappears (Smalley 1994: 37):

> When source-cause slips into hiding, identity becomes problematic, even impossible. Timbral qualities become phantoms and phantasms. Personalised visions during the imminent level suggest circuitous, labyrinthine trails to wider generic identities and to the extrinsic matrix. The spectromorphological traces which inspire such trail-finding can no longer be parcelled up in generalised physiognomic packages. Timbre becomes the timbre complex, and the timbre complex splits open to reveal disparate lives: the timbral nucleus dissolves, seeping through musical discourse. In struggling to maintain a timbral essence we are indeed obliged to penetrate the very nature of musical discourse.
> (Smalley 1994: 47)

Smalley's conception of timbre incorporates the advantages of frequency spectrum and ADSR analysis in an adjustment of difference-based and organological timbral definitions. This can include as well as enhance electroacoustic methods of composing. In 1986 Smalley had coined the term 'spectromorphology' as a compositional and analytical method specifically aimed at morphing elements of the spectral envelope and frequency spectrum. With spectromorphology, new timbres can be developed and operationalized that would be difficult to classify in more traditional systems of sound source and pitch (Smalley 1986: 68–80).

Multidimensionality or unquantifiability?

Psychoacoustic experiments show that it is not possible to qualify timbre through just one set of dimensions: tone colours are perceived on various scales including the areas between soft and hard, pure and rich, compact and scattered, full and empty, static and dynamic, as well as 'cross-modal' – i.e. synaesthetic – elements such as dull and bright, cold and warm, colourful and colourless (Sethares 2005: 28–30). In order to capture as many as possible of these various scales of evaluation, 'multidimensional' approaches have been adopted. John M. Grey developed the 'timbre space' model of a multidimensional scale that set a new standard for the quantification of timbral perception (Grey 1977; cf. Hajda et al. 1997: 284–6). In timbre-space experiments, listeners are presented with a number of opposing verbal qualifiers such as the above, and are asked to listen to acoustic and synthesized sound with specified frequency spectrums: the test subjects grade their listening experience along this scale varying from very similar to very dissimilar (Grey 1977: 1270–1; McAdams and Giordano 2016: 114). The results are then outlined against each other using statistical algorithms so that a two- or three-dimensional representation of timbral perception qualifiers can be plotted (Grey 1977: 1271–2; cf. Bregman 1990: 123–6, 481–8; Slawson 1985: 51–90, 134–43). This type of multidimensional scaling offers a way to quantify and visualize the difference thesis. Other multidimensional experiments test the organological sound source thesis through a combination of frequency spectrum and note envelope analysis with perception research (McAdams and Giordano 2016: 116–17).

Timbre's multidimensionality renders it difficult to make categorical distinctions between individual tone colours such as those employed in organology, and this makes it in turn impossible to represent timbre by way of objective schemata comparable to diatonic scales (Hajda et al. 1997: 257, 262–4; Smalley 1994: 36). The goal of multidimensional timbre research, therefore, is not described as finding a new timbral definition or discourse, but as increasing the predictability and control of timbral perception (McAdams and Giordano 2016: 120).

The objectivity of quantitative experiments on the perception of timbral frequency spectrums and timbral note envelopes, however, is fundamentally impeded in two ways. First, there is the problem of subjective perception: the test subjects will each hear and assess the sounds with which they are presented in different ways and in different terms. Psychoacoustic literature readily admits this problem: research articles often begin or end with a statement about the researchers' awareness of the subjectivity of timbral perception, as well as of the experiments' exclusive concentration on those elements that *are* quantifiable, thus leaving the unquantifiable elements out of consideration (e.g. Holmes 2011: 303–5; Howard and Angus 2009: 252; McAdams and Giordano 2016: 121; Sethares 2005: 30; Slawson 1985: 91–3; Taylor and Campbell 2001: 8.ii). Smalley neatly summarizes this predicament of psychoacoustic timbre research in the question 'Whose timbre?' (Smalley 1994: 35–6; cf. Clarke 2005: 192–4).

The second methodological problem inhibiting the validity of this kind of psychoacoustic timbre research is the fact that outcomes are restricted by the ongoing incompatibility of timbre and language: test subjects are encouraged to liken their timbral experience to words, even though there is no adequate (everyday or academic) discursive structure in which to capture this experience. These words, moreover, although they are employed to measure subjective experiences, were not chosen by the test subjects themselves but were chosen for them by the researchers. As a result, these research outcomes tell us nothing more and nothing less than that test subjects ticked pre-set boxes outlining extra-musical qualifiers such as 'warm', 'hard' or 'colourful' to describe an individually experienced quality of music that is known to defy verbal precision (e.g. Howard and Tyrrell 1997; Holmes 2011; Slawson 1985: 91–164). The ambivalence inherent to human emotion is implicitly dismissed in favour of fixed, and unilaterally preconceived, pigeonholes. Rather than providing insight into the musical, affective and cultural performativity of frequency spectrums or note envelopes and their relation to the word-defying sonic quality of timbre, therefore, such outcomes shine a light on the researchers' linguistic surroundings, vocabulary, and the ways in which such prescribed discourse – much more than the sonic event that is under scrutiny – shapes perception (cf. Hajda et al. 1997: 259). Passing comments such as 'there exists evidence that language affects the way people think about objects' (Zacharakis et al. 2014: 347), although a rare and welcome breath of fresh air in this data-saturated field, hardly scratch the surface of what has long been an area of philosophical debate. In order to counter grammatical, syntactic and semantic interference with the outcomes of multidimensional timbre research, some research projects have been conducted in different languages (Zacharakis et al. 2014: 340–1). Adding ever more timbre descriptors in ever more languages, however, arguably only increases the linguistic confusion around timbral evaluations, with different outcomes for different languages (Zacharakis et al. 2014: 346–51). Rather than providing evidence for the consistencies and inconsistencies of timbral assessment, this approach demonstrates the decisive importance of the cultural embeddedness of timbre evaluations, a factor that is not addressed in quantitative research.

In response to both these fundamental methodological and interpretative problems in psychoacoustic timbre research, a certain amount of criticism has arisen from within the field of psychoacoustics itself (Hajda et al. 1997; Holmes 2011; Siedenburg et al. 2016). Kai Siedenburg and his fellow authors propose that researchers, prior to embarking on their experiments, ask themselves straightforward questions such as 'What kind of knowledge is pursued?' and, if, a cognitive component is involved, 'Is it based on subjective judgements … or absolute identification or classification?' (2016: 37–8). Perhaps if these questions are implemented in experimental methodologies, psychoacoustic research on timbre could offer insights into the larger issue – a truly 'multidimensional' definition of timbre that encompasses its various productive, perceptual and performative aspects. As it stands, the field raises more questions than it answers.

Because of its inherent contradiction of the (explicitly acknowledged) qualitative imprecision of subjective value judgements on the one hand, and the (equally explicitly acknowledged) quantitative probing of what is only part of the topic of research on the other, Michel Chion contends that psychoacoustics is 'a bizarre unit' (2016: 23; cf. Chapter 4). Without going so far as to dismiss it altogether, the usefulness of these psychoacoustic measurements can be seriously questioned. The experiments document, in non-sonic metaphors, what certain ears and certain subjectivities perceive in certain cultural contexts, but omit the fact that not all ears, subjectivities and cultures perceive the same thing – let alone evaluate it in any comparable manner – and they fail to illuminate how this perception is processed through musical and cultural contexts, and in which ways these metaphors are able to relate – if at all – to sonic perceptions. Psychoacoustic experimentation, in short, attempts to quantify a quality, and that is a challenging task at the very least.

Psychophysics and neurophysics

The perception of sound in general, and timbre specifically, by the human ear and brain is more objectively quantifiable than that assessed by listener subjectivity (leaving aside, for the moment, the entanglement of subjectivity and neuro-activity). Both types of sound perception have been extensively studied and offer insights into the ways in which vibrating sound waves carrying sonic energy are transmitted into the neuro-system as electronic signals. From the neuro-system, auditory data are processed as cognitive data, impetuses for movement, and communicative or emotional responses.

Psychophysics of the ear

The ear is a threefold system of vibrational energy conversion and transmission consisting of the outer, middle and inner ear (Howard and Angus 2009: 73–89; Howard and Tyrrell 1997: 65–7; Parker 2009: 28–33; Slawson 1985: 93–4).

The outer ear, which is the visible part of the ear, functions as a resonance chamber responding to acoustic vibrations. It reflects, refracts and diffracts sound waves as they come in. Auditory signals then pass through the auditory canal, the concha, to the eardrum or tympanic membrane, which is a fibrous and elastic interface that converts acoustic pressure variations into mechanical vibrations (Howard and Angus 2009: 74–6; Parker 2009: 29–30).

The middle ear, which houses the ossicle bones (malleus, incus and stapes, more commonly known as hammer, anvil and stirrup), has the double function of transmitting movement from the tympanic membrane to the inner ear and protecting the hearing system from loudness damage. The malleus and the incus form a miniature lever system that transports the acoustic vibrations moving the tympanic membrane as mechanical movement to the stapes, which then transmits this movement to the inner ear. In the process of this energy transmission, the velocity of vibration is balanced out by the sensitive ossicle bones to modify pressures from outer ear to inner ear and avoid energy loss (Howard and Angus 2009: 76–9; Parker 2009: 30–2).

The inner ear itself consists of the cochlea, a snail-shaped tube structure lined with perilymph fluid, which is set into motion by the movement of the middle ear stapes against the oval window at the base of the cochlea. The inner part of the cochlea houses the basilar membrane, which carries out frequency analyses of any input sounds while vibrating along with the perilymph lining of the cochlea. The organ of Corti, which consists of about 30,000 hair cells each containing 12 to 40 hair cilia, converts the mechanical vibrations transmitted by the middle ear into electronic nerve signals. The soft tectorial membrane that is stretched out over the cilia is connected to auditory nerves leading into the brain (Howard and Angus 2009: 79–89; Parker 2009: 32–3).

The human ear is not able to perceive all sounds, and it does not perceive all sounds exactly as they occur acoustically. The critical band in the ear for perceived frequencies is between 20 and 20,000 Hz, with the upper range dropping from the age of twenty to potentially as low as 8 Hz by the age of eighty. Sensitivity to sound amplitude and loudness is related to frequency perception, and similarly alters with ageing. The critical band filters frequency input, which has an impact on the perception of such musical elements as harmony and melody, dynamics and musical interaction, timbre and orchestration. Moreover, the critical band for frequency, amplitude and loudness informs the subjectivity of pitch, loudness and timbre perception (Howard and Angus 2009: 83–100, 142–50). Hearing, then, is just as subjective from a psychophysical perspective as it is from a psychoacoustic perspective, as it is tied to highly individual limits and variations.

Neurophysics of the brain

Curt Sachs notes in his organology that the sound of the glass organ, the short-lived Romantic instrument that is also known as the glass (h)armonica, can lead to nerve damage due to the high harmonics in its timbre. The armonica is a lost timbre that Sachs describes as 'supersensible and without essence' and that has been used, interestingly, in operatic 'mad scenes' such as that in Donizetti's *Lucia di Lammermoor* (Sachs 1930: 75, 77–8). This highly debatable but amusing part of organological history illustrates the connections between the human ear and the brain, emotional response to music and its historical repercussions for psychopathology.

The auditory nerve is connected to the auditory cortex, which is located on either side of the brain in the upper part of the temporal lobe. The electronic signals transmitted by the organ of Corti are transported to multiple areas in the auditory cortex which are organized according to frequency range, and which are active in the identification of musical pitch. Besides frequency classes, the auditory cortex also processes type of resonance, pitch class, rhythm and tempo, and timbral difference (Levitin 2006: 81–91, 264–5; Slawson 1985: 100–15, 120–34). The individual differences in musical perception, which are initiated by individual physiological differences in the human ear, are then enlarged by the fact that no two auditory cortices function in exactly the same way.

The neural processing in the auditory cortex immediately initiates large-scale cognitive, motor and limbic brain circuitry across the brain (Alluri et al. 2012; Reiterer et al. 2008: 4, 8; Levitin 2006: 264–5). Hearing music is known to trigger neural activity and neurochemical changes in all areas of the human brain, and to increase psychological and mental health and well-being (Chanda and Levitin 2013; Levitin 2006: 165–88). Timbre has a special place in these auditory neuro-processes. While auditory data in general are processed quickly in the brain, there is evidence that the perception of timbre is faster than the perception of, for instance, pitch (Plazak and Huron 2011). Timbral data are used to identify sound sources, sonic environments, location and navigation (Fales 2002: 61–3; Giordano and McAdams 2010); moreover, neuropsychological research suggests that timbre is instrumental in the affective processing of music (Hailstone et al. 2009; Levitin 2006: 235–6). When listening activity is visualized with the help of functional Magnetic Resonance Imaging (fMRI) equipment these timbral neuro-processes can be studied in more detail. fMRI analyses show that while the frequency spectrum and loudness aspects of musical timbre are processed slightly more actively in the right hemisphere of the brain, other aspects such as timbral differentiation and temporal analysis pertaining to the ADSR envelope are processed in the left hemisphere (Reiterer et al. 2008: 2, 4–5). Moreover, these analyses reveal the activation of the language centre in the brain called Broca's area when test subjects were asked to perform timbral tasks pertaining to language such as the discrimination of timbral changes in relation to phonemes and vowels (Reiterer et al. 2008: 1, 7–8). Timbre, thus, appears to be just as diffuse and ambiguous on a neural level as it is on acoustic, psychoacoustic and psychophysical levels: all we know is that it operates in various dimensions, and that its precise operationality and processing is subject to individual differences.

To complicate timbral matters further, research on auditory neuropathways has shown that while the ear and the brain often work in tandem, there are also certain discrepancies between the two kinds of aural data processing. The brain may sometimes 'deceive' the ear: in cases of simultaneous and sometimes binaural frequencies, notes and timbres, the brain will tell the subject that illusory frequencies and timbres are heard which do not originate in the actual acoustic situation but are an effect of ear-brain interaction (Deutsch 1998; Howard and Angus 2009: 258–74; Levitin 2006: 95–108; Sethares 2005: 49–50; Slawson 1985: 94–100, 149–51). These effects often have elusive names: Bregman's timbrally fused 'chimeric percepts' and Diana Deutsch's 'octave illusion' are famous examples of the fascination that the subjectivity of sound perception still holds even in the most empirical of research domains (Bregman 1990: 44–60; Deutsch 1974). Besides the observation that ears and brains are literally individually wired, this type of auditory illusion provides evidence that the perceiving subjectivity which impedes psychoacoustic research on timbre runs deep, and that this is hard (if not itself illusory) to compensate by the statistical averages that timbre-space scaling seeks to achieve. It is based on such observations that Cornelia Fales has proposed that timbre is a perceptual 'paradox' (2002).

But how objective and how complete can neurophysical timbre research be? Like psychoacoustic research, neuroscientific experiments are conducted on the basis of unqualified timbre definitions (Alluri et al. 2012: 3677; Reiterer et al. 2008: 2). Because of the cost associated with these experiments, they are often carried out with very few test subjects, and repeat experiments are often restricted due to the same financial reasons. The tests themselves, moreover, are able to identify aural brain activity, but not aural processing, interpretation or cultural embedding: instead, researchers revert to listener feedback consisting of the same preconceived metaphors that are used in psychoacoustics. Hearing is a fundamentally untrustworthy sense, and neurophysics is able, at best, to offer objective evidence of its subjectivity.

Ecology

Coming to the end of this chapter, which has explored the various material elements involved in timbre production, timbre acoustics and timbre perception, it has become clear that all three areas are highly unstable, and that any quantifications of them can only be considered reflections of their subjectivity (cf. Fales 2005: 157–9). Is it possible at all to conduct research on timbre, let alone to define it? In view of the expansive and expanding list of factors that contribute – each in their own, decisive way – to the production, the materiality, the sound, the perception, the neuroscience and the interpretation of timbre, any attempt at a working definition would have to comprise all of its components and dimensions. Timbre is a single and singular sound event that in itself consists of a multiplicity of contributing factors, and any theory of timbre should be multifaceted and dynamic enough to encompass the manifold material, perceptual and aesthetic complexities of this phenomenon.

A useful way of thinking about timbre is offered by Eric F. Clarke's 'ecology of listening' (2005; cf. Hajda et al. 1997: 266, 300). Adapting the notion of affordances that James J. Gibson developed for the analysis of visual perception to a musical context, Clarke proposes to consider musical entities such as instruments, tonality and keys, production technology, as well as listeners, as offering affordances such as playing, melodic and harmonic development, virtual environments, and music-related subject positions (2005: 36–8; Gibson 1986: 127–37). This approach enables a view of music not only as an integrated part of its cultural, technological and social environment but also allows insight into the ways in which music functions within and, importantly, *with* that environment. Clarke's ecological definition of musical perception diverges sharply from that of psychoacoustics. He criticizes psychoacoustics' reliance on arbitrary metaphors and its negation of the differences between attentive and inattentive listening, habituated and unconscious listening, analytic and random listening (2005: 192-3). Instead of the psychoacoustic idea that listening experiences can be captured by way of post-factum adjectives attributed by recipients of preselected examples, Clarke proposes a dynamic definition of musical perception as a form of 'resonance' that is 'not passive: it is a perceiving organism's active exploratory engagement with its environment' which is operative through the ecological triad of perception, learning, and adaptation (ibid.: 19, 20-5). Listeners, he argues, are part of a musical ecosystem, and as such they are in continuous interaction with musical and technological entities in a mutual exchange of affordances that can play out on cultural, social and emotional planes: perceptual systems, in this view, are marked not by passivity and stasis but by constant change and 'plasticity' (ibid.: 25).

Clarke's approach has proved fruitful in a number of areas of musicology and has been employed, among others, by Allan F. Moore in analyses of studio recording and the perception of popular music (2012: 12-16, 243-8). The notion of musical ecology is also a useful tool to conceptualize the heterogeneous agencies involved in timbral production and perception. If we consider timbre as a musical ecology in and of itself – as the spectral composers of the 1970s did (cf. Grisey 2000: 2; Cendo 2010) – the manifold interactions between instrumental and vocal sound sources, acoustic surroundings, studio production, human physiology and neurology, and the various social, cultural and emotional interpretations charted by psychoacoustics fall into place. 'Timbre is an inconsistent amalgam of various data … There is not "a" piano timbre', Michel Chion asserts (2016: 173): piano timbres – plural – are not a given, but they emerge from their ecological contexts and engagements (cf. Fink, Wallmark and Latour 2018: 9).

My aesthetic experience of Petra Noskaiová's vocal timbre in the 'Benedicamus' performance in Leipzig, and the recording of that timbre on the *Cathedrals* CD, cannot be ascribed to any single source or agency: it is the variable outcome of the simultaneous interactions happening in each of the listening situations. In the live situation, Noskaiová's timbre emerged between her singing physiology, the acoustics of the Leipzig Schauspielhaus, the cultural environment of the *Wave-Gotik-Treffen*, the social environment of the Goth subculture, my auditory physiology and the way in which that was coloured by my own subjective, musical and cultural background. In the recorded situation, the theatre acoustics are replaced by studio recording and production, the listening situation is replaced by my headphones, and the social and cultural situation depend on where I am and how I am feeling. In both cases, both Noskaiová and I are part of an organic and complex ecosystem that entangles a multitude of factors in a multitude of ways (cf. Clarke 2005: 22). In both cases, timbre – both on the micro-ecological level of sound production and on the macro-ecological level of sound perception – is the singular outcome of these complex interactions.

This brief overview of the VocaMe ecology, however, also makes it evident that one aspect of timbre is still missing from the timbral ecologies outlined in this chapter: timbre's musical context, both in terms of composition and performance, adds a significant facet to its micro-ecology. From the perspective of composition, the concrete sound of a timbre depends on its place in musical design. Orchestrational context can change timbre: a solo violin produces a slightly different sonority than the fused timbre of a violin section in a chamber music or symphonic ecosystem. Musical texture, too, impacts on timbre: for instance, the choral voices in Ligeti's *Requiem*, with its thick, saturated texture, have a very different timbre than the choral voices in Lassus's 'Ave Regina Coelorum', with its transparent polyphonic lines (cf. McAdams and Goodchild 2017). In the VocaMe 'Benedicamus', the lucid organum texture of the composition, with the lower voices and hurdy-gurdy moving mostly in homophonous falsobordone blocks, creates a harmonious ground over which Noskaiová's mezzo soprano floats and explores the limits of timbral expression in soloistic extravagance. This purely musical micro-ecological building block of her timbre contributes to my aesthetic experience in at least as crucial a measure as the materiality of her vocal instrument and of studio acoustics.

From the micro-ecological perspective of performance, the concrete sound of a timbre depends on a number of factors besides the materiality of the sound source producing it. 'What physics represents as the sum of sine waves is heard as the character of a sound in all its specificity', says Aden Evens, and this includes specific performative qualia as well as quantifiable properties: 'the middle C of a Steinway and not a Bösendorfer, the bowing technique of Yo-Yo Ma and no other. The "sound" of a sound is its timbre, which contracts its multi-layered complexity into a distinctive quality' (Evens 2005: 5–6). As the example of Yo-Yo Ma's bowing technique illustrates, aspects of articulation have a major impact on timbral outcome: the use of vibrato and coloratura, staccato and legato, portamento and glissando, crescendo and diminuendo, violin *sul tasto* or pizzicato can each change the timbre of an instrument or voice (cf. Holmes 2011: 309–13). Although these timbral variations only occur in fleeting moments and cannot be easily measured and captured, or indeed reproduced, they are crucial for timbral perception. Their ephemerality, indeed, arguably contributes to their aesthetic impact. Noskaiová's evanescent use of portamento, articulation and dynamics was mentioned earlier; in a similar way, it is the almost casual passing through a series of subtle vocal portamentos and flutters (next to the ever so slightly, but somehow forgivably flat violin glissandi) that renders Dolly Parton's performance of 'Jolene' inimitable and unforgettable. Pierre Schaeffer, as one of the few researchers to recognize the importance of these performative factors for timbre, classifies these invariables in the aptly named timbral subcategory of 'allure' (2017: 437–8, 443–6).

Performative timbral blend (closely related to, but even more ephemeral than compositional timbral blend) is a micro-ecological aspect of tone colour that is entirely dependent on musical contingencies. There is an incidental magic about the coming together of individual voices or instruments whose frequency spectrums and musical intuitions resonate and harmonize. The female voices and Renaissance instruments that together constitute VocaMe's remarkable sound are a result of this performance ecological interaction; a similar effect was achieved when Dolly Parton, Emmylou Harris and Linda Ronstadt decided to sing Appalachian mountain songs together on their 1987 collaborative project *Trio*. The success of that album was due only in part to the three singers' accumulated fame: it was the incidental fact of timbral blend that made this project stand out over their solo work. The mixture of their three vocal timbres added an unexpected extra depth to each of their own – each exceptionally accomplished, each supremely suitable to this particular type of song, and yet each very differently coloured – voices. A soprano, a mezzo soprano and an alto voice created an unpredictably rich timbral micro-ecology: three timbres blended into one emergent new timbre.

Timbre, thus, can be understood both as part of a cultural, social and perceptual macro-ecosystem, and it constitutes a productive, acoustic and musical micro-ecosystem in and of itself, and both these dimensions of timbral ecology consist of continually interactive entities (cf. Chapter 4 for an analysis of this timbral interaction). It is impossible to understand timbre as a fixed or static object: travelling between sound source, acoustics, the ear, the brain, and social, cultural and subjective contexts, and adapting itself along the way, timbre is changeable, nomadic and fluid. Its singularity is located, precisely but ungraspably, in the chance outcome of each ecological interaction.

Timbre: A working definition

Each of the sections in this chapter has shown that timbre, as a music-aesthetic phenomenon, connects concrete quantifiable facts and ephemeral qualia. The elusive quality of sonorous difference can be described as instrumental materiality, but organology needs adjectives such as 'soft, dreamy, warm' (Sachs 1930: 274) to complete its descriptions. Timbre is meticulously produced and modified in actual and virtual acoustic environments, but acoustic design and studio production lack an adequate vocabulary to discuss the quality around which all its efforts revolve (Moylan 2007: 157). Psychoacoustics acknowledges the incontestable subjectivity of timbral perception and reverts to metaphoric circumlocution to assess it; and the psychophysics and neurophysics of timbre provide physical evidence that the perception of timbre is not just individually variable, but often untrustworthy.

It is impossible to construct a concise and unambiguous definition of timbre. Tone colour can only be described as always, and necessarily, contingent and emergent. It results from an incidental ecological convergence of heterogeneous circumstances including sound source materiality, actual and virtual acoustic circumstances, frequency spectrums and duration, physiological and neural perception, and musical and performative contingencies. The resulting sonic event is unpredictable, unstable and unrepeatable: it changes over time, it shares variables with other sonic phenomena but is significantly marked by invariables, and it is absolutely context-dependent. My first attempt at a working definition of timbre must therefore be accompanied by a list of paradoxes:

1. The material origin and the much-less-material interpretation of timbre are entwined.
2. Timbre is an objective quantity *and* a subjective quality.
3. Timbre is an ecological multiplicity *and* an unrepeatable singularity.

At the root of these paradoxes is the inseparability of timbre's materiality in production and its less material aspects in perception; the *technè* of timbral creation versus the ephemerality of timbral experience (cf. Hajda et al. 1997: 302). In the following chapters I will explore the paradoxical simultaneity of these apparent opposites in timbral aesthetics. I will begin my exploration, in the next chapter, with the non-sonic, subjective metaphors that are used even in the area most attached to objective quantitative data, psychoacoustics. Why does the statement 'this is a warm saxophone timbre' convey so much more than the observation 'this is a saxophone timbre'? VocaMe's work has received accolades such as 'angel voices' and 'the sound of light' in the international press (VocaMe). Such colourful metaphors are not used in acoustic or psychoacoustic research on timbral perception, but they are far more appropriate than 'breath control', 'female' or 'warm', as they convey the apparent audience consensus that the ensemble's voices reach for the sublime. What is the elusive *something* that metaphor adds to objective observation, and how does it relate to the undeniably material sonority of timbre?

2

Index, icon, grain

As timbre lacks a clear and concise objective definition, most communication about the phenomenon takes the linguistic detour of subjectively coloured metaphors. Such timbral imagery and its relations to sonic, musical and extra-musical identities and significations can fruitfully be explored through the Peircean semiotics of index, icon and symbol. Timbre can function as an index for a sound source: the grinding timbre at the beginning of Black Sabbath's 'Iron Man' points to its own origin, a 1964 Gibson SG guitar with a Dallas-Arbiter Rangemaster treble booster pedal. Timbre can also be an icon that denotes an aspect of both source and sound: Tony Iommi's guitar timbre could be said to share the metallic quality and strength of iron with the protagonist in the song's lyrics, and is therefore a sonic metaphor. Timbre can, moreover, function as a symbol that connotes associations: the guitar tends to be seen as a masculine instrument, so the song's lyric protagonist must be masculine too (cf. Shadrack 2017b).

Timbral metaphor, as a linguistic construction describing a sonic phenomenon, often functions in a slightly different way to its literary counterpart. In many cases the symbolic connotation of a timbre seems to return to timbral sound sources: in the case of 'Iron Man', this would happen if listeners assume that the guitarist who is able to produce such a sound must himself also be strong as iron and masculine as a superhero (cf. Walser 1993: 1–3, 116). In this way, timbral symbols can reveal the conventions from which the symbolic associations originate. These can appear irrational and even random when unpacked: the instrument sounds metallic (?), iron's main quality is that it is strong (?), this strength is a quality that iron shares with men (??), guitars and superheroes are as masculine as iron (??), and so it is perfectly logical to assume that the guitar itself, the guitarist and the Iron Man, and by extension the other band members are all as strong and masculine as iron (???).

This chapter argues that the use of tone colour imagery – even if it is often irrational and random – has distinct advantages over organological and empirical definitions of timbre. And there are certain aspects of timbre that continue to seep through even the multifarious cracks left open by metaphor. The ways in which timbre exceeds metaphors pointing to sound source or connotation are investigated through a reading of Roland Barthes's 'grain of the voice' and Mladen Dolar's vocal *objet petit a*.

Timbral index: From 'the real me' to *plus-de-c(h)oeur*

Indexing the real me

In July 2016, one of the world's largest banks announced that it was going to use voice recognition as a biometric method for customer identification and security (Belton 2016). Besides speech patterns and intonation, timbre is the key ingredient for such a 'voiceprint', which is as unique to individuals as fingerprints (Belton 2016; cf. Yarnall 2017a: 568–9). Vocal timbre can identify the person that produces it by virtue of its unique physical properties. The shape of someone's pharynx, the muscles around her larynx, the condition of her diaphragm, the thickness of her tongue, the shape and position of her teeth, the size of her head cavities, her torso musculature: all of these factors together create a singular sonorous convergence of wave forms, formants and harmonics – so singular, indeed, that it can be used as an official identifier (cf. Howard 2005). The uniqueness of vocal timbre, moreover, is not just a quantitative personal identifier. Singing pedagogy recognizes that timbre is also an important qualifier of vocal self-identity: singers have been documented describing the development, training and maturation of their vocal timbre as a journey towards 'the "real" me', which can be read here as a singer's 'real' voice, a timbre inalienably hers (Yarnall 2017a: 571, 577–8).

Not only human voices possess a timbral fingerprint. An oboe timbre is identifiable as 'oboe' because the particularities of its material, shape and mechanics lead to a sound distinct from other instruments. Each individual oboist, moreover, will use her own body to produce breathing, embouchure and fingering, which generates an 'oboeprint' unique to this instrumentalist (cf. Howard and Angus 2009: 232–3). In a more layered form of timbral identity, each studio producer will generate a 'sonicprint' of unique timbral qualities such as live room acoustics and isolation panels, microphone use and amplification, equalizing, compression and reverb, all of which identify the 'sound' of an individual producer or a particular studio (Camilleri 2010: 210).

The physical circumstances leading to timbral difference afford a timbrally demarcated form of sonic identity (McAdams 2001: iii). In Charles S. Peirce's semiotic terms, therefore, timbre can work as an index to sound source. The materiality of a timbre helps us identify aspects of its origin: we can distinguish brass from woodwind through their bright versus husky timbres; we can tell from Nat King Cole's gravelly voice that he smoked cigarettes; we can identify the timbres of LinnDrum machines in Prince's early work. A material approach to timbre based on such physical properties has inspired important methodological innovations in musicology. Allowing a movement away from score analysis, materialist phenomenology affords a turn towards the musicking body that was overlooked in traditional musicological approaches. It has led to significant insights regarding the political performativity of gendered, ethnic and queer voices (e.g. Abbate 1993, Bonenfant 2010; Eidsheim 2015; Middleton 2006). Extending such an anthropocentric carnal phenomenology to non-human voices, Don Ihde argues that 'every material thing has a voice' (Ihde 2007: 190). Analysing the sound of striking a wooden lectern with a knuckle alongside the sound of an oboe within that of an orchestra, Ihde observes that the voices of things index their materiality, their shapes and internal dimensions. He argues that all of these should be considered identities, but explicitly non-human and non-textual identities:

> The voices of things are not the voices of language. For what the voices of things bespeak is a kind of direct sound of their natures: materiality, density, interiority, relations within experienced space, outward hollows and shapes; complex, multidimensioned, often unheard in potential richness, but spoken in the voices of things.
>
> (Ihde 2007: 192)

From these observations Ihde concludes that timbre, which he terms 'expressivity', represents 'the *who* of voice' (Ihde 2007: 195). The physical origins of timbre, in this theory, convey a clear material identity: strings are the identity of stringed instruments, wood is that of woodwinds, and metal is that of brass instruments. These timbral identities can be understood and employed as forms of indexical 'sonic signs' in Jean-Jacques Nattiez's sonic adjustment of Peirce's categories (Nattiez 1990: 3–8). Sonic signs have no relation to language, and offer a way of understanding musical communication on a purely sound-based level.

Emily Dolan has compellingly demonstrated how Joseph Haydn's sensitivity to instrumental sonorities was crucial for the development of orchestration as a timbral form of art (2013: 90–135). She argues that Haydn's vision of instruments as 'characters' led to the employment of timbral identity in the creation of a 'republic of sound' in the eighteenth-century orchestra in which each voice could be heard individually (ibid.: 148, 136–79). From at the latest the mid-eighteenth century on, in this view, composers were able to allocate certain identities – however non-linguistic and however undefined beyond a purely sonic level – to their works through the defining act of choosing orchestration. A work for string quartet has a different 'identity' from a work for woodwind quartet due to the organizing choice of instruments, and an aria for alto produces a different sonic sign from an aria for bass. This compositional allocation of sonic identities through orchestration became ever more varied over the course of the nineteenth century, as the symphonic orchestra's colours increased exponentially (cf. Dolan 2013: 211–57). Musical impressionism and expressionism further explored the abstract complexities of such sonic identities, with timbral choices focused more and more on intangible qualities such as colour, temperature or touch (Fleury 1996: 117–37). This development ultimately culminated in Schoenberg's 'tone colour melody', in which timbral identity existed only on the ephemeral, and metaphorical, level of colour: more strongly than instrumental materialism, it was now the abstract connotations evoked by sonorous qualities that defined a timbre (cf. Chapter 3).

The indexical definition of timbre thus gradually gave way to a much more elusive, and much less firmly grounded, form of sonic identity based on metaphorical notions such as colour. This development away from a definition of timbre as a materially fixed identity illustrates the instability of timbral ontology based on indexicality, an ontology whose flaws were definitively disclosed by the timbral agency of sound technology.

Im/possibilities of the *objet sonore*

Chapter 1 introduced the ways in which the development of sound technology as a twentieth-century compositional tool led to further diminution of indexical timbral identity (for an empirical approach to this problem cf. Fales 2005). Sound technology highlights the problems inherent to notions of timbre-as-index in at least three ways.

First, the fact of recorded sound produces what R. Murray Schafer has termed 'schizophonia', the separation of sound from sound origin that leaves the physical index for a sonic sign absent from its aural occurrence (1994: 90–1). It is for schizophonic reasons that Friedrich Kittler asserts that the gramophone robbed voice of its physical identity: when the source of sound is absent, its indexical identity disappears also, and so '[n]obody knows who is singing' (1999: 37). But Kittler still called it voice, which implies that even a sound without origin must have, in Ihde's terms, a *'who'* (2007: 195), a certain sonic identity, although that *who* appears as physically removed. In his Lacanian approach to media theory, Kittler attributes this absent identity to the psychoanalytic realm of the 'impossible Real' (1999: 46).

Kittler's polarization of sonic identity into either direct presence or absolute absence is problematic. Recording technology proves simply that sonic physicality is not as straightforward as acoustic sound seems to suggest: in schizophonia, the material origin of a sound appears to be at a remove from its aural manifestation. That remove certainly complicates, but does not eradicate, all-too direct notions of timbral indexicality: with the cause of sound removed, its 'who' or 'what' may not always be clearly identifiable but is evidently in existence. The indexicality-by-proxy of recorded sound causes unease. The discomfort of hearing sound without a clear index demonstrates that perceptions of sonic materiality are often tied to symbolic framing: the importance of being able to name a sound's index helps listeners grasp it, to let the symbolic structure of language control its ephemeral presence. Without a name, without the symbolic order, our grasp of the phenomenon slips, and we ascribe it to the uneasiness of the 'impossible Real'. But the trouble is that sound and music – whether recorded or acoustic – are neither restricted to material presence nor to intangible absence. And because of that paradoxical ontological position, they are able (much like the *objet petit a*, which is discussed below), to both conform to and elude symbolic coding, to both defy and allude to the Lacanian Real (cf. Cox 2011: 153–5). Schizophonia does nothing more and nothing less than bring this sonic paradox to the foreground.

The second problem pertaining to timbral indexing that sound technology has brought to attention is the instability of timbre-as-identity. If it is already evident from both acoustic practice and scientific measurement that it is impossible to achieve 'a' piano, string or vocal timbre (Chion 2016: 173; Schaeffer 2017: 33–45; Smalley 1994: 37–8; cf. Chapter 1), this knowledge is further strengthened by the endless heterogeneity of technologically enhanced timbre (Schaeffer 2017: 36–7). Studio technology is able to manipulate and distort recorded timbres. We can change reverb tails to obfuscate acoustic setting as a recognizable property of timbral identity, which can alter our identification of a rock singer into that of an opera-orientated singer, as is the case in the reception of Within Temptation's singer Sharon den Adel, whose vocals are always treated with generous reverb. We can also alter sound waves so that pitch becomes an irrelevant factor as a timbral attribute, as is the case in underground electronic dance music which often uses timbre as a rhythmical agent whose pitch plays no real role in the compositional outline of tracks (Perevedentseva 2018; cf. Fales 2005: 160–1): think of the pounding timbres in dubstep, dark industrial or deathstep as examples. And we can distort frequency spectrums in such a way that human voices sound machinic. In this case some listeners may attribute a machinic indexical identity to them, as has become commonplace at least since the Daleks in *Dr Who*: but rather than confirming the existence of an integral sonic essence, that practice betrays an essentialist desire to attribute indexical identity on the part of listeners. At most, the technological manipulation of timbre provides timbral indexing with new parameters: the identification of timbre through sound source now includes not just instrumental but also technological indexes. Again, the desire to discern indexes must not be confused with the existence of stable sonic identities. In Jimi Hendrix's 'Voodoo Child (Slight Return)', for instance, we do not just hear a right-hand Fender Stratocaster restrung for the left hand, but also two cross-wired Marshall Super Lead 1959 amplifiers, a 1968 King Vox-Wah pedal, and a Fuzz Face pedal. Even with the precise set-up, however, it can still be hard to recreate the 'Hendrix' timbre, which was identifiable but far from stable even within the artist's own oeuvre. And if we add Chas Chandler's studio production to the live sound, the ecological layeredness of the timbral index becomes more complex and less clearly identifiable. Who is to say that what we hear here is a guitar timbre at all, or that the sound indexes any concrete material source? Is this one source or are there many? How relevant is the identity of sound source at all for the timbres in this track?

The third and perhaps most important technological complication of timbral indexing is the fact that sound technology enables the creation of completely new, machine-made timbres that bear no relation whatsoever to acoustic timbres, not even manipulated ones (cf. Schaeffer 2017: 36–9). With this technological affordance, the search for timbral index loses any bearing. It moves from irrelevant to outright ludicrous in the case of, for instance, Asche's dark industrial track 'Doom' or Marcus Schmickler's laptop composition

'Rekursi'. These digital works both present pulsations of unknown sounds that transform every possibility of melody, harmony and rhythm to a plane of timbral immanence in which prior parameters are long forgone. It does not matter which digital technology produced these sounds, which human programmed the sonic vectors at work here, whether these timbres should be considered information or matter, or to which particular republic of sound they may contribute – 'Doom' is popular on Goth dance floors, 'Rekursi' appeared on a CD accompanying a collection of essays on the Deleuzo-Guattarian implications of electronic sound (Kleiner and Szepanski 2003). The question of these timbres' indexes, identities and appropriations is more than just beside the point. Both tracks are propelled forward by the singular agency of timbre, and that driving force does not point back to a material origin, but rather affords an ongoing motion. Timbre here is no longer a static material identity tied to origin, but comprises an ever-evolving, not necessarily material, becoming.

The obfuscation of timbral materiality and index is arguably the greatest revolution of twentieth-century Western music, and one that was almost entirely afforded by sound technology. Sound synthesis changed the sound of music forever: 'With synthesizers', Jean-François Lyotard notes, 'musicians have access to an infinite continuum of sound-nuances' (1991: 141). While the rich outcomes of the technological timbre revolution have been celebrated across genres of 'art' and 'popular' music, it has also substantially complicated the epistemology of timbre – or perhaps it has revealed that that epistemology was always more complex than we thought it was (cf. Dolan 2013: 53–89). With the schizophonic, destabilizing and rhizomatic affordances of sound technology explicating the always-already immaterial, unstable and vectral aspects of timbre, it is no longer possible to think timbre-as-index only (cf. Evens 2005: 1–24). But neither is it possible, conversely, to understand it as a completely sourceless manifestation of the Lacanian Real or another form of immaterial absolute, or as lacking any stability at all, or as immanence alone. Timbre *does* have material sources, and they *are* audible, whether we recognize them or not. Sound technology simply highlights the problematic fact – as already observed in the discussion of Curt Sachs's organology in Chapter 1 – that hearing timbre also exceeds those sources, and thereby appears to exceed traditional materiality.

The ambiguity and complexity of material timbral identity that are at the heart of this paradox drove Pierre Schaeffer's endeavours to achieve a pure electronic sound that was to be free from connotations. In the diary-like document *À la Recherche d'une Musique Concrète*, Schaeffer details his timbral quest – 'j'emporte des timbres' (1952: 12) – outside the 'great monotony' of explicit sonic identity (ibid.: 12–14). 'Sonorous material itself possesses an inexhaustible fertility', he states, but this fertility can only be achieved when sound is stripped of all the accumulated clutter of traceable origin and acquired connotation (ibid.: 23). Frustrated, Schaeffer complains that such unspoilt timbres are hard to find, and he famously set out to create them himself. He stripped the attack and decay elements of the tone envelope that lead to instrumental identification in order to get to the 'body' of a timbral object (ibid.: 213–25; Schaeffer 2017: 164–89, 424–30). Schaeffer's experiments eventually led him to the development, in his *Traité des Objets Musicaux*, of the *objet sonore*: a timbral object that is liberated from the identifying constrictions of its physical origin (2017: 15–17, 33–4, 205–19). 'Doom' and 'Rekursi' could be described as ever-evolving *objets sonores*, and one imagines that Schaeffer would have been quite happy with Asche's and Schmickler's timbral experiments.

Schaeffer's ontologies and taxonomies of sound contradict themselves at many points. The *objet sonore* can be revealed in what Schaeffer calls 'acousmatics', which is pure sound without a discernible origin and whose key characteristic is timbre (2017: 64–9). Acousmatic sound can be approached through a 'reduced listening' to the phenomenological epoché of sound alone: this would enable a perception of sound as an *objet sonore*, as sourceless timbre only (ibid.: 276–84; cf. Kane 2014: 36–7). While it is difficult to think of phenomenological circumstances that would permit such an epoché, acousmatic sound is a problematic, oxymoronic concept in and of itself. Acousmatics seeks to exclude the material conditions inherent to the ontology of sound but at the same time claims to be based on 'one material cause' (Schaeffer 2017: 66): acousmatic listening, in this way, is somehow both a materialist phenomenology and an idealism that wishes to leave 'sound in-itself' intact.

On this paradoxical premise, Schaeffer considers timbre ontologically either as identity or as sonorous cause (ibid.: 41–5, 232–43). While looking to move beyond indexical timbral identity by way of the *objet sonore*, he simultaneously confirmed the existence of such an identity through the same causal listening that he aimed to replace by a new, non-causal and non-interpretative kind of listening. His reduced listening posits a decontextualized hearing which listens to 'sound' alone – meaning specifically timbre – without any reference to cause, affect or meaning (ibid.: 109, 212–14, 279–80; cf. Chion 2016: 169–73). Schaeffer expresses the wish that the reduced listener will no longer be a 'prisoner of timbres' (Schaeffer 2017: 282). The reader, meanwhile, is the prisoner of

Schaeffer's contradictions: she is to listen to material causes but un-identify them, she is to hear timbre-in-itself but unhear it as a sonic entity.

The ontological and phenomenological problems with Schaeffer's approach become most evident in those cases where the composer finds it difficult to free himself from timbral connotation, meaning and identity. He was recorded on French radio in 1968 saying that

> [w]e learned to associate the lute with the Middle Ages, plainsong with the monastery ... the viola da gamba with courtly dress. How can we really not expect to also find that music in the twentieth century relates to machines and masses, the electron and calculators?

As a result of its many inherent problems, Schaeffer's project has met with harsh criticism. Brian Kane outright dismisses the 'improvised ontology' of Schaeffer's early writing (Kane 2014: 16–17, 30–3), Nattiez asserts that the *Traité* 'precipitates us backwards into that old, nasty, normative rut of traditional musicology' (1990: 97), and Seth Kim-Cohen repeatedly rebukes Schaeffer for his 'essentialism' (2009: 29, 127; cf. Kane 2014: 39) – the same essentialism that motivates the attribution of timbral identities to non-human voices such as that of the Daleks. In binary readings of timbral materiality such as Schaeffer's, the physicality of sound is taken as a form of identity: because timbre indexes the material body that produces it, that body is considered the identity of timbre. Schaeffer aimed to supersede such materialist essentialism through an idealist striving for a timbral Thing-in-itself (cf. Kim-Cohen 2009: 243–4; cf. Chapter 3 below for a more extensive discussion of timbral idealism in Schaeffer and others) but was continuously stopped in his tracks by the materiality that is undeniably and persistently present in timbre.

Although it is important to recognize the problems raised by Schaeffer's attempts to bypass timbral materiality, his endeavours make a telling case for the complexities of the subject. In a remarkably nuanced reading of Schaeffer's work, Michel Chion notes that the theory of the *objet sonore* does not 'hide its contradictions, putting front and center the entire problem of the dialectics of listening' (2016: 186). By doing so, Schaeffer implicitly acknowledged that timbral performativity is neither only material nor entirely immaterial, as it moves from an ontic into a phenomenological realm which includes less obviously material aspects such as the memory of earlier hearings of a timbre. Chion's own 'acoulogy', in an attempt to move away from this problem, aims to extract the sound-object from the confines of Schaefferian reduced listening (ibid.: 191–2). A strictly material acoulogy would be problematic, as phenomenology of listening does not only affect the ear but also other senses and, moreover, does not only play out in the material but also in the less material realm (ibid.: 192–211).

Following the lines of Chion's acoulogy, I would suggest that timbre, as a particular aspect of sound, should not be studied in its materiality alone (cf. Chapter 4 for a timbral acoulogy). A reduction of timbre to materiality – as well as, on the opposite side of the spectrum, a reduced listening to timbre 'in-itself' – is impossible for the three reasons outlined above: even schizophonic timbre does not lose any of its material or immaterial performativity; timbre is not stable and not traceable to a static source; and its organic, inherent changeability renders the question of physical origin irrelevant. On the basis of its material instability, Chion goes on to dismiss timbre altogether as a useful analytical category, but that seems as radical a notion as Kittler's reverting to the 'impossible real' (Chion 2011; Chion 2016: 174). Rather than dismissing either timbre's materiality or timbre altogether because of their instability, I would argue that the seemingly unsolvable problem of timbral materiality and indexicality invites nuanced, non-binary approaches. There is no point in denying the ontological and epistemological validity of timbral materiality, just as there is no point denying those validities of timbre's less material aspects. The materiality of timbre, however, although it can be understood as an index to sonic origin, cannot be equated with causal identity: not because timbre is (or should be) an intangible *objet sonore*, but because such a reading does not take into account other, equally important aspects of the timbral experience.

The paradoxes embedded in timbral indexicality and identity as they were highlighted through twentieth-century electronic and digital music, moreover, necessitate a rethinking of timbral identity prior to, and separate from, the presence of music technology: if all of this is true for electronic timbres, the validity of these considerations should also be tested for acoustic timbres. If the sonic quality of timbre is not solely dependent on the source that produces it or on the medium that transmits it, how can we define instrumental or vocal timbre beyond 'clarinet' or 'alto'? With voice, moreover, there is an added layer of difficulty: the person producing a timbre becomes, in popular perception, part of what constitutes material timbral identity. The identity of vocal timbre is often seen as comprising not just the material source of that timbre – the body of the singer, their vocal tract, breath control and so on – but also the subjectivity of the singer, their personality, personal history and cultural background. Sometimes this is also the case for instrumental and electronic timbres, as the brief discussion of Black Sabbath's 'Iron Man' in the introduction to this chapter shows. In such timbral assessments, material identity is taken a step further than sound source alone: timbre's sonic 'identity', problematic as that concept is when understood through indexing alone, now also appears to include the material context of that sound source. If it is impossible to define timbral identity as index, how should we interpret such widespread notions?

Beyond indexes

The problems arising through the conflation of timbre, sound source and personal identity can be demonstrated by means of a comparison between the practice and reception of singing 'original' and 'cover' versions. These concepts are revealing in and of themselves. The notion of an 'original version' is based on an indefensible definition of the musical work based on the formalist idea of *Werktreue* (cf. Goehr 2004: 140-9). This conception of the musical work includes the aim to reproduce composer intention and to adherence to a rigid musical structure, a rigid set of timbres pointing to a rigid set of performers, and a rigid performance setting which aims to produce what Lydia Goehr criticizes as 'the perfect performance of music' which 'takes the *of* seriously' (ibid.: 141). These rigid parameters can be altered by the 'original' artists, for instance when they change the instrumental timbres of a track or when they swap electronic timbres to acoustic ones (the so-called 'acoustic version'): but as soon as another *vocal* timbre enters the soundscape, the same song is understood to be a 'cover' version. The voices in U2's, Mary J. Blige's, and Johnny Cash's performances of the track 'One' certainly index Bono Vox, Blige, and Cash, but that does not mean that the vocal timbres in these songs identify only them: such an understanding (which is pervasive among fans) dismisses any elements of timbral performativity that are not related to subjectivity, including the ecstasy in Bono's tenor, the versatile colours in Blige's alto, and the bare minimalism of Cash's bass (cf. Smith 2008: 96-7). Reducing these timbres to the persons producing them is a form of materialist essentialism leading to a conflation of the musical and the extra-musical in popular imagination (cf. Kim-Cohen 2009: 144-8). By extending that essentialism to personal identity, such readings disregard all notions of identity as performative, fluid and evolving. Timbre, moreover, is as interactive, malleable and unpredictable as identity, and pinning it down into material stasis is just as irrelevant as the idea of static identity. The history of the alleged 'rasp' in black voices, which led to 'blackvoice' performances, serves as a poignant reminder that an essentialist definition of timbre can have serious political implications (Smith 2008: 134–53).

Classical music tends to perform 'cover versions' more often than not, and vocal timbre in this praxis is less often considered the sonic equivalent of the singer's identity (cf. Frith 1996: 186–7). In singing pedagogy, the voice tends to be regarded as an instrument, which can be nourished, trained and transmitted by the singer. In this approach, the singer's person does not necessarily converge with her voice: voice is 'a vessel, an instrument in an impartial case' (Yarnall 2017a: 570). During a tutorial for a singing audition for which I was nervous, my singing teacher urged me to 'leave Isabella outside in the car' on the basis that 'the voice is lovely, let it go!' The explicit disconnection between 'the voice' and the person of the singer here, with the latter negatively influencing the other, is a familiar one in vocal pedagogy. The use of impersonal article rather than personal pronoun for 'the voice', which is an independent agency that the person must 'let go', indicates a marked distinction between the sound, the sound source and the person who happens to operate the sound source (cf. Goehr 2004: 121–2). Singers' identification of the voice as 'the real me' identifies a singing self which does not coincide with personal identity but rather signals a separation between the body, the vocal instrument it houses and the subjectivity which explores the voice to create sound (Yarnall 2017a: 570–1, 577–8). This strange double bind between singer and voice far surpasses the voice's 'split condition' as identified by sound theorists such as Steven Connor (2000: 6–7). This split condition is based on the fact that voice defines an individual 'because it draws me into coincidence with myself' but also leaves the self — which is defined as the body in these readings — as sound waves ripple away from the speaker's origin (ibid.: 7).

Such co-occurrence of voice-as-self and voice-outside-self acquires a slightly different dimension for singing voices than for the speaking voices that Connor discusses. The musical voice is, to a significant degree, distinct from the singer's person as an instrument with which she has a close physical relation: the singer as a person cohabits with her voice within her body. The possessor of a singing voice may choose to train that instrument for singing, or she may not. In the latter case this leads to a 'split condition' that is markedly different from the one proposed by Connor.

> *I have a conversation with a young woman in possession of a soprano voice of Wagnerian proportions. The timbres (plural, multiple, heterogeneous) constituting her speaking voice signpost every colour of a dramatic soprano: a diaphragm*

strong enough to carry the weight of a role such as Brünnhilde, a pharynx the size of an echo chamber, a perfect mask placement, and a rich and warm high head resonance. Listening to her speaking draws my musical ear to her voice like a moth to a flame: all it desires is to hear her sing. But she does not sing. This woman has a different agency, a different will, than her own voice and my ear each have. She is not sure whether she wants to pursue a career in opera: she has been a successful conservatoire student and has sung some interesting roles – including, in fact, Brünnhilde – but is not convinced that the competitive world of opera will make her happy. Although I (as a person) agree with her (as a person), my ears, excited by every sound she speaks, keep begging her voice to sing. And it is not only me who separates her personality from her voice (and my own personality from my own ears), she does so herself: she feels an ethical tension, a feeling of guilt almost, to have decided not to dedicate her life to this vocal gift.

This anecdote illustrates the problem that occurs in non-musical theories of voice. This woman *is* not her singing voice. In many ways she has nothing to do with it: it emanates from her body, but she does not, as Connor suggests, coincide with it. Voice does not equal physical or subjective identity. Joan Sutherland writes that 'My voice was obviously God-given and I have tried to give of myself honestly' (Major 1987: 7). Quantitative research into the timbral development of singers shows that the voice may appear to the singer almost like an identity that exists within herself, which does *or does not* coincide with the self-identity that she is used to: 'This very familiar "person" within a singer is like a mirror, and when the mirror reflects an image that is unexpected, it brings about a re-evaluation of "Who am I?"' (Yarnall 2017a: 568–9). The vocal 'real me', then, does not equate to the subjective 'me'. Although a singer's emotions and instincts enhance her musical performance, she will detach her personal self, to a certain degree, from those emotions and the way they play out in her voice. Even in extremely emotive performances such as Billie Holiday's 'Strange Fruit' or Jacques Brel's 'Ne me quitte pas' there will have been a certain detachment between Holiday's and Brel's personality and their performances: not only is it physically almost impossible to sing with one's throat literally choked up but such intense emotional involvement, moreover, also poses the risk of losing concentration and musical engagement with such elements as pitch, timing, articulation, and, importantly, timbre. There is a careful balance to be struck, in vocal performance, between creative emotional engagement and subjective critical distance: both need to be present, both can strengthen but also complicate each other (cf. Frith 1996: 186–91).

In her strictly corporeal reading of voice, Nina Eidsheim criticizes this distanced approach to vocal pedagogy. Emphasizing that singers are human beings with physical bodies that produce their voice, she contests the idea that there is such a thing as an ideal timbre for jazz, rock music, or especially classical music, which she maintains is driven by the normativity of 'timbral alignment' (2015: 135). Instead, she proposes what she calls 'sound-based' and 'action-based' singing pedagogies that are based upon the singer as an evolving, interacting material subjectivity (ibid.: 140–8). Eidsheim's materialist essentialism – just like the reasoning around timbral identity in cover versions – surmises that voice is an index for body, which in turn is understood as an index for subject. But while there is doubtlessly truth in both presuppositions, while it is true that Cash's version of 'One' indexes Cash, this exclusively material focus does not allow space for timbre's body- and matter-independent agency, for its performative fluidity, and moreover the ambivalence and surprise of timbre as an expenditure of materiality, or for its *plus-de-corps*, as Mladen Dolar has argued:

> One could use a French pun, and say that the voice is *plus-de-corps*: both the surplus of the body, a bodily excess, and the no-more-body, the end of the corporeal, the spirituality of the corporeal, so that it embodies the very coincidence of the quintessential corporeality and the soul.
>
> (Dolar 2006: 71)

The choral voice demonstrates the ways in which vocal timbre exceeds corporeal identity and subjectivity, and in that sense sublimates the *plus-de-corps* that Dolar describes. It has often been pointed out that choral singing requires all choristers to sing, as it were, with 'one voice', a singular timbre that emanates from however many bodies there are in the choir. This blending of the individual vocal timbres of all the singers in a choir can only be achieved by the most interactive form of listening. This 'mutuality of sound' (Liimola 2000: 151) is not unique to choir singing, but is characteristic of all forms of collective music performance, and it always affects timbral outcomes: think, for instance, of the perfect timbral blend of Billie Holiday's voice and Bunny Berigan's trumpet in their 1936 version of Gershwin's 'Summertime', which is only achieved through intense and interactive musicking. While such solo vocal timbres still bear the semblance of personality, however (and therefore often get equated with personal identity), the choral voice can appear uniform. In the tradition of English boy choirs, the united choral voice has been taken to unprecedented heights, and the resulting choral timbre has as many admirers as it has critics. Both groups tend to refer to the boy choir timbre as 'white' (Day 2000: 125). The perceived 'colourlessness' of this timbre indicates a lack of personality or individuality in the sonority: this appears to correspond with the ambition, in the English choral tradition, to focus on the creation of one unified sound rather than on the convergence of individually audible sounds. But that correspondence only works if we take timbre to index personality, and the example of cover versions shows that that index is tenuous at best. Why would a uniform choral timbre have less 'personality' than a solo timbre? Why should timbre equal personality in the first place? Johan Sundberg has detailed the physiology of singing in his often-cited work *The Science of the Singing Voice* (1987). Extensive empirical research and quantitative data show that the voices in a choir adjust their vowel shaping, pitch, and with that their timbre to each other and to the overall choir sound in a manner that is both incomparable to solo singing and largely unconscious (Sundberg 1987: 141–5). 'The voice' is an instrument, and the singer its vessel: its physical source, but not, or at least not only, equivalent to a personal identity.

The soprano singing next to me in the Renaissance Choir England is a professional singer who sometimes performs solos in the choral repertoire. When singing chorally, her voice blends perfectly with those of the other first sopranos, creating the choral voice our conductor wishes to elicit: the section sings with 'one voice' in which no individual differences are audible. But when she sings solos such as that in Poulenc's *Gloria*, her timbre undergoes a sudden change. It expands, deepens and effortlessly soars over the thirty-four voices of the choir and the grand piano accompaniment, audible across any performance acoustics through the 'sine tone purity' that characterizes the soprano soloist (Feldman 2015: 99). Sometimes the transformation occurs within the space of one bar, when she changes from her choir voice to her solo voice (cf. Sundberg 1987: 141–3). The same body and the same personality produce both sonorities, and yet, standing next to her as she achieves this remarkable timbral change, I am suddenly aware of a completely different voice in my left ear, which in essentialist readings would mean a completely different personal identity.

Timbre cannot be defined as 'the *who* of voice' (Ihde 2007: 195), although it is generated by the *what* of voice. It is an index, but it is importantly also more than that – and perhaps that is precisely why timbre touches upon the imaginary, both for those who listen to it externally and for those who perceive it internally. The soprano in my choir describes her solo voice as 'a flower that unfolds' from her choral voice (personal communication). I'd like to amend Dolar's pun: vocal timbre is *plus-de-c(h)oeur*, the surplus of the choir, the spilling out of the choir's body, and also the excess of the heart of the singer, emerging from her body and entangled with her subjectivity but extending far beyond them.

Indexical paradox

The intricate connections and disconnections between body, subjectivity and timbre have been described by black metal auto-ethnographer Jasmine Hazel Shadrack. Her exploration of screaming shows the ambivalence and instability of the relation between timbral source and timbral outcome, between singing vessel and singing subjectivity:

> The physical act of screaming, as a singular performative component, allows my trauma a voice. It is a vicious, enraged scream that with every cry vomits forth moments of hurt, pain and humiliation and in so doing, I reclaim my subjectivity, I take ownership. It is mine. I feel the blood hammering through my veins, the rush of air flooding me between verses, my diaphragm pushing the scream out until, by the end of the song, I am physically empty; I am nothingness. My performance body is every singular part as its whole, all working together to let loose this other-worldly, pained unsound (Thacker 179) … Yes, it is a noise rather than a melody line and the process of 'emptying out' is valuable but there rests a liminal territory in which, rather than it representing a form of mindlessness, I find a temporal voidic plateau for me to spit out my plague, its temporality becoming an extension of me for that timbral moment … When I am on stage, I feel the other-worldly effects of that performance. I feel possessed by the music as it passes through me. I am a conduit of timbres.
>
> (Shadrack 2017a: 11–13)

Shadrack voices her subjective trauma through an emphatically embodied timbre, but while she personally identifies with that vocal timbre she is also explicitly distanced from 'the voice' – in the same way that Brel is distanced from the pain in 'Ne me quitte pas' – to the extent that the performance becomes an other-worldly void and her body as well as her subjectivity nothing but 'a conduit of timbres'. Even in the most fluid, performative definition of the concept, Shadrack's timbrally demarcated form of sonic identity is not the same as subjective identity. Timbre is not exclusively an index for a corporeal source nor exclusively an acousmatic *objet sonore*. It is both, and it is neither, and both/neither at the same time. It is a tangible and ungraspable form of sonic becoming, a rhizome, a multiplicity.

Rather than forcing a choice between various possible manifestations of timbral materiality, an understanding of timbre must be based on the acknowledgement that timbre demonstrates the complex entanglement of sonic ontology and sonic phenomenology, and that it challenges music epistemology because of that entanglement. Just like my search for a working definition of timbre in the previous chapter, therefore, my exploration of timbral indexes can only end in an extension of the list of paradoxes:

4. The timbral event *does and does not* function as an index:
   a. timbre *is and is not* stable
   b. in its in/stability it *is and is not* material
   c. the im/material timbral event *does and does not* represent sonic identity

Even if the origin of a timbre is confusing or unknown, however, we give it names and invent metaphors to describe it – colourful names, poetic images, metaphors that tickle the imagination. Timbral adjectives and metaphors can help musicians, listeners and scholars of music process the elusiveness of timbre: finding language for musical experience can, as Michel Chion notes, 'empower listening' even if the language we find is deliberately vague in order to match the ephemerality of the quality we are describing (Chion 2016: 225). A flower that unfolds. A temporal voidic plateau. What functions do the names and identities we ascribe to timbre have other than that of metaphor?

Timbral icons: From synaesthetic displacement to veiled precision

Adjective and metaphor

If timbre does not exclusively point to physical identity, it does often seem to function as a musical sign that is, in Peirce's terms, more an icon than an index. In what is sometimes called 'semantic listening' to timbre, the indexically derived forms of sonorous 'identity' discussed above are carried over from individual instruments and voices to other forms of musical and extra-musical identity, moving indexical relations into an iconic domain and leading to timbral adjectives and metaphors. Programme music capitalizes on this iconic function of tone colour the brightness associated with a flute timbre is carried over to the brightness of morning in 'Morning Mood' from Edvard Grieg's *Peer Gynt Suite*; the elegance of the oboe timbre, the stateliness of the French horn timbre, and the melancholy often attributed to these timbres are all carried over to those of a swan in Pyotr Ilyitch Tchaikovsky's *Swan Lake*. These extra-musical icons, in turn, often become symbols that are seemingly independent of indexical relations. The flute theme from Grieg's 'Morning Mood', for instance, was whistled by a couple of strawberries swimming around in yoghurt in a 1980s Dutch television commercial that was based on the apparent equation of flute, whistling, morning moods, and having yoghurt for breakfast.

The pervasiveness of timbral icons has everything to do with the fact that timbre is so difficult to capture in words. It is notoriously hard to find adequate descriptors for timbre without relying on formants, harmonics, spectrograms and other scientific quantifiers, and so we turn to metaphor. This can lead to tenuous equations: the problems arising in psychoacoustic and neuroscientific research through an over-reliance on timbral metaphor were discussed in Chapter 1. The most telling instance of timbre's metaphorical elusiveness is doubtlessly the synaesthetically displaced synonym that is its most often-used linguistic representative: it seems counterintuitive to attribute visual qualia to a sonic phenomenon, but we do not hesitate to use 'tone colour' to denote timbre. Sometimes we turn to onomatopoeia, imitating the sound of a timbre rather than attempting to describe it. Through timbral onomatopoeia, language is enriched with words that have no literal meaning but exist only for their emulative ring: chirp, wicky-wicky, badoom-tish. More often than onomatopoeias, we use figurative language to describe, instead of timbre *qua* sound, the connotations that timbre evokes in us. Tone *qua* sound obviously cannot have colour, temperature or tactility: but imagery pertaining to colour and shade, light and darkness, warmth and cold, smoothness or gravelliness are a good approximation of the sonic experience it conveys in the absence of a more concrete timbral discourse. A church organ thunders, a hoarse voice is sexy, Leonard Cohen's vocal timbre gets described as a 'velour foghorn'. By comparison, strawberries swimming around in yoghurt as a visualization (or 'cross-modal descriptor' as it is called in psychoacoustics, Sethares 2005: 28–30) of flute or whistling timbres is as legitimate an icon as any. Timbral adjectives and metaphors are arbitrary icons that are often not even remotely related to sound.

Because of the shaping power of discourse, however, the linguistic icon can gradually detach itself from the sonic index, eventually leading metaphor to become not just a discursive replacement of sonic experience but a persuasive guide to its perception, production and use. My choir's conductor told us not to sing a certain passage like 'wall to wall magnolia' but rather like 'a thunderstorm over the Yorkshire Moors', and the collective choral timbre immediately transformed in response. Timbral metaphor has the capacity to shape timbral production.

So strong is the guiding agency of timbral metaphor that it proves an important factor not just in the perception, but also in the creation of timbre. Susan Yarnall asserts that timbral metaphor is an important element of vocal pedagogy. Tone colour imagery can be used to examine the difference between internal and external hearing, which in pedagogical practice often means the difference between the student's perception of their own voice and the teacher's perception of that same voice (2017a: 569–71). Evaluating the metaphors used by singers to describe their own vocal timbre can help address the tension discussed above between timbral identity as *sound source* on the one hand, and timbral identity as *personal identity* on the other. When these two forms of timbral identity are conflated, vocal self-indexing based on the inner perception of timbre can lead to anxiety: when a student perceives her own voice as unpleasant, she may turn her vocal self-assessment against herself. Tone colour metaphors, Yarnall argues, can help ease this anxiety by separating the two types of timbral perception. Explicating inner (student) and external (teacher) hearing experiences through adjective and metaphor can guide students in their discovery of their own timbral range and versatility, as well as help establish personal vocal goals (ibid.: 573–4). Such timbral goals diverge importantly from the 'ideal timbre' of traditional vocal pedagogy that Eidsheim criticizes as an unnatural aim formulated by convention, and therefore a potential cause for psychological stress and vocal duress in students (Eidsheim 2015: 136–40). Instead, when expressed in subjective 'timbre words' that result from a dialogue between student and teacher, these goals can provide flexible aims based simultaneously on the student's inner hearing, the teacher's perception, a realistic assessment of the vocal instrument and the student's own timbral ambitions. In this dialogue between voice, student and teacher, 'metaphors ... can and should act as *intensifiers* rather than comparators' (Yarnall 2017b, italics in original).

Timbre's resistance to language, the wealth of imagery that it yields as a result, and the guiding influence of this imagery on timbral production and perception have inspired composers and music theorists at least since early Modernity. There is strong evidence from German baroque music theory and composing that timbral difference was employed to signify different identities and meanings during this period. These were often interpreted in an allegorical way. Renate Steiger discovered an emblem by Johann Saubert from 1629 which indicates that the soprano voice should signify the faithful soul, the alto voice stood for prayer, the tenor held the biblical word (e.g. the evangelist's role in baroque passions and cantatas) and the bass represented the fundament of religion, the word of God or the voice of Jesus (Steiger 2002: 119–25). We can hear in many baroque compositions that this emblem reflected compositional practices of the time. Like vocal timbres, instrumental timbres had their own allegorical symbolism. The opening sinfonia of Johan Sebastian Bach's cantata *Gottes Zeit ist die allerbeste Zeit* (BWV 106), also called the 'Actus Tragicus', was set for two alto recorders and two viola da gambas. Recorders were called 'flauto dolce', soft flute, at the time, and Bach often used their 'soft' timbre to evoke connotations of the soul's passage into the heavenly kingdom (Lasocki 2001: I.1, III.3.iii). The recorder timbre and its eschatological connotations are combined with those of the viola da gamba, an instrument often used by baroque composers in the context of lamentations and by Bach to specifically indicate the bittersweet emotions evoked by Christ as King of Sorrows (Woodfield and Robinson 2001: 7). Timbral metaphor, in this case, guides timbral symbolism. Although the 'softness' ascribed to the recorder timbre and the 'hushed' sound of the viola da gamba have nothing to do with theology, they evoked religious connotations which became timbral metaphors; and these in turn lead to the use of alto recorder and viola da gamba as symbols for eschatological bliss and sorrow – with the bittersweet ensemble timbre of the 'Actus Tragicus' as an aesthetic result.

The timbral chain of connotation, metaphor and symbolism has been present in composing and listening from early Modernity on. The examples are manifold: the trombone as the Devil's instrument from early opera to Berlioz's *Symphonie Fantastique*; the trumpet as symbol of heroism from Bach's *Christmas Oratorio* to Wagner's *Ring* cycle; the harpsichord's evolving connotations from theology to domesticity to cinematic Gothic horror; the list goes on. Each of these forms of timbral iconicity are evidence of the rippling performativity that is present in the affective encounter between the sonic event of tone colour and the human imaginary. The encounter with the unstable sonic non-object that is timbre affords a perplexity, an aporia in aesthetic experience which may become fruitful in a profusion of imagery, an abundance of words attempting to capture this aesthetic singularity (cf. Chapter 3).

Metaphorical reversal

Timbral icons differ significantly from linguistic ones, both in their synaesthetic layering and in their semiotic functioning. An interesting illustration of this dissimilarity can be found in the existence of voice banks used for commercials and voiceovers. Websites such as voiceovers.co.uk offer broadcasters and companies the profiles of a range of voice actors, and each voice is described by a set of characteristics. Besides the accents that each actor can use, these sites mostly list the timbral specificities of the voices and their connotations. 'Friendly', 'natural' and 'trustworthy' are regularly used timbral descriptors, and this invites some thought. Perhaps a timbre could be described, with some effort, as 'natural' – as opposed to artificial or forced – but 'friendly' and 'trustworthy' definitely are not sonic qualities. More than merely describing a sound, these adjectives state an expectation about the character of the source of that sound. From their role as metaphors for vocal timbres, thus, they simultaneously also function as symbols for the personality through which the companies hiring the actors hope to achieve profit – and, by extension, for the product on sale.

Like the 'iron' and 'masculine' guitar in Black Sabbath's 'Iron Man', these voice banks are a case in point for the habitual transferral of timbral metaphor to the personality of the sound source, with the signified moving from icon back to index in a sort of semiotic reversal. Part of the semiosis is similar to the two-way process of correspondence occurring in verbal icons: metaphor can describe the trombone timbre as devilish, and in turn we may perceive the auditory phenomenon of trombone timbre as devilish (Erickson 2009: 12). In timbral icons, however, not two but three components are involved: (1) the sound source pointed out by timbre-as-index, in this example a brass instrument; (2) the trombone timbre produced by that sound source; and (3) the 'devilish' metaphor describing that timbre. Iconicity, in this case, does not only appear when words describe sound (component 3, devilish, describing component 2, trombone timbre) but also when sound in its own right becomes a sonic icon describing the material object that is its index (component 2, trombone timbre, describing component 1, brass instrument, by virtue of component 3, devilish). Besides timbre as sonic index *pointing to* sound source, this metaphorical reversal also puts timbre in the role of sonic icon *describing* the sound source: the mere sound of the trombone timbre now describes the brass instrument as devilish, only because linguistic convention has used that metaphor for that sound. Commercial voice banks demonstrate the traps of this process. First, as argued above, the very notion of timbral index is debatable, as timbre is contingent, unstable and singular: so, the idea that timbral icons would be able to pin down the characters of sound sources is simply unrealistic. Second, the fact that male voices are predominantly described as 'authoritative', 'corporate' and 'cool' while female voices tend to be assessed as 'mumsy', 'sassy' and 'a bit foxy' painfully reveal the cultural conventions from which such timbral icons originate and on which companies capitalize.

When the practical and political caveats of timbral iconicity have been met, however, there are situations in which tone colour imagery can have its uses. In film, television and video game composing, timbral icons are crucial conveyors of non-visual information to spectators. Claudia Gorbman argues that film music 'wards off the displeasure of uncertain signification', helping the viewer understand the cinematic narrative by giving them explicit aural cues as to its intended meaning (1987: 58). Adapting Roland Barthes's semiotic terminology, Gorbman describes this type of explicit musical signification as *ancrage*, the emphatic linking together of visual and musical material (ibid.: 58–9). As it is the purpose of *ancrage* to be unambiguous, film composing has developed a musical language that defies the incompatibility of music and signification. By virtue of their subservient functionality, film and television music are designed to solidify musical connotations, even to turn metaphor into cliché, so that viewers understand precisely what is happening on screen. As timbre plays a major role in this process, the most indescribable of musical qualities thus turns, ironically, into a stabilized sign. The harpsichord's now unshakeable cinematic reputation as a signifier of Gothic horror has already been mentioned; violins in film soundtracks often signal sweeping romance; and brass points to epic heroism. The conventional audiovisual connectedness of percussive colours and orientalism, or of digital timbres and alien evildoers, shows the dangers of collating (arbitrary) timbral icon with (debatable) timbral index: like the 'sassy' female voiceover, these cinematic timbral clichés spring from a materialist sonic essentialism, and are operationalized in a metaphorical reversal that does neither signifier nor signified any justice.

Precision in veils

Despite its obvious pitfalls, the metaphorical chain of timbral description and signification, operative as it is in the precarious borderlands where music and language meet, has the guiding quality inherent to any metaphorical process. It is important to repeat that it is precisely because of its sonic elusiveness that timbre evades the symbolic order of language, and is consequently only captured by proxy, in the shape of metaphor. Lost in translation between musical experience and linguistic communication, the metaphors we invent to make both ends meet can turn vagueness into precision – and they can be useful in musical pedagogy and timbre creation. Metaphor is a linguistic veil that is as shady as the sonic quality it attempts to describe, but I would argue that precisely its vagueness is the reason why metaphor *can* be an adequate signifier for timbre.

A constructive deployment of verbal limitations in the face of timbral multiplicity is noticeable, for instance, in the ways in which musical genres are defined. Musical genre can quite easily be identified through timbre (Tagg 2013: 306–8). Robert Walser argues that timbre has an important signalling function in popular music genres: 'Before any lyrics can be comprehended, before harmonic or rhythmic patterns are established, timbre instantly signals genre and affect' (1993: 41; cf. Zak 2001: 64–5). Specifically, Walser observes that a large part of the genre definition of metal is determined by the timbres of vocal grunt and guitar distortion, with the latter adding lower harmonics to the power chord (1993: 41–4; cf. Berger and Fales 2005: 187–97); interestingly, the genre name 'heavy metal' itself is a compound metaphor for the timbral qualities that are considered most characteristic in this music (Berger and Fales 2005: 182–7). The genres of shoegaze, dub, country, and funk are similarly recognizable by the timbral attributes that determine their 'sound': in this case, those timbral attributes are the instrumental means of guitar pedals, the productive means of reverb, and the distinctive articulations of vocal twang and slapped bass guitar. Similarly, Tony Visconti has stated that compression is 'the *sound* of rock', by which he points to the same genre-identifying agency of timbre (quoted in Zak 2001: 124). (The list goes on, crossing over from genre to era, from music to multimedia: early historical performance practice was recognizable by its period instruments and a vocal style inspired by Emma Kirkby's crystal-clear soprano; 1980s pop music was characterized by Madonna-esque pinched vocal chords in female vocals and Duran Duran-style open-throated wispiness for males; Nordic Noir television shows tend to be preceded by fragile, breathy voices for their opening titles; survival horror video games are accompanied by ominous white noise drones; and so on.) The dominance of timbral metaphor in the nomenclature of these and other genres is telling of the complex signifying processes discussed here: processes, that is, in which timbre, language, culture and identity are intimately, and increasingly, entwined. If musical genre is, as Joshua Gunn has argued, a questionable category based on 'an assemblage of preferred adjectival codes' (1999: 36; cf. Walser 1993: 27–34), then it is no wonder that timbre, the quality of music that is shrouded in adjectives describing sonorous difference, is so crucial for genre.

The early development of Goth as a popular musical genre is a revealing illustration of the guiding effects of metaphorical chains around timbre and genre. The bands performing in London's Batcave stood out from late 1970s music in Britain because of their timbral orientation. With the guitar tones of post-punk, the vocal extravagance of glam rock, and the reverb effects of dub, bands like Bauhaus, Siouxsie and the Banshees, and The Cure created a new timbral blend that cannot be described any more precisely than through an assemblage of adjectives: it was hollow, ominous and dark. The timbral difference marking the sound of these bands started a process towards genre 'identity' that was based on the ways in which timbral perception is not just described in but is itself also qualified by metaphor. The process starts with the recognition of timbral difference: the bands performing in London's Batcave sounded different from other popular music at the time, and this sound could not be described with more precision than as hollow, ominous and dark. This leads to adjectival assemblage: we shall call this hollow, ominous and dark musical genre 'Goth'. Through the metaphorical shaping of timbral perception, the word 'Goth' subsequently began to indicate any timbres that sounded similarly hollow or ominous or dark: not only Bauhaus's use of reverb evoked Gothic ruins but L'Âme Immortelle's reverberating tracks do, too; not only Siouxsie Sioux's alto voice had Goth overtones but so does Suspiria's Matthew Carl Lucian's baritone; not only The Cure's production style had dark connotations but so does Rotersand's. The 'Goth' metaphor, finally, gradually became a symbol for genre identity: Goth is now a recognizable genre that is hollow, ominous, dark (and any other adjective added to the blend), and we carry over this assemblage of musical and extra-musical qualifications to musicians and fans alike. Unpacking this process reveals the ways in which the timbral metaphorical chain can be as compelling as it is problematic. Metaphor is an evidently imprecise signifier: this linguistic signifier, however, is used to identify qualities of sound that defy linguistic description, and as sound meets word in the no man's land separating their immediate realms, it does so with the surprising precision of what Gumbrecht calls 'atmosphere, Stimmung, mood' (Gumbrecht 2012). Goth is an eminently *dark* music, and, with all the elusive precision of vagueness, the atmosphere of this visual metaphor matches the mood of the timbres that carved out a singular space for it within the soundscape of popular music (cf. Van Elferen 2018).

Iconic paradox

The omnipresent visual, tactile and olfactory imagery of tone colour, thus, is more than a collection of sensorily mismatched descriptions for an indescribable sonic quality. Timbre metaphors, Dennis Smalley notes, 'are not to be scoffed at. They are verbal signs that essential qualities have been recognised' (Smalley 1994: 36). Icons can convey in words the veiled precision that characterizes the sonic phenomenon of timbre. The reversed semiotic agency of metaphor, moreover, can in turn guide timbral perception and creation. In combination with an essentialist form of timbral indexing, this can lead to problems, as the voice bank example makes embarrassingly clear; but when the problems inherent to materialist essentialism have been met, timbral icons can enrich timbral experience. Again, I would argue that an understanding of timbre requires an acknowledgement of the paradoxes surrounding it. Kim-Cohen dismisses the convergence of the musical and the extra-musical in sonic icons, which he considers just the other side of the essentialist coin: metaphor, in his eyes, is as great a sin against sonic ontology as the supposition of a material *objet sonore* (Kim-Cohen 2009: 29, 127, 148, 259; cf. Cox 2011: 147–8, 157). But metaphorical practices do exist in the everyday life of tone colour, and they do inform timbre's sound and performativity: to dismiss them is to dismiss a part of tone colour's musical and cultural circulation. Timbre's non/indexical ontology cannot be separated from its non/iconic discursive circulation. Rather than on the exclusivity implied in Schaeffer's and Eidsheim's index-only theorization of timbre, in Gorbman's and Gunn's icon-only approach, and in Kim-Cohen's 'neither-nor' vantage point, I would suggest that a realistic approach to tone colour would have to be based on the inclusivity of accumulation, even if that means an accumulation of paradoxes. And so it is necessary to add the paradoxes of timbral icons to those of timbral indexes listed in the previous paragraph:

5. The timbral event *does and does not* function as an icon:
    a. Words *cannot but can* describe timbre
    b. timbre *does not but does* relate to the extra-musical

The grain of the voice: Icon back to index, and beyond

Roland Barthes's influential essay 'The grain of the voice' theorizes voice, vocal identity, musical signification, and timbre. The essay begins with frustrated exclamations about language's inability to convey music or musical experience in any other ways than either factual description or metaphorical circumlocution: 'Are we condemned to the adjective? Are we reduced to the dilemma of either the predicable or the ineffable?' (1977: 180). In an attempt to break free from the entrapments of language, Barthes sets out to renew critical attention for the purely sonic aspects of music. Discourse about music carries the imminent danger of devolving into a self-perpetuating linguistic loop that loses its connection to the musical: when we use metaphor upon metaphor, words about music are at risk of becoming words about words. Barthes aims to repair the metaphorical displacement of musical discourse by redirecting the music-aesthetic focus from language to the *excess* of language afforded by musical experience (ibid.: 180). In order to do so, he analyses the vocal performance of two singers: Dietrich Fischer-Dieskau, whom he considers technically accomplished but not gripping, and Charles Panzéra, whom he considers technically less perfect but emotionally gripping and aesthetically pleasing. The choice to address vocal rather than instrumental music, in this case, is not necessarily a fortunate one. Vocal music mostly contains words, and Barthes does not distinguish between the functional level of the words *about* music that he wishes to surpass from that of the words sung *in* music. His aim is to overcome words altogether in speaking about music but using the example of music-with-words adds to the challenge he sets himself.

Although Barthes recognizes that music is not comparable to language, he does consistently discuss music as a signifying praxis. This in itself is a highly contestable assumption. It has often been argued, both in musicology and in philosophy, that seeking for any form of signification in music is beside the point (cf. Nattiez 1990: 102–29; cf. Nancy 2007: 7–8, 13, 27). Contemporary musicology has shifted its attention from the distanced reflection on music to the immediate and activity of *doing* music, or 'musicking' as Christopher Small has famously called it (1998: 9–18; cf. Cook 2013). Barthes, who was writing his essays on music decades before the development of such 'drastic' musicologies (Abbate 2004: 508–11), has a more nuanced view on the subject than it would seem at first glance. He asserts that musical utterances should not be understood as fixed signs, but as continual deferrals of signification. Music therefore marks the very limits of signification: in his essay 'Rasch', Barthes writes that 'music is a field of signifying [*signifiance*] and not a system of signs' (1985: 308). Understanding music as a field of *signifiance*, the infinitely shimmering process by which text exceeds signification, Barthes does however continue to place music firmly in the domain of semiotics. Even if he argues that musical *signifiance* occupies the very outer boundaries of signifying, his position excludes other, less textual understandings of music and musicking.

Music's *signifiance*, Barthes contends, revolves around the performing body: 'the referent ... is the body. The body passes into music without any relay but the signifier' (1985: 308). He discerns a tension between language and body in the vocal performance of what he considers to be aesthetically pleasing singers. Despite the misleading fact that it often performs language, Barthes notes, voice represents more than language alone (1977: 182). This is not a very new insight for musicians and musicologists. If voice represented only language, vocal timbre would simply not matter, and there would be no difference between two versions of the same song, say Jacques Brel's and Nina Simone's renderings of 'Ne me quitte pas'. While the popular appreciation of 'cover versions' discussed above focuses on indexicality alone, Barthes adds the words that are being sung to his approach of such parallel performances: he uses them to address not just the difference between two bodies, but between two bodies singing words. Transposing Julia Kristeva's notion of geno-text into the musical realm as 'geno-song', Barthes defines the grain of the voice as 'the encounter between a language and a voice' that is able to overcome the pheno-text being sung (ibid.: 182, 181). Barthes's grain of the voice is built on Schaeffer's usage of grain as the 'sound matter' of timbre (Schaeffer 2017: 437) but adds a specific agency to it: in Barthes's vocal grain, the 'sound matter' audible in voice must be heard as corporeality rubbing out linguistic signification. In this way, Barthes maintains, vocal performance ultimately does not point to the language that is being sung, but to the body that sings it. Musical *signifiance*, he argues, is sublimated in the grain of the voice which should be understood as 'the body in the voice as it sings, the hand as it writes, the limb as it performs' (1977: 188). Barthes considers such emergent corporeality to be a form both of musical identity and of musicking quality: the grain, he contends, is what differentiates a good singer from a bad singer, with good singers making audible something of their own body in performance.

Barthes's assertion that a good singing voice can point to the musical identity of the singer is surprising in the light of his own earlier writing. By stating that the materiality in the grain of the voice equals 'the emergence of text in the work', he appears to move back to the discursive displacements that he wants to surpass, even if we accept that 'text' does not necessarily refer to language (1977: 188). Although it is based on music's excess of linguistic signification and fixed identity in geno-song – not every singer has a 'grain' – his reading not only reduces 'good' voices to singing subjectivities but also returns to, and blends, indexical and iconic relations in voice. Carolyn Abbate critiques this remarkable U-turn, stating that '[r]ather than killing the author, Barthes proposes the rebirth of an author "inside" the artwork, one that reveals herself in the "grain" of the voice(s) that speak what we read (hear)' (1993: 232).

Although the material aspects of timbre are undeniable, moreover, that materiality is not the same as musical identity – Barthes regresses not just to 'texts' and their 'authors' here, but also to materialist essentialism. Nina Simone and Jacques Brel were both terrific singers, both with a tangible grain: but does that help us understand vocal performance, or indeed the vocal performance of language? Simone's rendering of 'Ne me quitte pas' does not only point to Simone; Brel's version does not only point to Brel; it does not matter who wrote the 'original version' and who 'covered' it; and my statement that both are terrific singers with tangible grain is hardly useful beyond what it says about my personal aesthetic preferences. Conflating vocal icon (words about music) with linguistic content (words being sung), and equating corporeality (the body that musicks) with musicality (the capacity to musick), Barthes's essay unapologetically privileges corporeal index over any other aspect of vocal performance. In stating that only good singers have grain, moreover, he elevates the audibility of corporeality-equated-with-musicality to the status of aesthetic icon described in the same 'ineffable' qualifiers he set out to overcome (1977: 180) – 'truth', 'hallucination', 'the infinite' (ibid.: 184). This part of the essay adds normativity to materialist essentialism: Panzéra's vocal performance is assumed to point to Panzéra's body, and therefore Panzéra is assumed to be the better singer. Barthes's reading of vocal performance, despite its carefully outlined caveats, thus incorporates all the problems inherent to popular assessments of cover versions, and to the reversal of musical qualia from sound source to timbre and back via timbral metaphor.

'The grain of the voice' is sometimes taken as a theorization of timbre. While timbre is certainly an important manifestation of the grain's ephemeral performativity, Barthes explicitly states than the grain of the voice is 'not – or is not merely – its timbre' (ibid.: 185). What is confusing, however, is that just a few pages before this passage he defined the grain of the voice as 'the materiality of the body speaking its mother tongue' (ibid.: 182). This oddly leads back both to two things he claims to surpass: 'the materiality of the body' is exactly the physiological, and causal, definition of timbre that Schaeffer struggled with, and 'speaking its mother tongue' indicates, if not some form of language or signifying system, the type of metaphor against which he fulminates in the opening of the article.

Despite – and arguably thanks to – its problems, Barthes's essay offers an important intermediary step on our road towards an understanding of timbre. The essay highlights the delicate relations between music and icon on the one hand and music and index on the other, illustrating how these semiotic tools can provide helpful ways of thinking about music as well as where their usefulness reaches its limits. And exactly because his understanding of musical iconicity and musical indexicality seem to fold back in on themselves, exactly because of the contradictions within the essay, Barthes's 'grain of the voice' offers a view of music, voice and timbre that necessitates an openness to the paradox and excess implied in musical aesthetics. His apparently confused approach to timbre, in particular, would seem to confirm that timbre presents a paradox: it unites the material ontology of corporeal causality and the immaterial ineffability of metaphor.

Barthes's openness to the paradoxes of musical, vocal and timbral epistemology is especially noticeable when he describes his own music-aesthetic experience. In these sections he leaves space for the excess of signification in voice, the aesthetics of excess located beyond the corporeal causality that he finds in voice. He frames this excess as a form of sublime aporia, a dissolution in *jouissance*: 'The climactic pleasure hoped for is not going to reinforce – to express – [the] subject but, on the contrary, to lose it' (ibid.: 188). While this could be read as another contradiction, I think Barthes's ambiguity here reveals that he wished to break open the rift between the fixity of musical embodiment and the infinity of musical experience – an infinity that reduces the shimmering of *signifiance* to a faint memory. Jonathan Dunsby notes that 'Barthes is challenging us through a remarkable epistemological premiss to learn from our listening' (2009: 129). The grain of the voice, both as an essay and as a concept, is inconsistent because what Barthes is trying to describe is inconsistent. Voice is ambiguously embodied and it is an ambiguous signifier, and the aesthetic experience of that voice is even more ambiguous. The aesthetics of voice is the experience of loss: the loss of sonorous stability, of material fixity, and of any relation to signification. And at the heart of that loss – in the *jouissance* that Barthes mentions – lies the paradox of timbre.

The individual instruments of oboe and violin (and the musicians playing them) in J.S. Bach's concerto in C minor (BWV 1060), or the two individual guitars and personalities of Gary Moore and B.B. King in their 1992 performance of Roy Hawkins's 'The Thrill is Gone' arguably play a very limited material or personal role in either musical event. Both works, however dissimilar in their historical, musical and cultural contexts, are driven by nothing but a *jouissance* in timbral interplay: two instruments alternating on the same melodies, copying each other in timbral echo, each adding their own tone colours and flavours to often very simple repeated motifs. Very similar in procedure to compositions by Varèse, Xenakis and Ligeti, timbre here is a musical structuring device rather than a sign, and the result, in both cases, is actual tone colour melody (for more examples of timbral structuring see Deutsch 1998: 301–11, 317–19; Actor-Project; on *Klangfarbenmelodie* cf. Chapter 3). Similarly, it is only the aesthetic pleasure in sonorous difference between timbres – our drastic enjoyment of timbre's most basic property as difference – which guides our listening to these pieces. If timbral difference affords identities here, those identities are certainly not limited to bodies or text. These two musical events illustrate precisely how timbre exceeds the boundaries of corporeality, identity and signification, and endorses, rather, a mindless *jouissance* in musical difference that is free from the constraints of language and embodiment, signification and identity: they afford an excess of all of these things that is free from the corporeal entanglement of Barthes's grain. Timbre simultaneously points, as an index, to the material cause of sound as 'the body in the voice as it sings' (Barthes 1977: 188) or the wood in the oboe as it plays and so on; and, as an icon, to an ineffable aspect of sound that is fetishized, as Brian Kane notes, as an 'aesthetic object in its own right' (2014: 209). Since it is difficult if not impossible to distinguish any boundaries between timbre-as-index and timbre-as-icon, it has to be understood as a sonic event *and* as an aesthetic event, *and* as the excess of both. One and the same timbre may appear as index for a physical sound cause, as icon for an extra-musicality, and as a tangibly grainy but unattainably elusive void. Timbre marks a loss that coincides with desire.

The timbral void: Lack, surplus, desire

Barthes's assertion that the grain of a voice identifies the possessor of that voice is the subject of the episode 'The Big Lockout' of British sitcom *Black Books* (Channel 4, 2000). Or rather, the pitfalls of that assertion. Fran Katzenjammer (Tamsin Greig) finds herself irresistibly drawn towards the voice of a man she knows, Howell Granger (Peter Serafinowicz), but does not find his appearance or character in the least attractive. Mildly repulsed by Howell's flesh and blood, Fran learns to her great excitement that he will be reading the shipping forecast on the radio. She has a very pleasurable evening alone with her radio but finds herself wanting more of that timbre and calls Howell on the phone. A phone voice is still disembodied, and Fran is able to extend her timbral pleasure. She responds rather loudly, Howell is puzzled by the *jouissance* in her phone voice, and hilarity ensues.

This *Black Books* episode hinges on the ambivalence of vocal embodiment, which manifests in the fact that Howell Granger 'confuses' Fran. It is commonplace to assume that the grain of a voice *does* bear a correlation to the body, and by extension even the personality, of the speaker or singer – but this assumption often turns out to be ill-founded. The woman possessing a 'mumsy' voice on the voiceover website may never have had any maternal feelings; the trombone may not have anything to do with devils; and the man with the 'trustworthy' voice may be a con. Timbral reversal is a trap, and most people are aware of its incongruities; but it could be argued that precisely the ambivalence of vocal timbre is enjoyable. Voice, whether in a face-to-face situation or a mediated context, generates the undeniable sensation of something that is present but invisible, tangible but just out of reach, and it raises the enjoyable possibility to inscribe any listener fantasy or desire onto its sonic appearance (cf. Kane 2014: 180–6). Acousmatic voice heightens this potential. In schizophonic voices such as Howell's in *Black Books*, vocal embodiment and vocal signification are redundant categories: in acousmatic sound, only timbre matters. Fran Katzenjammer can only experience *jouissance* in this voice by explicitly un-indexing Howell's voice, reducing it to an *objet sonore* that is a sexy timbre only. Surrounded and touched by timbre, she can project her desires onto its unattainable presence: this vocal timbre is free from Howell Granger's body, free from the shipping forecast's linguistic signification, and free from the corporeal groundedness of the Barthesian grain.

In his *Dumbstruck: A Cultural History of Ventriloquism*, Steven Connor theorizes the mysterious attraction of one acousmatic voice in particular: that of ventriloquism.

> I suggest that the dissociated voice is a recurrent source of excess, menace and awe. Because it is a category of excess, a figure of nonfigurability, it has no one meaning ... Nor is the ventriloquial voice pure exorbitance or disruption; like the neurotic symptom, it is both wound and cure, enigma and explication, trauma and therapy.
>
> (Connor 2000)

Offering stark instances of the dissociation between timbre and sound source, the acousmatic voice is a compelling demonstration of the limits of Barthes's grain: voice, precisely in its timbre, exceeds the confines of the body that is its cause and of the signifying systems in which it is audible.

The case of acousmatic voice also reveals the boundaries of Schaeffer's *objet sonore*. Because human hearing wants to find the origin of sound, acousmatic sound prompts hearers to find or invent an invisible source. Schaeffer's two concepts are phenomenologically irreconcilable with one another: there can be no 'pure' *objet sonore* as long as there are human ears to hear it, as human perception finds it difficult to accept the possibility of acousmatic sound. As Connor states, the sourceless voice is both wound and cure: it simultaneously signals lack and wills into existence an explanation for that lack, and it does not matter if that explanation is scientific (acoustic analysis), fantastic (Fran Katzenjammer's bodiless lover), or supernatural (the ghostly voices in horror literature and cinema). Imagining sound sources, inventing whichever sonic cause our desire wishes to project onto the delightful ambivalence of the present absent, is the therapy that revels in never quite curing a pleasurable rupture – the aporia of listening, the loss of the self that Barthes wilfully leaves untouched and untheorized, the beyond of the grain.

The pleasure of experiencing this rupture, of the projection of desire onto sound, is not exclusive to ventriloquism or to acousmatic voice. The causally dissociated voice merely foregrounds the excess that is always present in sound, in voice, and specifically in timbre. Even if we can see the source of a sound, and know the details of its genesis, our listening experience is not limited to what we see, to what we know or to how we interpret sound. On the contrary, as the following example illustrates.

> *Antony and the Johnsons' 'Deeper than love'*[1] *begins with angular, jagged violin and cello motifs falling and rising into an accompaniment of soft G# minor and E major piano chords, cross stick drum, and a male voice that whisper-sings the words 'fall deeper'. Antony Hegarty's alto voice and a flute enter this sparse setting that continues to negotiate major and minor harmonies, with the flute playing alternating B and G sharp semibreves. The voice, in* sotto voce head register, *sings and sighs, toils and trembles above the instruments. The chorus introduces a stirring up of sounds and spirit: the harmony now moves via D# to G# major, the cello plays an agitated melody, the full drum kit is employed in rolls and*

---

[1] The track can be found on https://www.youtube.com/watch?v=VyU2SeT9Qgc.

fourth-beat accents, and the flute briefly flutters in higher regions. The vocal line is pitched upwards here, its expression moving from a sad to an imploring tone. After the chorus the verses are repeated, but the mood has changed. The cello's low octave double to the violin is more pronounced; the voice is now louder, with more chest resonance, sounding at once hollow, desperate, and somehow angry. Long 'aaaahs' resonate in the corner of the soundbox. The end of the track is set off by a grand pause after which the lead voice sings sustained phrases, repeated almost like mantras – 'Hold on, let go, fall deeper even than love' – against a background of sustained violins and fading piano chords confirming B major. The song does not really end, but slowly dissipates as the voice leads the listener, falling, down into a world of wide reverb and white noise, or maybe wind or sea?

Everything is unusual about this track, unsettling even. The lyrics are mysterious: the tormented persona, whose 'old blood' spills 'from between cracked fingers', seems to be struggling towards an idealized state 'deeper than love' just beyond description and reach. The wavering between major and minor harmonies in the verses, the modulation in the pained chorus, and the overall musical form of the song make it stand out from popular music conventions. By far the most unusual aspect of the song is the intensity of timbral combinations. The instruments in 'Deeper than Love' are carefully chosen for their colours, and the resulting palette bypasses every convention: strings and flutes do not often play such a large role in popular music; flutes do not often play such low pitches or such long notes throughout an entire track; the drum kit is employed more as orchestral percussion than as a rock drum; but most importantly, Hegarty's voice is unlike any other voice in popular or classical music. Its range is that of an alto, but its timbre does not resemble that of a female singer or that of a male contralto, which makes indexing a matter of confusion rather than causality. Singing its enigmatic lines, the voice is light, vulnerable, fragile in the first verse. Come the first chorus, however, something else is added, and that something else is not just the audible factors of increased volume and diaphragm support. The vulnerability is still there, but it now has the sharp edge, the violence almost, of desperation and of anger. Hegarty's voice has the uncanny capacity to tremble in deepest humility but at the same time to be powerful and menacing, and this ambivalence is heightened by its gender-defiant sonority. This is a timbre that pushes music and listeners far beyond the ordinary, even if its cause is visible and known.

The band's eponymous first album, from which 'Deeper than Love' is taken, came out in 2000 and gained critical and popular acclaim. The album featured nine tracks, every song intensely emotional and richly orchestrated. Hegarty, who is currently known as Anohni (names, identities, words, metaphors), has been openly transgender from the early stages of her career, with many of the band's song lyrics showing a non-binary approach to gender and sexuality. 'Frankenstein' from the EP Hope There's Someone (2005), for instance, opens with the line 'when I was a young boy' and moves to 'now that I'm a grown woman'.

But it is not Anohni's body or her lyrics that send audiences reeling. It is not the indexical question of whether she is a young boy or a grown woman or both, or the iconic question of whether she is vulnerable or angry, that captivates the bodies and souls of those who hear her. Nor even is it the tangible grain of her musicking voice leading back to her transgender corporeality. It is the strangely haunting timbre of that voice in the face of which such icons as 'vulnerable', 'angry', 'haunting' and indeed 'grain' are merely metaphors. Words have no relevance for timbre – they do not inhabit the same realm.

Anohni's voice is universally known to evoke shivers, goose bumps and tears. 'The musicians wept. The audience wept. The taxi driver wept.' (Charlie Blake, personal communication). Index, icon and grain bear no relation to the excess, the lack, the void that is timbre.

Timbre is operative through excess, a spilling over of the boundaries of indexicality and iconicity. It is embodied and it may signify, but it is importantly also an exhaustion of both, an exceeding of embodiment and signification. Anohni's vocal timbre is an illustration of how problematic notions of timbral identity and signification are – her voice illustrates how timbre simultaneously affirms and defies even the most ephemeral of them. To hear this timbre as the voice of transgender is an essentialist pinning down of Anohni's musicality; to interpret it as fragile or imploring is to capture its boundless musical expression in the symbolic chains of language. The timbres in this track are not signs. They are merely sounds. Not even that – they are the difference between sounds, and the negation that defines them extends to their musical performativity.

For all its physical presence, then, timbre remains a negative, a void. But precisely because it is simultaneously so undeniably present and so resistant to indexicality and iconicity, this void is crucial for musical aesthetics. Timbre is the first thing that strikes – tangibly, physically strikes – listeners in musical experience, and its sway sets in motion the drastic, unconscious flow of musical immersion. Because of its powerful performativity, listeners project meanings onto its *tabula rasa*. Timbre appears to signify because we desire to fill its presence-that-is-absence with meaning: its excess spills out of the gap that defines it.

This aspect of vocal timbre has been theorized by Mladen Dolar, whose book *A Voice and Nothing More* (2006) begins where Barthes's essay ended: with the voice's relation to language and corporeality. Like Barthes does, Mladen Dolar states that a reduction of voice to text 'does away with its living presence, with its flesh and blood' (ibid.: 19). In terms of signification, Dolar emphatically steps away from phonology, which he claims 'stabs the voice with the signifying dagger' (ibid.: 19). But he diverges sharply from Barthes in his assessment of vocal embodiment. Dolar states that

> formulas like those proposed by Barthes – le grain de la voix, the grain of the voice, 'the materiality of the body speaking its mother tongue', 'the body in the singing voice', and so on … will never do. The problem is that the voice cannot be pinned to a body, or be seen as an emanation of the body, without a paradox.
>
> (Ibid.: 197, n. 10)

Dolar recognizes the voice's detachment from the body that produces it, arguing, in the section quoted earlier in this chapter, that voice is a *'plus-de-corps'* as it marks both the excess and the outside of corporeality (ibid.: 71). He even goes so far as to say that the voice, as it represents the rift between the interior and the exterior of the body, must be seen as the flesh or materiality of 'the soul' (ibid.: 70). Occupying this paradoxical position at the very point of division between inside and outside of both embodiment and subjectivity, Dolar then argues, voice represents the surplus of materiality and language that Jacques Lacan calls the *objet petit a*:

> So the voice stands at a paradoxical and ambiguous topological spot, at the intersection of language and the body, but this intersection belongs to neither. *What language and the body have in common is the voice, but the voice is part neither of language nor of the body.* The voice stems from the body, but is not its part, and it upholds language without belonging to it, yet, in this paradoxical topology, this is the only point they share—and this is the topology of *objet petit a*. This is where we could put Lacan's pet scheme of the intersection of two circles to use in a new application: the circle of language and the circle of the body, their intersection being extimate to both … For what Lacan called *objet petit a*—to put it simply—does not coincide with any existing thing, although it is always evoked only by bits of materiality, attached to them as an invisible, inaudible appendage, yet not amalgamated with them: it is both evoked and covered, enveloped by them, for 'in itself' it is just a void.
>
> (Ibid.: 73–4, italics in original)

Dolar's assessment sheds some light on the questions regarding the voice's paradoxical relation to language and embodiment that were left open by Barthes. This relation is marked by a surplus – the excess of the voice – that can be, in psychoanalytical terms, traced back to the extimacy of the Lacanian *objet petit a*. Lacan usually explained the *objet petit a* in relation to the gaze, describing the desire for something (or, more appropriately, some Thing) in the other that is lacking in the self or the present as the driver of the gaze (Lacan 1977: 104, 112, 267–70): the *objet petit a* is both the object and the cause of desire, and as such it can never be fulfilled (ibid.: 77, 103–4). On occasion, however, he did state that the voice, too, can function as an *objet petit a* for listeners, as the perceivable something in the Other (ibid.: 242); it is this reading of it that Dolar applies to the voice by the example of the HMV 'His Master's Voice' campaign (Dolar 2006: 74–81; cf. Kane 2014: 206–14).

Like Barthes, Dolar studies the human voice with a relative disregard for the role that its timbre plays in the psychoanalytical contexts he outlines. The psychoanalytical preoccupation with subjectivity determines his thought: in his search for 'the nature of the subject implied in [voice]', Dolar's conception of the voice does, at times, his objections to Barthes notwithstanding, coincide with the interior subject (Dolar 2006: 23). He argues that a large part of the voice's significance lies in its political and ethical impact (ibid.: 83–124). Here psychoanalysis follows a similar trajectory to carnal phenomenologies of voice, and curiously curves back to the areas from which it claims to step away. When Dolar does discuss timbre, therefore, it is unsurprising that he describes it, based on traditional notions of timbre as sonic difference originating from material difference, as the 'individuality' of the voice (ibid.: 22). The human subjectivity that Dolar finds in vocal timbre is as much a reduction to corporeality and identity as Barthes's 'grain of the voice' and Ihde's 'the who of voice'.

When we translate Dolar's ideas about the voice to timbre, however, interesting vistas are opened. Like Barthes, Dolar notes that voice exceeds language and signification. Although both identify the non-linguistic signification that voice could have through corporeality, they both leave space for the loss of signification in voice. While Barthes frames this excess as aporia (cf. Dunsby 2009: 130–1), Dolar, following Lacan, theorizes it as the unattainable object-cause of desire (2006: 71–4). I would argue that this excess, this aporia, this *objet petit a* in voice is operative precisely in timbre – the timbre of voice, in this case, but also of instrumental and electronic timbres – because timbre brings to the foreground the paradoxical relation between the material and immaterial aspects of sonic phenomenology that both Barthes and Dolar find so fascinating. The idea that vocal timbre works as a lack which triggers *jouissance* (Lacan 2007: 178) would explain listeners' eager inscriptions of meanings – inscribed signifieds which have to be understood as fantasies of meaning – onto this tangibly present but ephemeral quality of sound. These inscriptions are not indexing or iconic practices, and they should not be taken as evidence of timbral indexicality or iconicity. On the contrary: they are evidence that timbre, while it causally points to an index and can be circumscribed via the linguistic artifice of metaphor, simultaneously also exceeds both categories, and thus, from a psychoanalytic perspective, assumes the role of unattainable object-cause of desire. When the timbral *objet petit a* is vocal, the desire it evokes is caused by the speaking or singing Other, and the listener's aural fantasy will be projected onto them (Fran Katzenjammer in *Black Books*); in the case of instrumental and electronic timbres, desire and fantasy are extended to the non-human realm (Goths dancing to Asche's 'Doom').

My exchange, above, with a dramatic soprano who is reluctant to sing can be understood in this manner. My musical ears wanted some Thing from her voice that had nothing to do with her corporeality, her subjectivity or her speaking. Although it was triggered by those material circumstances, my desire was in excess of them and hinged on lack: it was sparked and driven only by the surplus *jouissance* audible in her timbre, and although my rational self knew that voice has no necessary connection with personality (and so I did not explicate my desire), my psychological self was concerned with her personally (and so my desire implicitly framed the potential of her timbre as an *objet petit a*).

The paradoxes of timbral indexes, icons and excess

The stepwise assessment of timbre's most frequently occurring discursive representations can only lead to the recognition that its key characteristics are marked by ambivalence. This chapter has yielded a list of paradoxes that could be added to the list compiled in the previous chapter – the timbral event *does and does not* function as an index, and it *does and does not* function as an icon. The open ending of timbre-as-excess in Barthes's and Dolar's theories of voice adds another paradox:

6. Timbre is able to evoke aporia or function as an *objet petit a*:
    a. it exceeds indexicality and iconicity, as surplus *and* lack.

Timbre's accumulative paradoxes are difficult to overcome. Perhaps the important point to make here is that they should not be overcome. Perhaps a theory of timbre is only possible if it does not just account for, but is based on, the same paradoxes that make this musical quality so hard to grasp. Because these paradoxes are instrumental for timbre's role in musical appreciation I would argue that such a theory would have to be developed as an aesthetics of timbre.

Steven Shaviro notices that Dolar's psychoanalytical focus overlooks the 'aesthetics of the voice', which he deems key to an understanding of the topic (Shaviro). Judging from the list of individual singers he names as examples of such an aesthetic, he refers to vocal timbre here: rather than an assessment of the meanings of voice, Shaviro desires an assessment of the more immediate, 'purely sonic' – i.e. timbral – aspects of voice and their appreciation. Shaviro pinpoints precisely what is lacking not just in Dolar's book, but in many existing theories of timbre outside of the empirical fields studied in Chapter 1, which tend to be based on one or more of the timbral characteristics explored in this chapter. A theory based on the aesthetics of timbre could acknowledge, include and operationalize the paradoxes at the root of timbral ontology and discourse.

The aesthetics of timbre revolve around gaps: those between production and performance, difference and identity, index and icon, no-sign and signification, lack and surplus. The aesthetic moment of timbre is brief and powerful. Reverting once again to visual metaphor, timbre occurs to the listener in a manner comparable to turning a photo negative to light, within the event of the evaporation of the image. Timbral aesthetics is so powerful *because of* its immediate evaporation: tone colour establishes an aesthetics of the moment, of the event. This evental aesthetics is marked by what can only be described as present absence: while timbre is audibly and tangibly present, the experience of this presence indicates the absence of anything concrete, anybody in particular. But it is precisely that abyss, the alluring gap that timbre inhabits, that affects us. Hunter Hunt-Hendrix describes the 'haptic void' of black metal timbres as an assault on the senses that is overwhelmingly present in its bewildering absence:

> Extremity as a concept that is inherently bound in violence and horror exists sonically and aesthetically; the distortion of the guitars and vocals and

jackhammer drumming gives the timbral assault that exceeds its boundaries and exists as the haptic void, the hypothetical total or maximal level of intensity.
(Hunt-Hendrix 2010: 55)

In a similar albeit slightly less colourful manner, Shaviro argues that the aesthetic experience of voice leads listeners into a 'labyrinth' (Shaviro). The plane of immanence established by timbral becoming is the core of its aesthetic attraction, and this is why the meanings attributed to it will always be as vague as they are compelling: the *plus-de-c(h)oeur* awakened by an enchanting soprano voice as it emerges from a choir, the dark mood of Goth music, the grain of the voice that evokes unattainable desires in listeners, or the unknown emotion that is somehow 'deeper than love' in Antony and the Johnson's unusual timbres. Timbre's aesthetic significance is that of an intensified here and now, a time and place engendered by the drastic event of musical difference. And even the event of timbre itself is paradoxical, as its temporal ephemerality contradicts the seeming infinity of its immersion. It is the finitude of the tone colour event, the ephemerality of its occurrence, the series of gaps it establishes, that defines it as an aesthetic quality. Amending the extimacy of the *objet petit a* that Dolar describes, which is tied to subjectivity by way of desire, timbral aesthetics must be thought of as a more layered type of outside: the outside of present absence which coexists with the inscriptive process operated by desire.

Before moving on to the epistemological complexity of timbral aesthetics itself in Chapters 4 and 5, Chapter 3 explores the ways in which the surplus and lack of timbral indexes and icons lead to the timbral sublime, the alluring gap that is the core of the timbral aesthetic event.

3

Excess, sublime, lure

In her rich cultural history of the castrato, Martha Feldman cites eighteenth- and nineteenth-century reviews of castrati performances. Feldman is struck by the way in which the reviewers are caught in a 'tumble of metaphoric densities' (2015: 105–9): the castrato voice was described as sweet, full, rounded, silvery, golden, crystalline, angelic, heavenly and uncanny. Through an extensive study of the castrato vocal apparatus, contemporary newspaper reviews, printed vocal exercises used by castrati, as well as the few remaining castrati recordings, she tries to tease out the embodied vocal praxes that created these lost timbres (ibid.: 79–132). Castrato timbre is a noteworthy example of the ways in which tone colour exceeds the realms of indexicality and iconicity as outlined in the previous chapter. This timbre is the index to a very specific body onto which lack is both physically and imaginatively inscribed, but a detailed knowledge of that corporeality does not explain the legendary allure of the castrato timbre. The linguistic icons 'angelic', 'heavenly' and – because of the ambiguity of the castrato's genderedness – 'uncanny' (ibid.: 123–4, 128) negate the horrifying psychical procedures from which these voices originated and hinted, instead, at an ephemeral, divine or ghostly disembodiment. These descriptions raise the uneasy possibility that there may be a connection between the corporeal horror of the castrato index and the perceived sublimity of its aesthetic experience. One reason why these timbral 'palimpsests' of endless inscriptive openness are so fascinating is precisely that they are physically as well as aesthetically unattainable for most people (ibid.: 132): as it will now forever remain out of reach, the castrato timbre has itself become a lack, and is left to the hazy borderlands of retrospective aural imagination. The castrato timbre is an aesthetic *objet-a* in which we fetishize a sonic object-cause of desire that is no longer present. Combining Schaeffer's and Dolar's thought, the castrato voice is the ultimate *objet sonore petit a*: forever acousmatic, forever inapproachable, forever sublime, locked in nostalgic horror or horrific nostalgia.

This chapter explores the aesthetics of timbral excess and sublimity. It argues that although the materiality of timbre – as explored in Chapter 1 and in the discussion of Barthes's 'grain' in Chapter 2 – is always present in its concrete sound and its perception, the aesthetic appreciation of tone colour is characterized as much by an awareness of that materiality as by a flight into immateriality. Surpassing even the most elated of linguistic metonymies, the pervasive inscription of sublimity in tone colour is just as irrepressible in timbral aesthetics as the tangibility of sound source.

Excess and gaps

Jean-Luc Nancy's treatise *Listening* (2007) questions the differences between hearing and listening to sound and music. The treatise argues that language, time and self bear no discernible relevance to sonic experience, as the event of hearing sound, and especially music, are not related to verbal signifying systems and redefine both temporality and subjectivity in exclusive relation to the sonic event. Having evacuated the plane of listening from traditional structuring mechanisms, Nancy asks himself what we listen to when we do not attribute meaning to sound, when we do not worry about time and self. Listening to raw, non-coded sound finds its epitome, Nancy contends, in listening to timbre (2007: 36). Albeit very similar to Schaeffer's *objet sonore* in definition, Nancy's version of timbre as non-referential sound, which he describes as 'the very resonance of the sonorous', is much less concrete than the sonic objects that Schaeffer crafted (ibid.: 40). Nancy is unreservedly idealist in his assessment of timbre: 'Timbre is the resonance of sound: or sound itself' (ibid.: 40). Although such a description of timbre finds no evidence in physics or musicology, it is not difficult to see the philosophical grounds for Nancy's observation. Timbre cannot be defined as a 'single datum', but presents and unites, rather, a heterogeneity of components (ibid.: 41). As Chapter 1 asserted, timbre's material ontology can best be described as a convergence of sound source physicality, frequency spectrum, live or virtual acoustics, production technology and musical contingencies. And as Chapter 2 subsequently argued, what seems an evident effect of timbre's phenomenology – its sensory reception verbalized into index or icon – can only be described in a bewildering accumulation of paradoxes: timbre continually confirms as well as negates its own indexicality, and it yields as well as eludes the fixity of iconic representation. Timbre is an ever-present but ever-evolving, frustratingly opaque and fascinatingly excessive aspect of sonic events. Nancy's response to this timbral predicament is to revert to the idealism of Schaefferian reduced listening: he defines timbre at its most basic level as the inalienable, entwined materiality of sonic cause and sonic manifestation, 'the resonance of sound', which he does not hesitate to refer to as sound 'itself'. But he then goes on to use the term 'resonance' both on a material and a metaphorical level, using it both to indicate the resonating of frequency spectrums in air and the experiential resonance of perceived tone colours inside listener subjectivity. Here the material indexes of timbral ontology and the iconization of timbral phenomenology find themselves conflated yet again. When unfolded, Nancy's seemingly straightforward reduction – timbre is sound itself – conceals layer upon layer of accumulated paradoxes.

Nancy's 'resonance' could be read as an attempt to include timbre's manifold paradoxes. He recognizes that timbre is in excess of material origin, arguing that it resounds as much outward and *from* the body of its cause, as inward and *within* the body of the listener. Exceeding ontological grounding, timbre reaches into the phenomenologies of sense, hearing and listening (ibid.: 40). But it does not sit comfortably in traditional phenomenology either, as here, too, its sonic and sensory instability exceeds the limits of perception. Timbre is not merely heard, it is also felt, in both senses of that word: in its corporeal and mental resonance, Nancy contends, it contributes to and shapes subjectivities. The necessary subjectivity of timbral perception is one reason for timbre's perpetual excess of verbal description, linguistic signification and empirical quantification: this sonic event is corporeally and emotionally felt as part of me and my relation to the outside world, and therefore it is as much in process as my subjectivity and the world. I cannot grasp the extent of timbre's touch, but at the same time I am necessarily entwined with it (ibid.: 40–1; cf. Vogels 2017). Timbre does not just entangle and invert the relations between index and icon, but it also implicates listening subjectivities in the entwinement of its ongoing sonic and sensory becoming. Here Nancy's reduction of timbral resonance turns, suddenly and sharply, from indexical ontology and iconized phenomenology to a form of sonic extimacy.

Timbre now appears to the subject like a Kantian Thing that is no longer reducible to the ontology of a material sound wave or the phenomenology of a grain:

> I would say that timbre is communication of the incommunicable: provided it is understood that the incommunicable is nothing other, in a perfectly logical way, than communication itself, that thing by which a subject makes an echo – of self, of the other, it's all one – it's all one in the plural.
>
> (Nancy 2007: 41)

Nancy's concept of timbre as 'sound itself' has evolved to sound *in-itself*, the sound of an absolute other resonating in Plato's cave through which the listener creates an echo (echo) of self and other (self other other self), but all in one (all one one one one one). Timbre, then, is not just constantly in excess – of index and icon, of referentiality and body – but is, rather, itself the process and the resonance of excess. Timbre's resistance to ontological or phenomenological definition accordingly leads Nancy to redefine timbral resonance in terms of surplus and expenditure as 'my body beaten by its sense of body, what we used to call its soul' (ibid.: 43). In Mladen Dolar's terms, Nancy's version of timbre is a sonic *objet petit a* (Dolar 2006: 73–4; cf. Chapter 2): the fact of timbre is irresistible to him precisely in its impossible unification of tangible immediacy and ineffable elusiveness (Nancy 2007: 58), that is to say he is both philosophically and mindlessly lured by the unattainable non-object that is present in all sonority. As he ultimately describes it in a manner more related to the Kantian supersensible than to ontological cause or phenomenological epoché, timbre appears to function for Nancy as a noumenon.

Nancy's noumenal assessment of timbre (like Barthes's ecstatic descriptions of his own listening experience) should not be discarded because of its seemingly unquantifiable premise. There is, in musicking, an element of the ineffable, even if the musical ineffable has not been the subject of philosophical debate since the waning of post-Kantian idealism and German Romanticism in musical aesthetics (cf. Chapter 5). In a philosophical dialogue with Hanslick and Wagner, Lydia Goehr has sought to renegotiate the presence of the noumenal and the ineffable in music. Contesting the musicologically engrained, dualist distinction between the 'purely musical' and the 'extramusical', or formalism and transcendentalism, Goehr approaches musical aesthetics through the non-binary perspective of 'doubleness'. She argues that music can be understood simultaneously as a Hanslickean auditory phenomenon and as an audible manifestation of the Schopenhauerean transcendental (Goehr 2004: 28–9, 37–8, 201–7). The transcendental part of music's meta/physical 'doubleness' is what she refers to as the 'extra', the gap between concept and idealist Thing-in-itself which is not accounted for by a dualist approach to music's formalistically or scientifically quantifiable properties (ibid.: 38, 64). Goehr uses unreservedly Romantic language for the 'inexpressible or unknowable' in music, the surplus that appears in Nancy's essay as the 'incommunicable', and which has been excluded from the philosophy of music as well as from wider philosophical discourses since, at the latest, poststructuralism (ibid.: 136, cf. 29–31).

As Goehr's 'doubleness' mediates music's exceeding the limits of the speakable and the knowable, it is closely related to the sublime, which itself is the experience of these limits (Brillenburgh Wurth 2009: 20). In musical experience, Goehr contends following Schopenhauer, there is always the knowing that we are on the brink of something transcendental, something absolute, but this knowing is accompanied by the simultaneous realization that this Thing is unattainable, beyond the reach of the physical (2004: 119). What remains is the sublime:

> We are left only with the sublime (and, therefore, double-edged) knowledge of the unavoidable suffering of our insatiable wills but also of our desire and ability to escape this realization by any means possible, even if only temporarily.
>
> (Ibid.: 26)

The recognizable but unknowable presence of the transcendental in music, Goehr argues, evokes 'a moment of fundamental doubt' (ibid.: 42) which manifests as an 'aesthetic reaching' (ibid.: 27, 112, 123). The deliberate separation of this doubt and this reaching from Enlightenment rationality was the key impetus of the Romanticism that ultimately inspired Wagner (ibid.: 42).

Goehr does not limit her exploration of aesthetic doubleness to the nineteenth century. She finds the same oppositions and the same doubleness in contemporary music aesthetics and in the debates surrounding performance practice. Whether musicians and critics are inspired by formalist notions of historically perfect authenticity (*Werktreue*) or rather follow postmodern impulses towards the imperfect, each performance of music shows the same inherent convergence of musical and extra-musical elements, the same paradoxical presence of the transcendental within even the most rationally grounded form of musicking (ibid.: 132–73). The key concepts she uses to identify this convergence are 'musicality' and 'musical expression' (ibid.: 118–31). With these concepts she pinpoints that particular instinct possessed by any musicking human being that enables them to distinguish, as a musical version of the Kantian *a priori*, what a certain phrase, melody or rhythm wants, what it needs to be drawn out of an instrument or voice. Musicality is the intuitive knowledge of how music sings and does so autonomously (Chapter 4 will theorize this peculiar musical agency, through vital materialism, as music-power). Goehr speaks about this musical *a priori* in intentionally vague terms:

> I have recalled all those appeals 'to heart and soul' to demonstrate deliberately the noticeable lack of terminology for the residue that cannot be captured in empirical terms. That there is this lack reveals the 'negative' character of the domain of the 'inexpressible'.
>
> (Ibid.: 129)

The physical techniques that musicians employ, Goehr contends, are always counterbalanced by 'musicality': this musical *a priori*, the possession of an inner ear to music and the capacity to translate into performance what music *wants*, the ability to translate music's autonomous voice, is what she calls 'expression'. The moment of expression is the topology of music-aesthetic doubleness, the reaching that she theorizes: 'the literally musical becomes extra- or metaphorically musical. For this transfiguration, this aesthetic reaching, the two elements are at every moment required' (ibid.: 123). This aesthetic reaching, moreover, takes place both on a practical and a philosophical plane: it is the reaching across the binary of musical autonomy in the formalist sense and music's engagement with the extra-musical in Schopenhauer's sense, which Goehr sees exemplified in the debates between Hanslick's 'metaphysically constrained' and Wagner's 'metaphysically inflated' music-aesthetic positions (ibid.: 64). Goehr's philosophical doubleness, thus, deploys the gaps between these two opposed strands of thinking not just as a methodological bridge but also, itself, as the aesthetic location of music. Music formalistically refers to itself and it simultaneously also transcendentally intervenes in the extra-musical. The 'limit of philosophy' in the title of her book is the very fact of this simultaneity in musical aesthetics: the autonomous voice of music, she argues, establishes itself in this unspeakable reaching across, this musical expression (ibid.: 17, 46, 92).

Goehr's non-binarism in musicality offers a significant step towards an understanding of the paradoxes of timbre. Timbre, the previous chapter argued, is the very nexus of musical excess: it points indexically to the materiality of sound and defies it, it is an indispensable but highly unstable part of music's internal and external vectors, it can be hinted at by the most colourful of verbal icons but eludes even the most ephemeral of them, and it presents the object-cause of desire in the listening experience. In its simultaneous affirmation and excess of all these practically and philosophically opposing positions, timbral aesthetics occupies the gaps that Goehr describes. Timbre, in many ways, epitomizes the aesthetic reaching she proposes: with its extreme aesthetic stretch between the quantifiably physical, the purely musical and the transcendentally extra-musical, timbre *is* the 'residue' (ibid.: 129) of musical aesthetics and philosophy that inhabits the questioning gap, the moment of transfiguration into the meta/physical. The paradoxes inherent to timbre's epistemology render reductions – Schaeffer's *objet sonore*, Barthes's grain, Nancy's resonance – difficult if not impossible. Timbre leaves gaps: but these gaps invite a 'reaching' across binaries rather than a musical or philosophical polarization.

The following paragraphs explore the timbral gap, the inexpressible reaching in timbre. Our rational selves cast aside for the duration of listening, we wallow in that gap: following our ears' desires, savouring the *jouissance* of the philosophically off-limits, we lose ourselves in the timbral sublime.

Sehnsucht for the unknown: The timbral sublime

Like Schaeffer's creative striving for the (unattainable) *objet sonore*, Nancy's reflection on timbre as 'sound itself' is consistent with the aesthetic idealism that dominated music philosophy in the early Romantic age, and that culminated in the veneration of instrumental music as the highest form of art. In the Romantic idealism of the sublime, the paradoxes of timbre do not seem so strange.

In his 1757 treatise on the sublime, Edmund Burke reflects on the attraction of the ineffable. He describes the core of the sublime as lying in 'obscurity': the strongest emotions are evoked, he says, by art that does not give precise descriptions or depictions of its subject matter, but rather creates images shrouded in obscurity (1990: 54–5). As an example of such sublime obscurity he quotes Milton's description of Death in *Paradise Lost*, and states that in this fragment 'all is dark, uncertain, confused, terrible and sublime to the last degree' (ibid.: 55). It is the darkness, the circumlocution of metaphor, Burke contends, that affects readers most, and that elevates their emotions towards the sublime. Sublimity, he states, has everything to do with reaching for infinity, whether in words, painting, or sound: it 'is due to the terrible uncertainty of the thing described' (ibid.: 58). Different from Kant's philosophy of the sublime, where not knowing is posited as the undesirable epistemological opposite of knowing that is waiting to be resolved, Burke's version of the sublime capitalizes on the desirability of not knowing (Brillenburgh Wurth 2009: 47–52). He relates this not knowing directly to metaphysical infinity:

> The ideas of eternity, and infinity, are among the most affecting we have, and yet perhaps there is nothing of which we really understand so little, as of infinity and eternity.
>
> (Burke 1990: 57)

The epistemological uncertainty of the infinite stirs the imagination, Burke argues, and this is what evokes the twin imaginations of grand terror and grand beauty that constitute the sublime. In order to reach for the sublime, for this reason, art has to have an element of uncertainty that allows for the possible imagining of an unknowable beyond.

Burke describes sound as 'almost infinitely' capable of evoking the sublime (ibid.: 77–8). Although he would not have used the word timbre, which was only introduced by Rousseau in 1765 (cf. Chapter 1), it is interesting to note the timbral components of Burke's sonic sublime. He begins by discarding language as a component of the sonic sublime: language in sound, whether in speech, in song or in programmatic description, would prescribe too precise an interpretation of the sonic, and therefore inhibit the possibility of the unknowable (ibid.: 75, 77). It is 'by means altogether different' that sound has power over the human passions (ibid.: 75). Burke identifies four different ways in which the perception of sound can lead to a sublime experience: through loudness, suddenness, intermitting sound and animal cries (ibid.: 75–8). The excesses of loudness, suddenness and interrupted sound clearly point towards the terrifying beauty evoked by the infinite: a loud volume, for instance, 'amazes and confounds the imagination' (ibid.: 76). Within these excesses, it is timbre's indexical and iconic elusiveness that powerfully channels the infinite potential of sound. In the section 'Intermitting', Burke focuses on 'low, confused, uncertain sounds' (ibid.: 77). While 'low' could refer to volume or pitch – both closely related to timbre – 'confused' and 'uncertain' as qualities of sound can only refer to timbre, and it is this confusing timbre, Burke contends, that makes them sublime. He compares the absence of a clearly identifiable source in certain sounds to the absence of light that renders the darkness of night a vehicle for the sublime:

> I have already observed, that night increases our terror, more perhaps than anything else; it is our nature, when we do not know what may happen to us, to fear the worst that can happen; and hence it is, that uncertainty is so terrible, that we often seek to be rid of it, at the hazard of certain mischief. Now, some

low, confused, uncertain sounds, leave us in the same fearful anxiety concerning their causes, that no light, or an uncertain light, does concerning the objects that surround us.

(Ibid.: 76–7)

Timbre's capacity to obscure its own indexicality, thus, is a key quality of the sonic sublime, which, in Burke's hearing, manifests as an acousmatic sublime. Similarly, in the section on 'The cries of Animals' Burke emphasizes that particular 'modulations of sound' in animal sounds can evoke the sublime as they may not point to physical sources known to the listener (ibid.: 77). These 'modulations of sound' present unknown timbres, and their indexical evasiveness, again, leads to an experience of sublime terror and beauty.

The terrified and yearning imagination of the unknown in which the Burkean sublime manifests itself has been theorized by Kiene Brillenburgh Wurth as *Sehnsucht*. Brillenburgh Wurth argues that *Sehnsucht* is characterized by a desire that is not directed towards the fulfilment of a lack, but by 'the very disinterestedness of desire *qua* desire', or desire for its own sake that does not want well-defined objects, but rather an endless repetition of the affective drive of yearning itself and of the unfulfillable promise it offers (2009: 50). '*Sehnsucht* performs again and again a great outlook of becoming' (ibid.: 51). *Sehnsucht*'s 'paradoxical delight of indeterminacy', Brillenburgh Wurth asserts, is central to Burke's sublime (ibid.: 51). The Romantic notion of *Sehnsucht* offers perhaps a more adequate approach to timbral aesthetics than Dolar's theory of the vocal *objet petit a*: whereas the latter is directed inwards, seeking to identify the psychoanalytic vectors constituting listening subjectivity, the former is directed outwards, seeking to identify the shared characteristics of listeners' aesthetic reaching in timbral experience. While the *objet petit a*, in other words, elucidates listening subjectivity, *Sehnsucht* elucidates timbral aesthetics.

The philosophical attention to the sublime in the eighteenth century opened the door for a new aesthetics of music of which the remnants can be traced in twentieth and twenty-first century philosophy. Nancy finds in music a 'romantic' potential, namely its capacity to hint at an ineffable 'beyond-significance' which is not analysable through semantic structures or decodable as an affective language (2007: 58–9). This capacity of music was indeed crucial in Romantic philosophy and aesthetics. Brillenburgh Wurth argues that the sublime, in many ways, is in itself a musical effect, and that it was for this reason that music was such a central presence in eighteenth- and early nineteenth-century aesthetic philosophy. Music, she argues, is an 'empty sign': because of music's eternal deferral of referentiality and signification, the musical sublime is able to set listeners in an aporetic oscillation that remains – and must remain – without resolution (2009: 23–46). The musical sublime, therefore, is a 'repetitive sublime': as music's indeterminacy lacks the transcendental resolution required for the Kantian sublime, the driving force of musical *Sehnsucht* dictates that it lingers perpetually on the threshold of the infinite. In a distinctly Foucauldian line of reasoning, Brillenburgh Wurth contends that '[t]he limit *itself* always already negates its beyond … the threshold, the *limen* contains the void that we deem beyond it' (ibid.: 20; cf. Foucault 2000).

Timbre is doubtlessly the most liminal of all music's qualities. Hearing timbre is lingering on the threshold of a void: beyond the *limen* of timbre there is no clearly identifiable physicality, no concrete signification, and not even a premonition of meaning. The threshold of listening is the topology of timbral paradox, and our *Sehnsucht* for the awesome emptiness beyond dictates that we linger in its gap. It is not surprising, therefore, that timbre, specifically instrumental timbre – which most explicitly leaves words and human bodies behind in its sonic flight – became an important focus of German Romantic composers and music philosophers. Writers such as Wilhelm Wackenroder, Ludwig Tieck, Jean Paul, Novalis and E.T.A. Hoffmann all theorized instrumental music as evoking the wordless, incomprehensible aporia of sublime infinitude. Although it had the epistemological qualities of the Kantian noumenon, Brillenburgh Wurth argues, the sublime described by these authors bears a closer resemblance to the unresolved, eternally repetitive *Sehnsucht* inherent to the Burkean sublime (ibid.: 55–71). This led, from the late eighteenth century onwards, to an increasing urge towards the abandonment of words in music. Instead, symphonies and *Lieder ohne Worte* were the expression – in Goehr's sense of the musical *a priori* – of that which words can never say: the Burkean infinite evoked by the repetitive sublime of musical experience (cf. Brillenburgh Wurth 2009: 55–9). In his 1830 review of Beethoven's instrumental music, E.T.A. Hoffmann voices German Romanticism's instrumental sublime in language heavily laden with Burkean *Sehnsucht*:

> When we speak of music as an independent art, should we not always restrict our meaning to instrumental music, which, scorning every aid, every admixture of another art (the art of poetry), gives pure expression to music's specific nature, recognizable in this form alone? It is the most romantic of all arts – one might almost say, the only genuinely romantic one – for its sole subject is the infinite.

[M]usic discloses to man an unknown realm, a world that has nothing in common with the external sensual world that surrounds him, a world in which he leaves behind him all definite feelings to surrender himself to an inexpressible longing ... Beethoven's [instrumental] music sets in motion the lever of fear, of awe, of horror, of suffering, and wakens just that infinite longing which is the essence of romanticism.

(Hoffmann 1965: 35–7)

When Hoffmann and his contemporaries write about instrumental music, they do not necessarily mention timbre. Indeed, as Emily Dolan has demonstrated, the word timbre was not often explicitly used until well into the nineteenth century, and the words 'resonance', 'Ton' (tone/sonority), or 'Farbe' (colour) would be used instead (2013: 47–71). Hoffmann refers to the art of orchestration elsewhere as 'the mystique of instruments' and emphasizes that instrumentation could have an 'astonishing effect' on the listeners (cited in Dolan 2013: 166, 229). Instrumental timbres were described in a number of eighteenth- and early nineteenth-century treatises in terms of affective characters that could give individual colours to music but were not reducible to 'a tidy semiotic system' (Dolan 2013: 163). In other words, timbre does not signify but rather leaves listeners in what Burke would call the allusive 'obscurity' which is a condition for the experience of the sublime. The musical and aesthetic attention to timbre thus gave musical tone a form of autonomy – a voice, as Goehr would say – that could be utilized in the shaping of musical Beauty in the Kantian sense (cf. Dolan 2013: 148–67).

The fiercest contemporary proponent of this view was the philosopher Johann Gottfried Herder. Contesting Rameau's theories, Herder argues that musical aesthetics should not occupy itself with harmony, which is merely sound (*Schall*) and therefore a 'quantity' of music (2006: 92–4, 99–101). The true experience of music connects the first moment of tone (*Ton*) directly to the innermost depths of the soul (ibid.: 110–1): an aesthetic focus on this sensory and emotional immediacy, Herder argues, pinpoints the 'quality' inherent to musical experience rather than the superficial 'quantities' which tell us nothing about how music is perceived (ibid.: 95–8, 102–9). Although he is critical of Burke, who he contends did not have 'enough of an ear' to truly understand and appreciate the aesthetic impressions that music could make upon the human soul, Herder does agree with 'the Briton' that art should strive to reach for the sublime (ibid.: 103–5). He argues that music is able to achieve this elevation and profundity more than any other art form, and that it is specifically the individual qualities of certain tones – not the quantities of sound – that enable this capacity in music:

> You, who understand nothing but loudness and quietness, high and low pitches: pay attention to whether the sound of a flute and a shawm, of a lute and a violin, of a trumpet and a *Nachthorn* organ stop, do not have in any way, in the mixture of tones, where there cannot be loudness and quietness or high and low pitches, a specific mass of sound? Whether each of these sounds have the same effect on your sensitivity [*Empfindbarkeit*]? And if this is not the case, if there are bodies in which actual sound and counter-sound sleep, and others in which a yearning god of love, *Sehnsucht*, and lament is implicit – if there are instruments of which one bemoans the sounds of the entire world, the other one weeps, the third one resounds, the fourth forms a soft rumbling of waves, the fifth forms a rolling of tones – when each of these sounds furthermore has its own relation to our sensitivity: with this one we don't feel anything, with that one we are elevated, with another one we tremble and shudder: this one lulls us to sleep: that one inflames us to bravery and fury: a third one melts us to pity, to compassion, to love: this stings, this screams into the ear, this flows softly into us – where can I find words for it all? Who is the deaf person that could not feel this difference between sounds? and if he can feel it, then he must also admit that there is a distinct difference between individual tones … Sound is nothing but a dark admixture of tones.
>
> (Ibid.: 98–9)

Herder's use of the word 'tone' (*Ton*) to denote the specific qualities of individual sonorities points to 'what the Frenchman [presumably Rousseau] calls timbre' (ibid.: 95). He asserts that it is timbre – and decidedly not the quantifiable aspects of sound such as volume, pitch or harmony – that affects the emotions in an immediate, elating manner (cf. Dolan 2013: 77–8). With its strange simultaneity of elusive sonic qualities ('where can I find words for it all?') and undeniable differentiating effects over listener perception, the discovery of timbre as a crucial ingredient to musical experience marked what Dolan calls 'the birth of the aesthetic' in the eighteenth century (2013: 88). In Goehr's terms, moreover, it could be said that the aesthetic discovery of timbre also marked the philosophical birth of music's autonomous voice.

Philosophically entwined with the notion of the sublime, the timbrally embedded Romantic aesthetics of music was practically demarcated by the colours of instrumental music (cf. Bonds 2014: 103–17). Romantic instrumental music revolved for a large part around the expressive potential of timbre: listeners were captivated by instrumental differences forming ephemeral sonorous identities that existed only in the strokes of a violin or the passing sighs of woodwind. This could well evoke the sublimity of terror-delight: 'Beethoven's instrumental music', Hoffmann writes, 'opens up to us the realm of the monstrous and the immeasurable' (1965: 41). This focus on the sublime experience of instrumental timbre in early Romanticism led to what Carl Dahlhaus has somewhat dismissively described as an elated, metaphysically-inflected or esoteric discourse around instrumental music (1989: 88–96), but which Brillenburgh Wurth more accurately views as a reflection of the aesthetics of musical *Sehnsucht* and the Burkean sublime (2009: 59–67). As timbre was the quality of music able to express most unspeakably 'the infinite' that Hoffmann carved out as the sole subject of music, it is a form *par excellence* of the musically sublime in Brillenburgh Wurth's definition. Nancy's definition of timbre as 'sound itself' is therefore thoroughly Romantic (2007: 40): in musical idealism, instrumental timbre had the function of a musical Thing-in-itself, but a Thing whose incomprehensibility remained without resolution, evoking only the eternal rhythm of *Sehnsucht*.

While the early Romantic timbral sublime would not evoke anything more specific than the terrifying unknown, timbral expression was described in more detail over the course of the nineteenth century. The lyrical language that Hector Berlioz uses in his *Grand Traité d'Instrumentation et d'Orchestration Modernes* was mentioned in Chapter 1. His description of the flute timbre in Gluck's *Orphée* as the 'thousand-fold sublime wailing of a suffering, despairing shade of the departed' is interesting in this context (Berlioz 2002: 140). This kinship to the Burkean sublime (which Berlioz often finds in Gluck's orchestration) notwithstanding, the purpose of the treatise is to describe the expressive possibilities of specific instruments with as much precision as possible. Berlioz's aim is

> to show the range and certain essential details of the mechanism of each instrument, and then to examine the nature of the tone, particular character and expressive potential of each – a branch of study hitherto greatly neglected – and finally to consider the best ways of grouping them effectively.
>
> (Ibid.: 6)

Berlioz is keen to ascribe precise modes of expression and characteristics to individual instrumental timbres (cf. Dolan 2013: 213–19). The section in his treatise that discusses the clarinet, for instance, begins with an exploration of the timbral differences between clarinets and other reed instruments, in order to offer as precise a description as possible – albeit in metaphor – of the instrument's 'fuller, purer and more limpid voice' (Berlioz 2002: 117). After this general introduction, Berlioz proceeds to a description of the individual tone of each of the different clarinets. The lower the instrument is pitched, he asserts, 'the more veiled and melancholy its sound', whereas the higher instruments lack 'purity, sweetness and individuality' (ibid.: 122). The B flat instrument is the most 'appealing' of all clarinets, whereas the F instrument is 'screechy' and the C instrument can be 'harsh' (ibid.: 122). When well played, the clarinet's intermediate register is both tender and noble, and can be used for the expression of 'the most poetic thoughts and feelings' such as epic scenes, heroic love and ghostly 'half-shades of sound' (ibid.: 125). Pointing out the exemplary use of the clarinet in Weber's *Freischütz*, his own *Lélio*, Beethoven's Seventh Symphony and Sacchini's *Œdipe à Colonne*, Berlioz also explains why none of these excerpts could possibly have contained other wind instruments: a flute timbre would have been 'too weak' for that particular section in Beethoven's Seventh, and the use of oboes instead of clarinets in *Lélio* would have ruined the musical symbolism of 'love and purity' (ibid.: 126–31).

Berlioz's meticulous exploration of individual instrumental timbres illustrates how tone colours came to represent orchestrally embedded individualities in nineteenth-century instrumental music. As Berlioz's descriptions of the expressive possibilities of the clarinet timbre illustrate, however, these individualities of tone colour functioned as metaphorical approximations of intellectual concepts rather than as concrete signifiers of particular characters. This careful balance is illustrated, for instance, by the *idée fixe* in his own *Symphonie Fantastique* (1830). The *idée* wanders between various instrument groups and movements. Being 'a melody with the function but not the appearance of a theme', the various permutations of the *idée* are differentiated through rhythm and harmony, but most importantly in timbre, exploring the individual sonorous differences between various instruments (Dahlhaus 1989: 155). We could speculate, based on Berlioz's writings on orchestration, what these timbral individualities may signify, but that would be missing the point. Only the *idée*, the musical form, is fixed – not its identity, not its signifieds, which must remain as vague as the composer's passion, or the Thing that is Harriet-in-herself: a 'dream image', as the *Symphonie*'s programme announces, an ideal, a noumenon.

Berlioz's and similar treatises and practices pre-empted the organological classifications of Hornbostel-Sachs (cf. Chapter 1). They also led to what Dahlhaus calls 'the emancipation of timbre' in nineteenth-century music, which gave it 'an aesthetic raison d'être and significance of its own' (Dahlhaus 1989:

243). In Gustav Mahler's music, this emancipation of instrumental timbre – and with it the wordless, imprecise, aporetic expressive capacity of tone colour – reached a culmination (Sheinbaum 2005). Consider the 'fate' motif in the first movement of Mahler's Sixth Symphony (written in 1903, re-orchestrated by the composer before and after the first performance in 1906), in which A major in the trumpets changes to A minor in the oboes. The fact that it is difficult to imagine this harmonic motion the other way around, with major in the oboes leading to minor in the trumpets, indicates how timbral identity is simultaneously undeniably present in music, extremely hard to define and deeply culturally engrained. The 'fate' that names the motif is the unnameable fate of timbre.

The timbral noumenon of German Romanticism was thus marked by the 'doubleness' of musical autonomy that Goehr proposes: it was a noumenon that was not quite a noumenon, out of reach but tangibly perceivable, an abstract idea that however had – as Berlioz's treatise shows – technically analysable components, and that ultimately was both material and ineffable. Moreover, the aesthetic phenomenon of timbral doubleness also played an important role in the separation of two strands of music philosophy, as it was the elated discourse around the sublimities of instrumental music that led Hanslick to proclaim, in his *On the Musically Beautiful* (first edition 1854), that music should only be considered in relation to the musical and does not bear any inherent connection with the extra-musical. Subjective impressions, he contends, are merely 'old spectres' coming back to 'haunt us in broad daylight' (1986: 2). Note the juxtaposition between Hanslick's statement here and the obscurity of night that Burke sought in aesthetic experience: in the sobering light of day, ghosts do not arouse the terror-delight of the sublime, but are simply subjective associations, mere 'feelings' that have nothing, objectively, to do with musical beauty (ibid.: 8–27). In distancing itself explicitly from the idealist assessments of instrumental music that gave rise to Richard Wagner's absolute music and Schopenhauer's musical metaphysics (Bonds 2014: 129–40), Hanslick's formalism consolidated the post-Kantian split between the musical and the extra-musical, or the formal and the transcendental in music criticism (Goehr 2004: 6–26; Hamilton 2007: 82–9; cf. Chapter 5).

When viewed through the aesthetic lens of the sublime, the paradoxes around timbre's unstable indexicality and elusive iconicity that were explored in Chapter 2 acquire a different dimension. Rather than as frustrating, the elusiveness of timbre's material sources can now be read as advantageous to musical aesthetics: precisely the fact that we cannot determine whether a vocal timbre points to the singer's throat, her personality, or *something else*, or the fact that Jimi Hendrix's legendary guitar sound can never *quite* be reproduced, contributes to the unfathomable depth of these timbres in the listening experience. In the light of the Romantic sublime, moreover, timbral metonymy regains momentum: its necessarily imprecise verbal images shroud sonority in the obscurity that the listener craves (not) to hear. Her *Sehnsucht* desires to perceive, in the most indefinable of musical qualities, a hint of something beyond the known, a sonic figuration of what Dolar assesses as the psychoanalytic *objet petit a* but which was theorized by Burke and his contemporaries as the terror and fascination unified in sublime experience. Listening to timbre, from this perspective, is a form of the 'aesthetic reaching' that Goehr identifies in music (Goehr 2004: 123): this reaching for a 'beyond' accessible through music is engendered by timbre's 'doubleness', by the aesthetic gaps and philosophical residues it leaves between listening and cognition. It is interesting in this light that ethnomusicological research shows that timbral features are associated with the sacred, the other-worldly and rituality in an array of non-Western music (Fales 2002: 79–90).

The twentieth-century timbral imperative

The eighteenth-century aesthetics of the sublime helps us understand the conceptual paradoxes around timbre identified in the previous chapter, which pervaded timbral discourses since the inception of modern aesthetics. As briefly mentioned in Chapter 1, that inception itself was significantly influenced by the attention to timbre, which appears in Enlightenment philosophy as an unnameable or sublime aesthetic phenomenon. So important was timbre for Herder's aesthetics that he repeatedly urged composers, philosophers and listeners alike to return to the sensitivity of the ancient Greeks, who were able to 'hear tone where we only hear sound' (2006: 106–8). 'Oh coldness, oh misery', he exclaims in reflecting on the timbre-deaf ears of his contemporaries (ibid.: 106). If we were only able to actually hear timbre and understand fully its connection to our soul, he contends, we would no longer need metaphors when talking about music (ibid.: 107). Herder expresses the ardent desire that music composers and philosophers of his time could revive the timbral sublimity of the ancients:

> The inner shudder, the almighty feeling that would seize them [those who can only hear sound] would be inexplicable to them: they would know nothing that could work so ardently and deeply upon them in the entire nature of visible beings: they would believe it was ghosts, ghosts of heaven and earth, that were

drawn towards them by the chains of music, plunged from spheres and abysses; they would float around them; invisible, but all the more tangible [*empfindlicher*]: one would feel their presence and that would be the inner shudder, the deep feeling that grips them in tones! – – – Here I would wish that the philosopher of pleasant sonority [*Wohllaut*] had the magical power to make all these magical histories of the fervour of music come true in actual apparitions: and when he has understood the strength of individual accents, passions, tones, and musical elements, then he can!

(Ibid.: 112)

Herder's passionate plea for a manner of composing that is informed by the sublimity of timbre was overshadowed, in the nineteenth century, by the polemics between formalists and transcendentalists (Goehr 2004: 6–47). But his musical aesthetics pre-empted, in many ways, the idealist aesthetics of timbre as it was formulated by a number of twentieth-century composers, most notably Arnold Schoenberg, Pierre Schaeffer, Karlheinz Stockhausen and Pierre Boulez. Each following their own compositional, intellectual and aesthetic trajectory, these composers contributed significant elements to the ongoing idealist aesthetics of timbre.

The most important precursor of twentieth-century timbral aesthetics of composition was Claude Debussy. Debussy's work departed from the orchestrational traditions reflected in Berlioz's treatise, which dominated nineteenth-century thinking on the subject, in that his fascination with timbre was no longer oriented towards orchestral difference as a musical representation of certain identities, or as a suitable musical expression of certain meanings. Instead, Debussy and other French composers of the late nineteenth century considered each instrumental timbre as a fount of potential sonorous beauty, a much less defined agent of musical colour, light, mood and effects. (Fleury 1996: 120–2; cf. Debussy's letter to Charles Levadé from 4 September 1903, Lesure and Nichols 1987: 112; cf. Jensen 2014: 230–1). In his search for the musically 'Inexpressible which is the ideal of all art' (Lesure and Nichols 1987: 42), Debussy firmly believed that music – through timbre – was more capable of achieving the inexpressible than other art forms: 'Music consist of colours and rhythmicized time …' (Lesure and Nichols 1987: 154). He advises composers to focus on impressions and colours:

> Collect impressions. Don't be in a hurry to write them down. Because that's something that music can do better than painting: it can centralize variations of colour and light within in a single picture – a truth generally ignored, obvious as it is …

(Ibid.: 166)

The impressions transmitted in music were never precise, but always characterized by vagueness – the imprecise, synaesthetic approach to a mood mentioned in Chapter 2 as the veiled precision of timbral metaphor. In the programme notes for his *Nocturnes*, for instance, Debussy writes that the three movements 'Nuages', 'Fêtes' and 'Sirènes', should be taken not as precise prescriptions for the form of the pieces, but as indications of 'impressions and particular light effects'. These could, in the composer's words, vary as much as a cloudy sky, could be as dazzling and light as a summer party in progress, and have as many colours and movements as the sea (Holmes 1989: 62). These effects were achieved to a large extent by Debussy's innovative use of timbre: *Nocturne* is organized into timbral groupings that create timbral 'nuances', finding 'different combinations possible inside a single colour, as a painter might make a study in grey, for example (Lesure and Nichols 1987: 73, 75; cf. Fleury 1996: 123–7). Debussy's work was received with attention to and admiration for his mastery of timbral impressions and movement. When Stéphane Mallarmé, whose poem inspired Debussy's *Prélude à l'Après-Midi d'un Faune*, first heard the composition during its premiere performance in Paris on 22 December 1894, he wrote

> Sylvain d'haleine première
> Si la flute a réussi
> Ouïs toute la lumière
> Qu'y soufflera Debussy

> If the flute has played well, the primal woodland breath hears all the light that Debussy has inspired in it.
>
> (quoted in Holmes 1989: 48)

Fellow composer Vincent d'Indy commented that Debussy's opera *Pelléas et Mélisande*, which premiered in 1902, rolled out 'many-coloured waves of music' that revealed 'hidden meanings' (quoted ibid.: 66).

While Debussy experimented with tone colour in his compositions and wrote about them in his correspondence, he did not systematically document his ideas on the use and development of this musical parameter. Timbre was first theorized in its own right (that is, separately from orchestration) by Arnold Schoenberg, who dedicated a large part of his *Harmonielehre* and his composing to timbre. Schoenberg was a great admirer of Claude Debussy's timbral approach to musical expression (even though the feeling was far from mutual, Lesure and Nichols 1987: 292, 306). Debussy's timbral impressionism resonates, for

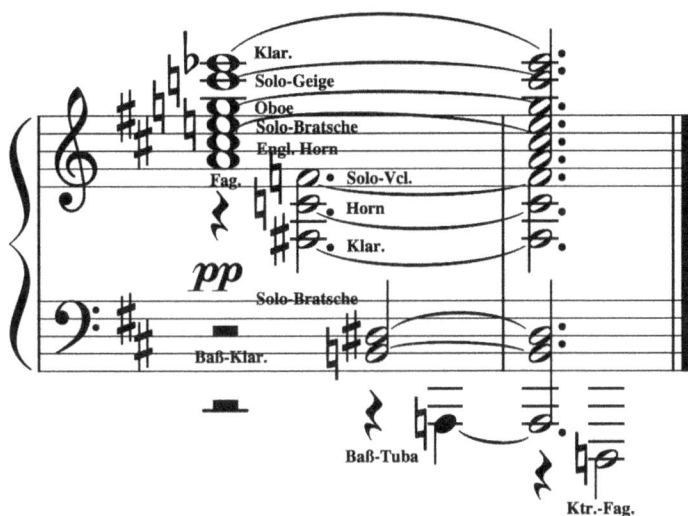

Figure 3.1 Arnold Schoenberg, chord group from *Erwartung* (1909).

instance, in the shifting orchestral colours, their subtle interplay, and the title of Schoenberg's 'Farben', No. 3 from his *Fünf Orchesterstücke* from 1909 (Op. 16). The subtitle of the piece is 'Summer Morning by a Lake: Chord Colours', which reflects the development of his compositional and theoretical focus on timbre during the late 1910s. In his *Harmonielehre* Schoenberg insists that timbre, which he consistently refers to as colour (*Farbe*), is the most important component of a tone, and that pitch is just one of its dimensions (Schoenberg 1922: 506). For this reason, some of the chords he writes seem to look like dissonant clusters but are in reality a close conglomeration of harmonics. As an example he describes a chord group from his monodrama *Erwartung* (Figure 3.1). By letting different instruments play each layer of the harmonic complex, Schoenberg illustrates that each tone consists of infinitely many tones, each of which can have their own timbral manifestation (ibid.: 502).

Insisting, like Debussy, that tone colour is capable of expressing the inexpressible, Schoenberg ends his treatise with the dream notion of *Klangfarbenmelodie*, literally 'tone colour melody'. The passage bears a remarkable kinship with the early Romantic discussions of musical sublimity discussed in the previous paragraph and with Herder's timbral ideals in particular:

> [This] has the appearance of a futuristic fantasy [which] I firmly believe is capable of heightening in an unprecedented manner the sensory, intellectual,

and spiritual pleasures offered by art. I firmly believe that it will bring us closer to the illusory stuff of our dreams; that it will expand our relationships to that which seems to us inanimate today, as we give life from our life to that which is temporarily dead for us, but dead only by virtue of the slight connection we have with it.

Tone colour melodies! How acute the senses that would be able to perceive them! How high the development of the spirit that could find pleasure in such subtle things!

(Ibid.: 507)

Early Romanticism reverberates throughout Schoenberg's timbral writing. The passage is very similar, for instance, to an account of Stamitz's instrumental music which was written in 1795 by Jean Paul: 'Each note seemed a celestial echo of his dream, answering to beings whom one did not see and did not hear ...' (Paul 1965: 27). Explicitly referring to tone colour melody as the music of the future, Schoenberg's treatise culminates here in what can only be described as a *timbral imperative*: the urgently formulated call on composers to focus on timbre as the highest possible form of musical expression. Like Herder, Schoenberg asserts that timbre is the most aesthetically powerful quality of music; like Herder, he considers timbre able to cross the gap between the sensory and the intellectual, or the quantitative and the qualitative; like Herder, he fervently wishes that future composers would deploy timbre to create music so intense that it seems as ineffable as a dream, as indescribable as a noumenon. With Schoenberg's timbral imperative, the timbral idealism of the early Romantic age re-emerged in the early twentieth century (cf. Steege 2012: 234–41).

Schoenberg's timbral thinking was followed by his pupils, among whom were Alban Berg and Anton Webern. A famous example is Webern's 1935 *Ricercar a 6*, an orchestration of the theme that forms the basis of J.S. Bach's *Musikalisches Opfer* (BWV 1079) in which the original melody becomes a true *Klangfarbenmelodie* as it moves through trombone, horn, harp, flute and violin, and opens unexpected colour vistas on Frederick the Great's melody (Figure 3.2).

Here the exploration of timbral identity and difference is the sole theme of musical composition and expression. It is interesting to realize that despite Webern's serialist compositional starting point, this treatment of timbre has equally strong roots in Romanticism: Webern engages here with Schoenberg's notion that tone colour can express the sublime 'illusory stuff of our dreams'.

Figure 3.2 Anton Webern, excerpt from *Ricercar a 6* (1935).

Although Pierre Schaeffer's 1950s and 1960s *musique concrète* departed radically and explicitly from twelve-tone technique and late Romanticism, Schaeffer, too, developed a timbral imperative. Chapter 2 discussed his search for a method of composition freed from connections to physical sources or habitually inscribed meanings in his search for new sounds to make new music. Schaeffer considered Schoenberg's striving after *Klangfarbenmelodie* a worthwhile effort but criticized the 'naive haste' with which it had been adopted by composers and audiences who lacked the appropriate means to discuss and document timbre (Schaeffer 2017: 30, 238–9): the word *Klangfarbenmelodie* itself, after all, reverts to visual icons to describe the phenomenon. Schaeffer's *Traité* aims to develop discursive and notational strategies for sound and specifically timbre in order to achieve new compositional and listening strategies. This would also engender the 'unusual refinement' required for true *Klangfarbenmelodie* (ibid.: 239).

Schaeffer's version of the timbral imperative was as much rooted in idealism as Schoenberg's. Basing himself on Husserl's phenomenological negotiation of transcendental idealism, Schaeffer defines the *objet sonore* as the meeting place between acoustic sound and sound 'in itself' (ibid.: 209). While acoustic sound is perceivable through aural impressions of the physical reality around us, the latter 'ideal object' of sound in-itself is 'unknowable' (ibid.: 206–7, 209; cf. Kane 2014: 32–4). The *objet sonore*, as a transcendental object that mediates between both, is accessible through the disengagement of the Husserlian phenomenological epoché (Schaeffer 2017: 206–12; cf. Kane 2014: 17–26): as 'the offspring of the epoché', the *objet sonore* is 'the coming together of an acoustic action and a listening intention', with this listening intention being the exclusion of any form of referential listening in order to approach the unknowable sound in-itself (Schaeffer 2017: 213):

> There is a sound object when I have achieved, both materially and mentally, an even more rigorous reduction than the acousmatic reduction: not only do I keep to the information given by my ear (physically, Pythagoras's veil would be enough to force me to do this); but this information now only concerns the sound event itself: I no longer try, through it, to get information about something else (the speaker or his thought). It is the sound itself I target and identify.
>
> (Ibid.: 211)

The *objet sonore* has harmonic, rhythmic and melodic properties, but their importance is dwarfed by that of timbre in its many dimensions, to which Schaeffer dedicates the majority of his writing. He was looking to concentrate composing, music criticism and listening on the sonic Thing-in-itself, and that idealist concentration necessitated a radical foregrounding of timbre as the key property of the sonic noumenon – even if this meant that the noumenon was now a decidedly *material* noumenon. The many criticisms that the *Traité* met, and that pointed out the fundamental contradictions between Schaeffer's materialism and his idealism, were discussed in Chapter 2. But those criticisms omit the observation that Schaeffer's sonic theory can be read as a practical, experimental version of the early Romantic timbral idealism that Schoenberg sought to revive. While maintaining the idealism that informed the earlier historical versions of the imperative by Herder and Schoenberg, Schaeffer refined the discourse around it through psychoacoustic analyses and sonic experiments, adjusted its practical manifestations to the era of technological sound production, and embedded it in sonic phenomenology. Whether we agree with his approach and his findings or not, it is important to note that Schaeffer's *Traité* marks the continuing presence and transformation of the idealist timbral imperative in twentieth-century musical thought. If the treatise, therefore, is 'essentially *normative*', then that normativity must be understood as the inevitable result of its aim to refine this imperative (Nattiez 1990: 97, italics in original).

At the same time as Schaeffer was carrying out timbral experiments in Paris, Karlheinz Stockhausen was trying to achieve timbral innovation in the WDR studios in Cologne, Germany. Stockhausen worked tirelessly on the creation of entirely new, electronically generated sounds. Although working on a different compositional basis and within the different praxis of the electronic studio, Stockhausen developed a timbral imperative that was similar in its idealist aesthetic to Schaeffer's: he emphasized time and time again that the composer of electronic music should strive to create new timbres which are free from any previous connotations. Like Schaeffer, he maintained that associations distract the listener's attention from 'the autonomy of each sound world' (Stockhausen 1963–1984, vol. 1: 143). In order to create such timbral autonomy, Stockhausen asserted, every sound has to be the 'result of a compositorial act' (ibid.: 142). In 'Four Criteria of Electronic Music' Stockhausen writes about this compositorial act in electronic music in a manner highly reminiscent of the ways in which Schoenberg discussed acoustic timbral expansion:

> If we understand that sounds can be composed, literally put together ... if we can compose these sounds, in the sense of the Latin *componere* meaning put together, then naturally we can also think in terms – note the quotation marks – of the 'decomposition' of a sound ... And whenever a component leaves the original pitch, naturally the timbre of the sound changes ... we now have a situation where the composition or the decomposition of a sound ... may be the theme itself, granted that by theme we mean the behaviour or life of the sound ... This change in perception will bring about incomparable changes in humanity in the next hundred years, spiritual and physiological.
> (Stockhausen 2000: 97–9)

Stockhausen's focus on 'the life of the sound' as electronic composition's 'theme itself' betrays the paradoxically idealist foundation of his material approach: it is a Kantian sound in-itself he is after, with timbre at its nexus. Schoenberg's transcendental wish reverberates in the spiritual and physiological 'widening of our perception' that he aims to achieve through this timbral approach (ibid.: 99) – 'How acute the senses that would be able to perceive them! How high the development of the spirit that could find pleasure in such subtle things!' (Schoenberg 1922: 507).

Stockhausen's 1955–56 composition *Gesang der Jünglinge* (*Song of the Youth*) is a celebrated example of his approach to electronic sound. The *Gesang* combines technological and human timbres. The work is composed for five groups of speakers which should be placed around the listener and consists of the musical dialogue between a recording of a boy soprano singing the words 'Preiset den Herren', electronically generated sine tones and electronic clicks. Stockhausen's own description of the work illustrates his timbral idealism: 'In the *Gesang der Jünglinge*, a unity of electronic – synthetic – and sung – natural – sounds has been achieved: an organic unity, which seemed to be a far utopia even three years ago' (Stockhausen 1963–1984, vol. 2: 49). To enhance the autonomy of his timbral 'utopias', Stockhausen created spaces and times that were specific for each composition. His careful arrangement of speakers in compositions like *Gesang der Jünglinge* led to a 'multi-layered spatiality' (Stockhausen 1963–1984, vol. 4: 380–90); moreover, his composing aimed to suspend time in what he called 'the eternity of every moment' or a 'time continuum' which could be achieved through the interaction between new timbres free of any associations (Stockhausen 1963–1984, vol. 1: 199; vol. 4: 361–70). Stockhausen's electronic music, then, brought into practice a timbral imperative that was not just marked by the idealism regarding autonomous timbre in-itself – he complained as late as 1973 that Schoenberg's dream of tone colour melody had still not been brought into practice (Stockhausen 1963–1984, vol. 3: 361) – but, like in Schaeffer's work, simultaneously also by the materialism of timbral embodiment and experimentation.

In the 1970s, a new type of tone colour melody was developed. The temporal development of sonic frequency spectrums was the main compositional parameter of the spectral music of IRCAM-based composers such as Gérard Grisey. Although 'sound', and not specifically timbre, was the key focus of spectral compositions, this new manner of composition changed timbral approaches as tone colour now became an 'ecology' in which the difference between sound and noise disappeared (Grisey 2000: 2–3; on timbral ecology cf. Chapter 1). This led Robert Reigle to declare that the only definition for spectral music is that it is guided by timbre (2008).

The next key iteration of the twentieth-century timbral imperative appears in the work and writing of Pierre Boulez. Reading Boulez's 1987 essay on timbre in parallel to the other timbral theories discussed here, the practical similarities and conceptual consistencies spanning across two centuries of Western timbral thought are striking. Using the exact same terminology as Herder did two centuries before him, Boulez wonders why the 'quantitative' and the 'qualitative' aspects of timbre tend to be separated from each other in musical thought, and comments that the quantitative approach fundamentally overlooks the musical appreciation and 'truly artistic value' of timbre (1987: 161–2). A purely qualitative approach, however, leads to 'the impossibility of linking instinctive feelings about the qualitative aspect to a more reasoned appraisal of the quantitative' (ibid.: 162). He mentions Berlioz's treatise on orchestration as an example of the latter but adds that he thinks Berlioz is rather too precise, too prescriptive in his assessment of the affective values that can be evoked by specific timbres (ibid.: 163).

Boulez notes the loss of understanding of this 'affectivity' of timbre as a 'signpost for the emotions' (ibid.: 162, 163), describing the development from timbre as static identity in baroque composing, through orchestral blocks and multiplicities of colour in the nineteenth century, to the timbral textures explored throughout the twentieth century (ibid.: 164). This development, he argues, has liberated composition from the constraints of fixed instrumental identities that impeded timbre's potential for infinite and diffuse expression. As an example he mentions Schoenberg's *Farben*, in which melody, harmony and rhythm have been stripped of their structuring function, leaving 'only timbre with its multiple identities' to create compositional cohesion (ibid.: 165).

Boulez's reading of timbral aesthetics shows idealist starting points similar to those of the other timbral composers. His idealism becomes especially evident when he attempts to define timbre. Finding it impossible to come to a one-dimensional definition of this multivalent, ever-changing, contiguous musical phenomenon, he argues that timbre connects inside and outside, identity and absence of identity:

> Timbre does not function on its own, but the acoustic illusion of timbre is brought out by the way the music is composed. From this I deduce two notions of timbre used in instrumental timbre: raw timbre and organized timbre. In the first case composition acts from the outside. In the second case it works from the inside of the sound-object. The reality and identity of the instrument can thus be enveloped in a network of ambiguities which either hides it within a fused sound-object or reveals it in its absolute state.
>
> (Ibid.: 169)

By 'raw' timbre, Boulez means the material indexicality of timbre: the wood of the violin's body, the strings, the hairs on the bow, the act of bowing. In idealist terms, 'raw' timbre is the appearance of timbre. By 'organized' timbre, on the contrary, he means something far more abstract: it can be found 'between the extremes of immediate perception and elusive perception', which plays with memory's multiple temporalities (ibid.: 169). This is what he calls the 'absolute state' of timbre, the timbral Thing-in-itself that cannot be described in words except through linguistic icons. It is for this reason that Boulez, when he tries to describe timbre as a musical language, asserts that 'timbre both explains and masks at the same time' (ibid.: 170): timbre both indexes its physical source and does something entirely different, something indescribable that is simultaneously 'multidimensional' and 'specific' (ibid.: 171). Even though it is informed by material practices of composing, and even though he wants to find identity and signification in timbre, Boulez's ambivalent assessment of tone colour tends more towards a numinous ineffable, a masked obscurity in Burke's terms, than towards the grain of a voice or an electronically achieved autonomous sound world: the 'sound-object' he describes is as much an idealist construct as Schaeffer's.

Like Herder, Schoenberg, Schaeffer and Stockhausen before him, Boulez urges composers to explore the expressive capacities of this still-uncharted territory of musical communication. His version of the timbral imperative focuses on how to optimize timbral expression in composition, rather than on how to achieve an abstract aesthetic ideal (Herder, Schoenberg) or on how to create electroacoustic experiments with new tone colours (Schaeffer, Stockhausen): 'From now on timbre, composition and acoustic setting should be linked by the same necessity, unique to the work in question' (Boulez 1987: 169, cf. 171). This aesthetic ideal, however, requires a careful balancing of elements that have the agency to resist the composer's will. Boulez mentions the *Klangfarbenmelodie* in Webern's Opus 10 as an example of timbre's remarkable independence of compositional forces:

> The more one wants to produce clarity, the more one risks ending up with obscurity. At a certain point, things go the other way: the more you explain the fundamental construction of a phrase by timbre, the more you make its totality difficult to perceive, because you have mixed different categories, which have a tendency to take their autonomy and tear up the continuity which, on the contrary, you wanted to preserve by over-explaining it.
>
> (Ibid.: 168)

Boulez's timbral philosophy, here, does not so much revert to the Romantic sublime as renegotiate elements of it. Burkean obscurity meets a need for rationalization here as timbral autonomy must be embedded in compositional structure. But as frustrated as Boulez is by the musical tensions and contradictions that timbre affords, he is also fascinated by its unknowability and uncontrollability. In an assessment of the various shapes that timbral paradox can take, he argues again and again that composers ought to capitalize exactly on timbre's capacity to create confusion. He mentions the gaps it inhabits between, for instance, the articulation and fusion of specific instrumental indexes, the identification and the impossibility of identification of these indexes, the presence and absence of the acoustic envelope that identifies timbre, the clarity and obscurity of expression and finally, in wonderfully oxymoronic language, between the 'hidden constant' and 'apparent diversity' that timbral textures can engender (ibid.: 167–9).

Throughout these twentieth-century readings of tone colour, the aesthetic persistence and conceptual stability of timbral idealism is remarkable. The evocative assessments of timbre's expressive potential by all these timbrally-orientated composers reflect a renegotiation, across almost the entire twentieth century, of the timbral imperative as it was developed by Herder in the later decades of the eighteenth century: although each developed in different compositional contexts – sometimes explicitly positioned against each other – Schoenberg's, Schaeffer's, Stockhausen's and Boulez's ideas about timbre each foreground the persistent distance between phenomenological appearance and noumenon. While Schoenberg and Boulez speak in abstract aesthetic language harkening back to Romantic idealism, Schaeffer and Stockhausen infuse this idealism with a new-found fondness for instruments inspired by the infinite possibilities of technology. The fact that these composers phrase their timbral aesthetics as an imperative arguably already implies a form of idealism: we must, imperatively, seek to approach the inapproachable, we must engage in what Goehr describes as 'aesthetic reaching' across the gaps with which timbre presents us (2004: 123). In Boulez's words, timbre requires aesthetics to reach across the gap between no-thing and identity:

> Timbre exists aesthetically when it is directly bound to the constitution of the musical object. On its own timbre is nothing, like a sound on its own is nothing. Obviously a sound has an identity; but this identity is not yet an aesthetic phenomenon. Aesthetic identity only appears if there is utilization, language and composition.
>
> (1987: 166)

Material re-enchantment

Despite the idealism shaping the timbral theories discussed in the previous paragraphs, Romanticism's intense interest in timbre as a sublime or noumenal Thing was consistently accompanied by the awareness that the allegedly unspeakable expressive power of timbre had a distinct material component.

Berlioz's treatise on orchestration, for instance, contains extensive sections on how *not* to play an instrument or how *not* to treat an orchestra. He asserts that most trumpeters should simply not even try to play trills as it is almost 'impracticable' and warns against the use of the bass trombone 'because of the fatigue experienced by even the most robust players' (2002: 188, 211).

Precisely because the idealism that has dominated timbral discourses for over two centuries recognizes the simultaneity of a sonic index and an ungraspable aural noumenon, moreover, its material components have been treated in surprisingly contradictory ways. On the one hand, organology and later (psycho)acoustics are predominantly quantitative branches of music research that do not necessarily engage with the qualitative or philosophical aspects of their subject matter. The focus on timbral identity in popular timbral discourses has led to the fetishization of material objects: think, for instance, of the symbolic value of historical instruments in 'authentic' performance practice, the fantastical prices paid for Stradivarius violins, or the idolization of Fender Stratocaster guitars used by Buddy Holly, Jimi Hendrix or Eric Clapton. On the other hand, and simultaneously, the sound made by such venerated instruments remains ungraspable, mysterious, sublime. However hard a viola player tries, she can never approach the sound of an actual baroque performance; neuroscientific and psychoacoustic studies are doomed to fail in their quest to identify the mysterious 'unattainable perfection' of the Stradivarius timbre (Sendin 2017); and the 'Slowhand' guitar timbre is elevated to divine status ('Clapton is God').

Since the 1950s, developments in music technology have yielded an intensified attention to timbre's material aspects. With technology it is possible not only to manipulate timbre but also to create entirely new, previously unheard tone colours (cf. Chapter 2): Schaeffer's and Stockhausen's experiments stretched the limits of electroacoustic timbre, and the work of spectral composers explored the extent to which full harmonic spectrums could be employed in composition. After Schoenberg's tone colour melody, with its clearly Romantic and idealist genesis, spectral music (in all its forms) is arguably the first purely material, and materialist, form of music with timbral variation as its key outcome.

As the rise of timbral materialism was accompanied by the democratization of compositional agency, the creation of new sounds has not been limited to research institutes and professional studios. In the early 1960s, theremin enthusiast Bob Moog and his partner Herbert Deutsch invented an affordable means to create new sounds with the help of a keyboard interface, which meant that timbral experiments could become both easier and cheaper (Pinch and Trocco 2004: 14ff.). Moog and Deutsch turned to 1950s *musique concrète* for inspiration on how to design unheard noises, and their 1964 invention the Moog synthesizer became a hugely popular extension of Schaeffer's efforts (Pinch and Trocco 2004: 36). Wendy Carlos, electronic music pioneer and creator of *Switched-On Bach*, contends that one of the great attractions of the Moog synthesizer was the fact that it could 'jump from timbre to timbre' (Pinch and Trocco 2004: 141).

Since the digitization of sound in the 1990s and the subsequent rise of file- and software sharing via the Internet, the ease of access, user friendliness and timbral versatility on which the Moog synthesizer built its success became an even more widespread phenomenon. Music software such as Ableton, Logic, Pro Tools and FL Studio is available to many people, and a simple Mac or PC can provide a studio for domestic musical creation. An interesting, relatively recent example of do-it-yourself timbre is provided by Low Frequency Oscillator (LFO) software and plug-ins, which enable users to change wave forms and to filter out or modulate frequencies. LFO software controls the length and shape of audio waves, so that effects like vibrato, tremolo, crescendo, glissando and distortion can be programmed into the timbre of a tone. LFO software implicitly answers to Schaeffer's and Stockhausen's versions of the timbral imperative and takes it forward in ways that they could not have foreseen: it enables home users to create wholly new, autonomous sound worlds which are then globally distributed via the Internet and further refined by swarms of networked do-it-yourself timbral composers. Despite the evident materiality of the timbre produced by LFO software, though, it is important to be aware of the immediate simultaneity of this timbral materiality with its less material, metaphorical counterpart: the timbre produced in painstakingly fiddly sessions with this software is the sole sonic identifier of the dubstep genre, in which basslines are given their characteristic 'wobble' with the help of LFO software. Effects like vibrato, tremolo, crescendo, glissando and distortion are employed to generate syncopated rhythms, which creates the unusual sound of timbre-led rhythmical patterns.

The technological developments that enriched the twentieth-century soundscape result in a form of timbral disenchantment: even though the ephemeral aspects of timbre are powerful and immersive, their evident materiality appears to defy Romantic aspirations to 'absolute' timbral sublimity. The (domestic) studio musician knows that timbre is not noumenal or inapproachable. On the contrary, it is the result of detailed technological labour on the shaping and manipulation of (to mention just a handful of the elements involved) acoustic design, microphone placement, reverb times, wiring, sound waves, harmonics, equalization and compression. This is not only true for electronically recorded and produced timbres but also for acoustics ones. The iconic timbre of a Stradivarius violin, for instance, indexes fine spruce, willow and maple wood cut at highly specific densities, and combined into a sophisticated acoustic design with elongated sound holes; the knowledge and craftsmanship required to create this unique instrumental timbre was developed through generations of Cremonese violin makers (Stoel and Borman 2008; cf. Strad3D). Making any string instrument – and especially such a sensitive violin as a Stradivarius – sing, moreover, requires not only highly advanced musicianship but also demands a lifetime of continuous study which in turn often takes the painful physical toll of a variety of playing-related musculoskeletal disorders (PRMDs, Zaza and Farewell 1997).

Nor is such disenchantment restricted to instrumental timbres, whether acoustic or electronic. Biologically generated timbres, including those emanating from such ineffable goddesses as 'La Divina' (Maria Callas) and 'La Stupenda' (Joan Sutherland), are equally the result of a combination of relentless corporeal labour, intense physical discomfort and personal sacrifice. Legend has it that Callas studied for five to six hours each day to maintain her *messa di voce*, and the effects that spectacular weight loss as well as her later dermatomyositis had on her 'divine' voice are well-documented. Aporetic descriptions of Sutherland's voice similarly fail to recognize the painstakingly corporeal origins of her performance: she suffered from chronic sinus infections and ear abscesses (Major 1987: 52–3) and had to produce her 'stupendous' timbre through sinuses which her doctor rather bluntly described as perpetually 'full of muck'. Opera musicology is in the process of overcoming the divide between traditional formalist musicology and new materialist approaches, with the work of scholars such as Carolyn Abbate, Nina Eidsheim and Laura Tunbridge inviting their score-minded colleagues to undertake more embodied appreciations of the repertoire and culture of opera. In an assessment of the relation between materiality in opera practice and opera studies, Jonathan Sterne has argued that operatic musicking not only fundamentally involves both the material and the transcendent but also bridges the gap between the two through the technicity that is at its core. He stresses that this technicity includes both technological performance aids such as microphones and singing techniques such as breath control and aural reception:

> Particularly in its most transcendent, riveting moments, the voice of the diva points to the artifice at the core of human life. This is not because operatic singing is in any way universal or transcendent, but because its transcendence cannot be anything other than a situated transcendence ... we risk forgetting the tremendous artifice necessary for that first bit of breath that constitutes the onset of the first note that we hear sung, and the last little ringing bits of decay in our ears, or in our memories. Technicity is of the diva, and all divas are made of it.
>
> (Sterne 2016: 164)

The necessary attention to the 'physical and psychological substance' of opera praxis (Bronfen and Straumann 2002: 216) has perhaps brought the diva, as a singing person, back to the realm of the human, but – as the elated language in YouTube comments, opera and CD reviews abundantly illustrates – it has hardly diminished what Sterne calls the 'transcendent, riveting' appeal of her voice (cf. Tunbridge 2014: 291). Listeners *want* to hear the sublime in timbre. The discomfort and PRMDs suffered by contemporary professional musicians do not compare to the immense physical, emotional and social sacrifices that castrati had to make, but in both cases material, corporeal pain is accepted as the musician's condition: and in both cases that sacrificial exchange culminates, specifically, in the achievement of a timbral sublime (Feldman 2015: 6–17, 105–9). In contemporary television culture, the vocal sublime seems to have undergone a renewed impulse with talent show judges howling ecstatically over the apparently ineffable vocal timbres of their candidates.

The ongoing attention to the sublimity of the diva, embodied though she or he may be, signals the heightened paradoxical status of timbre at the start of the twenty-first century: despite the exponential growth of creative, popular and scholarly attention to timbral materiality, the sublime ineffability ascribed to tone colour persists. Rather than adding to timbral disenchantment, the materiality of timbre tends to be included in the ascent towards sublimity. Material awareness in fact contributes to a form of timbral re-enchantment: diva fandom – whether in opera, popular music or televised talent shows – very much includes the veneration of the singing body, just like historical performance practice includes the veneration of period instruments. In a similar way, the recent resurgence of analogue sound shows that the timbres of 1960s and 1970s pop music have an ongoing appeal for composers and listeners which has led to a lively nostalgia culture organized around analogue recording and production equipment (Bennett 2012). 'Retromania', as Simon Reynolds calls it (2012), is a contemporary form of idealist attachment to a timbral noumenon that resembles the Romantic idealization of instrumental timbre.

In many ways a focus on timbral materiality simultaneously obscures the transcendental idealism that dominates the aesthetics of tone colour and instrumentalizes that same idealism. With the imbrication of timbral idealism and timbral materialism in contemporary theory and practice, the timbral paradoxes observed in Chapters 1 and 2 seem to persist. For how can a piece of wood, even one so artfully crafted as a centuries-old Cremonese violin, evoke in us the thrill that a Stradivarius timbre does? How can a voice sung through mucky cavities be stupendous? Awestruck, we direct our admiration to the impossibly material origin of the sound we do not want to comprehend: the woman whose body produces that voice, the instrument that generates the sonorities we cannot grasp, the studio equipment that creates those nostalgic sounds. And we capture that material index in icons of ineffability: the superior Strad, La Stupenda, Retromania.

Timbre's doubleness: Paradox, sublime, lure

The Romantic history of timbral idealism and its persistence throughout the age of technological re/production is the background to the paradoxes of timbral indexicality and iconicity outlined in the previous chapter. Rather than solving the questions raised there, however, the intellectual trajectory in which timbral thinking is embedded intensifies their poignancy. The paradoxes that are apparent on the concrete level of timbral indexes and icons are themselves rooted in the more fundamental paradoxes underlying timbral aesthetics. This adds two paradoxes to the list compiled in Chapters 1 and 2:

7. Timbre offers a simultaneously sublime *and* tangible aesthetic experience:

    a. the timbral imperative, from the eighteenth to the twenty-first century, urges composers to aspire to the noumenal *by way of* the material;
    b. it is for this reason that material timbral indexes and immaterial timbral icons mutually enchant each other.

8. Timbre can be understood through both idealism *and* materialism.

The now extensive list of aesthetic and practical timbral paradoxes would appear to obscure our understanding of tone colour. It is after identifying paradoxes closely related to these as the core problem of music epistemology that Lydia Goehr introduces her methodology of philosophical doubleness, a critical approach that is inclusive of the various aspects of music epistemological paradox and offers a multifaceted view of potential intellectual conflict:

> Doubleness supports a theory of open and critical practice. It closely recalls traditional dialectics, yet it does not depend upon establishing too strong a teleological development in which oppositions are brought to their (pre)determined syntheses. Instead, it serves more moderately to preserve both in theory and in practice the two or more sides of conflicts, sides that often serve one another by being at hand to be denied.
>
> (2004: 5)

Following Goehr's incentive, therefore, I would propose to instrumentalize timbral doubleness rather than attempting to brighten up its obscurity through the misleading light of binarism. A theory of timbral doubleness would take the shape of an 'immaterial materialism' entailing a convergence of the transcendental idealism and transcendental realism surrounding timbre. Even if such a convergence appears to be counterintuitive, it is the only possible starting point that meets the key prerequisite for a theory of timbre: its doubleness enables fluidity and mutualism between the numinous ineffability and the firm materiality that are the simultaneous qualities of timbral aesthetics.

While the full detail and range of such a theory of timbral doubleness will be the subject of the next two chapters, it can be outlined through a combination of Jean François Lyotard's, Vladimir Jankélévitch's and Carolyn Abbate's ideas regarding the sublime, the ineffable and the drastic aspects of musical experience. All three theorists describe the convergence of the material and the ideal in music, and all three emphasize that while this paradox poses serious epistemological questions, both elements are undeniably present in musical experience. The solution they offer is the doubleness of a material sublime, or a noumenal that is transcendentally accessible through hearing and touching music.

Only one of these three thinkers writes explicitly about timbre, and surprisingly he is not a musicologist. Citing Varèse, Boulez, Schaeffer and Grisey, Jean-François Lyotard argues that the technological revolutions in twentieth-century music have emancipated timbre from indexical signification. The creative agency of technology in composition and sonority has revealed that timbre, thus stripped down, lacks any index or any signified at all (Lyotard 1991: 167–76; cf. Lyotard 1996: 40). Lyotard asserts that contemporary music should for this reason be regarded as *Tonkunst* rather than as *Musik*. He understands *Tonkunst*, in a manner reminiscent of Herder, as 'the art of sound and/or tone' (1991: 167, cf. Lyotard 1996: 44). Formulating his own version of the timbral imperative, he argues that *Tonkunst* is a more direct form of art than traditional music: as it is based on wholly new sounds, it should help disclose new listening experiences and new emotions, and it affords a sonic art whose sole purpose it is to unveil 'the marvel of the sound-event alone' (1991: 174, 177; cf. Lyotard 1996: 40).

Timbre-led *Tonkunst* is able to engender such marvellous sonic experiences because timbre, as sound-event, is in and of itself free from indexical signification. Lyotard explicitly defines timbre in its most basic form as musical difference and hastens to add that this sonorous difference should not be equated with identity. He thereby pre-empts – and dismisses – the problematic equation of sound index and sonic identity discussed in the previous two chapters:

> Nuance and timbre are what differ and defer, what makes the difference between the note on the piano and the same note on the flute, and thus what also defer the identification of that note.
>
> (1991: 140)

Having established that the paradoxes in timbral aesthetics are not caused by a misunderstanding of timbre but are an integral part of timbre's own non-identity (cf. Bertola 2017: 598–9), Lyotard goes on to argue that these paradoxes and this non-identity are rooted in the question of timbre's im/materiality. He contends that timbre must be immaterial 'if it is envisaged under the regime of receptivity or intelligence' (1991: 140). But although listeners are mentally touched by timbre, this touch is also, and tangibly, a physical one, and so timbre must also be considered as a form of matter too: in a 'mindless state of mind', he argues, the mind is 'accessible to the material event, can be "touched" by it' (ibid.: 141). By acknowledging the paradoxical co-occurrence of materiality and immateriality in timbre, Lyotard is able to gain a simultaneous view (or hearing) of what Herder and Boulez refer to as the individually separated 'qualitative' and 'quantitative' aspects of timbre.

Lyotard's assessment affords an undisturbed sense of the obscurity of timbral doubleness, which he describes as the 'singular, incomparable quality' of timbre's access to the physical senses (ibid.: 140–1). He coins the phrase 'sound-feeling' (*sentiment sonore*) to describe the singularity of music's touch that opens up an 'ungraspable instant' between hearing and interpreting (ibid.: 176). In order to think through the effects and affects of being touched by sound-feeling, the essay 'Anima Minima' introduces the concept of *anima* or body/thought, a 'substance soul with the faculty of being affected', and which indeed only exists *as* affected (Lyotard 1997: 242). One of the key factors that encourage this substance-soul, the element of musical experience in which the *sentiment sonore* is concentrated and exploded, is the sublimely paradoxical force of timbre marking the 'mystery of sensation' (ibid.: 243, 249).

The fact that the timbral *sentiment sonore* keeps returning throughout Lyotard's work indicates how important the sound-feeling of tone colour was for his aesthetic philosophy. The concept grows and develops over the course of his writing. In the earlier essays, Lyotard advocates an explicitly sublime idealism of timbre: in the Kantian essay 'After the Sublime' he relates the ungraspable touch of timbre to 'the Thing' which is external to the signified, the mind and questioning (Lyotard 1991: 142). Mauro Fosco Bertola has noted that Lyotard's later work moves away from the strict Kantian separation between object and noumenon but retains a transcendental conception of timbre (Bertola 2017: 599–601). The transcendental philosophy of Lyotard's later work, I would argue, veers towards a more Burkean version of the sublime which is focused on the aporia of not knowing. In 'Anima Minima' he asserts, in explicit reference to Burke, that the sublime is as a form of excess, of an 'aesthetics at the limit' that engenders a 'sublime spasm' (Lyotard 1997: 240–1). Timbre, he says here, is itself a version of 'the unnameable' that lies beyond the limit of aesthetics (ibid.: 241). In 'Music and Postmodernity', Lyotard further refines his paradoxical and sublime assessment of tone colour defining the postmodern sublime as the 'absolutely aporetic', non-communicative, non-aim of all art (Lyotard 1996: 42). Such sublime art is able to affect mind and body at the same time because it does not address either but touches both:

> The enigma of this touch is that it affects thought at the same time as the body ...
> Now, to the extent that the arts especially, but also the sciences, are guided by the absolutely aporetic project of making matter felt or thought, they always suppose something that is not sensible or thinkable ... [that] is not even, in itself, the anticipation of its form, that ... does not obey any finality. It is not addressed to thought, nor is it addressed to the mind-body, to the sensibility.
> (Ibid.: 41, 42–3)

Tonkunst, which Lyotard defines in this essay as 'an art of timbre' (ibid.: 44), is the art that is most capable of approaching the postmodern sublime. Timbre, as 'sound-matter', is un-located between body and mind, materiality and immateriality. It bears no relation to any language, any identity or any signified, and is therefore able to engender in *anima* the immediate aporia that Lyotard considers the purpose of art:

> In striving for the ideal of causing the ear to sense sound-matter – timbre – freed from all destination, contemporary music pushes to the extreme its 'stake' in the aporia constitutive of all music: to make heard that which escapes in itself all hearing, to address what is not addressed.
>
> (Ibid.: 43)

Lyotard's postmodern timbral imperative, then, coincides with Herder's, Schoenberg's, Schaeffer's and Boulez's earlier versions in its aesthetic reaching for the sublime. It diverges from those earlier versions, however, in that it no longer holds to idealism alone, but rather combines transcendental idealism with transcendental realism in what he himself had referred to, in 'Matter and Time', as an 'immaterialist materialism' (Lyotard 1991: 45, 140; cf. Woodward 2016: 121, 133).

Vladimir Jankélévitch's book *Music and the Ineffable*, which appeared in French in 1961 and was translated into English by Carolyn Abbate in 2003, follows a similar trajectory as Lyotard's music-aesthetic writing, albeit from a more musicianly starting point. Jankélévitch was a musicologist and Bergsonian philosopher publishing on Ravel and Fauré who played piano with Roland Barthes. Like Lyotard, Jankélévitch wishes to approach in his writing the noumenal that is present in musical experience. As he is fully aware of the insufficiency and superfluousness of words in relation to the musical absolute, his philosophy takes the asymptotic shape of approaching but never quite reaching the Thing of music in-itself, which is the ineffable and untellable (cf. 2003: xiv, 71–6).

Jankélévitch's music philosophy acknowledges the paradoxes at the heart of music epistemology, and it attempts to work *with* rather than overcome them in a non-teleological dialectics of simultaneity that Goehr would qualify as doubleness (cf. Gallope 2012: 240). Michael Gallope notes that '[m]uch of his philosophy is preoccupied with a central paradox at the root of [music epistemological] dualism: that any presentation of *quoddity* (or the drastic) entails a necessarily *quidditive* (or gnostic and discursive) means of representation' (ibid.: 236). More than by this dualism, therefore, Jankélévitch's writing is marked by ambiguity: rather than an 'either-or', he advocates a 'both-and', a 'yes *and* no', even if the two elements he attempts to reconcile appear to be in diametrical opposition (2003: 68). In his reaching across the dualist divide, however, Jankélévitch's *Ineffable* increasingly privileges an immaterial understanding of music, to such an extent that the latter half of the book tends towards noumenal and even metaphysical interpretations of musical immersion (ibid.: 110, 127; cf. Lochhead 2012: 232–4).

In Jankélévitch's ineffable assessment of music, the subject-dissolving 'bewitchment' of musical experience is aided by the temporal dislocation prompted by such experience (2003: 2). Music creates its own time, and this time is characterized by a chronological disobedience that exceeds even Bergsonian *durée*. Bergson's concept of duration focuses on the absolute knowledge to which lived time enables access: as opposed to the relative or quantitative knowledge provided by the intellect, absolute or qualitative knowledge can only be provided by the intuitive awareness of the noumenal Thing-in-itself (cf. Lochhead 2012: 231–2). Jankélévitch, seeking the limits of this philosophy, attempts to reach beyond the dualism of Bergsonian temporality. He applies Bergson's ideas to music, arguing that musical experience is lived time giving immediate access to absolute knowledge, and adds to that a distinctly metaphysical flavour whose immanence, rather than strict transcendentalism, far surpasses Bergson's binaries (cf. ibid.). Jankélévitch argues that music escapes and transforms clock time as it possesses the subject-formative powers of temporality. Moreover, he asserts that that music is, in and of itself, a form of time: it provides 'an enchanted chronology, a melodious form of becoming, *time itself*' (2003: 70; cf. 51, 96, 120ff). In Jankélévitch's musical ineffable, Goehr's aesthetic reaching becomes a 'transphysical' reaching (ibid.: 76), and doubleness morphs from pervasive ambiguity to a metaphysical absolute.

There are striking resemblances between Jankélévitch's and Lyotard's assessments of the excess of signification, temporality and subjectivity in musical experience as it approaches the noumenal. Jankélévitch's 'ineffable' corresponds with Lyotard's 'absolute aporia', and in both cases this musically-induced state of perplexity surpasses ordinary temporality and even the finitude of (Heideggerean) being. Jankélévitch contends that 'we live music, as we "live" time, as a fertile experience, with the ontic participation of our entire being', and that this being is a form of endless becoming in 'a timeless Now' that annuls finitude (ibid.: 95, 127). In a very similar line of argument, Lyotard states that sound-feeling is 'perhaps the most elementary presence of time or to time, the "poorest" degree or state (although it is not a state) of being-time: *Durchlaufen*.' This *Durchlaufen* is a radical 'being-now' that is opposed to the finite being-there of *Dasein* and that is entirely subjected to the *durée* of music (Lyotard 1991: 176).

For both theorists, the phenomenological convergence of the sensible and the mental in musical experience is crucial for its excess of language and time. Jankélévitch states that music is 'more-than-phenomenal' as it simultaneously works upon and surpasses the senses (2003: 13); Lyotard contends that the sound-feeling of music is an '*archi-épochè* of sensation' in which the phenomenal crosses over into the mental (1997: 249). It is interesting to note that Lyotard uses the same phrase here as Pierre Schaeffer does in his *Traité*: but where Schaeffer sees the *objet sonore* as the noumenal 'offspring' of the sonorous epoché (2017: 213), Lyotard inverts this relation by asserting that the *experience of* the sonorous event is a meta/physical epoché. Timbre is the operative factor in this epochal experience for Lyotard, like it is for Schaeffer: 'timbre or nuance introduce a sort of infinity' (1991: 140).

Both Jankélévitch and Lyotard conceptualize the musical noumenal in Romantically sublime terms as the simultaneity of terror and pleasure in the stupefied aporia of non-comprehension. Where Lyotard emphasizes that this aporia is the goal of all arts, Jankélévitch wallows in its aesthetic experience, which he describes as 'a fruitful perplexity that is more ineffable than untellable' (2003: 96). This perplexity may bear fruit in the shape of the asymptotic verbosity of Jankélévitch's own writing, or that of the poetic imagery described in Chapter 2 above. The musical agency that evokes this aporia remains unapproachable in both philosophies. Lyotard asserts that timbre is a figuration of the musical unnameable, Jankélévitch keeps an even greater distance and only hints that '[m]usic in itself is an unknowable something' (Lyotard 1997: 241; Jankélévitch 2003: 102; cf. Lochhead 2012: 233).

This version of the musical sublime, which Lyotard envisages as *anima*'s experience of musical aporia through the *sentiment sonore*, and which Jankélévitch theorizes as the *Charme* of the musical noumenal (2003: 96; cf. Gallope 2012: 238–40; cf. Chapter 4) is marked by a transcendentalism that can be understood both in a philosophical and a theological sense. Jankélévitch's and Lyotard's theories of the musical sublime are based on the dualist grounds of ontological differences that can only be overcome by transcendence: the transcendence, in this case, from object to Thing, from the phenomenal to the noumenal. From the perspective of this particular kind of transcendentalism, the mysticism that appears to shine through in both philosophies is unsurprising

(Lochhead 2012: 231; Gallope 2012: 236, 238, 240). In mysticism, dualism is overcome in the mystical unification (*unio mystica*) between the human and the divine. Mystical union is temporary but infinite, it is sublime and terrifying, ineffable but fruitful, and it is induced by experiences that simultaneously stir the physical senses and the mental faculties: meditation, eroticism or music (Van Elferen 2009: 225–30). In Jankélévitch's philosophy, music serves the same function in these contemporary aesthetics of sublime aporia as it did in medieval and baroque *raptus mysticus*: 'Musical rapture is an escape from immanence … a soul enchanted by music, the almost-nothing, escapes its finitude' (2003: 127). While Jankélévitch and Lyotard both accept the doubleness of the material and the immaterial in music, in their attachment to the noumenal they both ultimately maintain the dualism that is the basis of the separation. 'One cannot get rid of the Thing' (Lyotard 1991: 143; cf. Bertola 2017: 600). Both attempt to overcome this dualism by allowing into their philosophy a form of 'surpassed transcendentalism' that would make Kant frown and Herder smile but may leave Goehr mildly disappointed.

Along with her translation into English of Jankélévitch's *Music and the Ineffable*, Carolyn Abbate's seminal article 'Music – Drastic or Gnostic?' (2004) introduced Jankélévitch's philosophy of the musical ineffable to a wider musicological readership. Focusing on the immediacy and eventness of musical experience, Abbate called for a musicology that researches the performative and corporeal aspects of playing and listening to music next to the more traditional hermeneutics of musical scores and historical facts. 'Drastic' musicology (Jankélévitch 2003: 77) does not occupy itself with the gnostic facts derived from scores, composer biographies and historical developments – there is 'nothing to think about', as Jankélévitch says (2003: 83) – but with such non-cognitive thoughts as 'doing this really fast is fun' (Abbate 2004: 511). It does not interpret music *after* the event of musicking but assesses music *in* the event of musicking: it focuses only on the infinitely stretched *now* that Jankélévitch and Lyotard describe. Within that *now*, drastic musicology addresses what Abbate calls 'musical performance's strangeness', in which 'unearthly' and 'earthy' qualities, that is its immaterial and material qualities – Lyotard would say *sentiment sonore* and *anima* – coexist (ibid.: 508). Abbate advocates a musicology that is both drastic *and* gnostic simply because musical aesthetics needs both kinds of assessment. The methodological bridge between the drastic and the gnostic is a practical, performance-orientated form of Goehr's philosophical doubleness: it connects material and immaterial, idealist and realist approaches to musicking without having to revert to the kind of transcendentalism that limits Lyotard's and Jankélévitch's dualistic philosophies.

In combination with Jankélévitch's and Lyotard's assessments of the musical and timbral sublime, moreover, Abbate's approach creates space for a theory of timbre that acknowledges and instrumentalizes the paradoxes of tone colour. With the gnostic and the drastic connected through performative eventness, the obscurity of timbral doubleness is no longer an obstacle, but simply an experiential given; the material and immaterial aspects of timbre are linked together in the drastic affectivity of the *sentiment sonore* (Lyotard 1991: 176); and the realism of timbral materiality blends with the idealism of the timbral sublime in the physical and mental 'timeless Now' of the drastic event (Jankélévitch 2003: 95). Timbre is a sublimely drastic quality of music: it has a powerful and immediate agency in which signification and embodiment as well as elusiveness and ephemerality play a role. In her study of Haydn's orchestral revolution, Emily Dolan contends that timbre is nothing more and nothing less than the human experience of sound: 'it is the concept to which we must turn to describe the immediacies of how sounds strike our ears, how they affect us' (2013: 87). Dolan's inadvertently Lyotardian definition of timbre underscores not only the convergence of matter and non-matter in timbre but also its immediacy, its physicality and its eventness. More than anything else, timbre is a sonorous event that is bound by the temporal and spatial contingencies of musicking and which, in its meta/physical '*archi-épochè* of sensation' (Lyotard 1997: 249), profoundly affects body and mind.

The lure of timbral paradox: Aesthetics itself

In combination with Goehr's music philosophical doubleness, Lyotard's, Jankélévitch's and Abbate's mediation between the sensory and mental, gnostic and drastic aspects of musical experience can help us understand some of the timbral paradoxes identified in Chapter 2. Timbral doubleness elucidates the precise imprecision of timbral icons and their relation to material timbral sound sources, it demystifies the enigmatic occurrence of timbre's *plus-de-corps* and its *plus-de-c(h)oeur*, it creates room for Barthes's elated language when he describes the sensual dimensions of Panzéra's voice, and it frees Dolar's vocal *objet petit a* from its psychoanalytical restrictions. But it does not solve the more fundamental paradoxes that were already outlined in Chapter 1: timbre is undeniably both material *technè* and immaterial excess, it is both objectively quantifiable and subjective qualia. Timbre is tangible and sublime, and it occupies the gap in between both.

The aporia of being physically and mentally touched by the *sentiment sonore* is stirred by the accumulation of paradoxes in timbral aesthetics. The timbral noumenon is a thing and a Thing, an object that is not an object. The terror and pleasure that this non-approachable but physically knowable no-Thing evokes can be traced back at least to the early Romantic era, to which Dolan argues timbre was key because 'ultimately timbre … is aesthetic attention itself' (2013: 89). Timbre lures listeners into the drastic non-time and non-space of musical aesthetics alone: to turn our ear to the timbral event is to embrace the paradoxical reality of a sublimely grainy singularity. Overwhelmed, all we have to express ourselves is the obscurity of metonymy. *Of course* we call Maria Callas 'La Divina': she is audibly human but her timbre transcends her corporeality. It lures us out of this world, makes us stand on the edge of something vast and overwhelming that we cannot and do not want to approach. The lure (closely related to Schaeffer's 'allure', cf. Chapter 1) of timbre is the self-perpetuating *Sehnsucht* of the Burkean sublime: the siren call of its doubleness entices us onto its limen, behind which lurks an unknowable void. The persistent aesthetic coexistence of timbral materialism and timbral idealism, thus, marks the nexus as well as the impossible lure of timbral paradox.

4

Vibration and vitality

Cloven: Paradox 0 and timbral binarism

The first three chapters of this book have discussed existing debates about timbre: debates concerning timbral quantities versus its qualia; about tone colour's capacity to signify and exceed indexes, icons, grain and desire; and about the sublimity and ineffability of timbral perception. Every single one of these debates appears to be open-ended and sometimes dichotomous, with mutually opposed – but equally valid – arguments and outcomes. Timbral theory is cloven by binarism, split broadly into materialist and realist approaches on the one hand, and metaphysical and idealist approaches on the other. While the former approaches are based on the firm, physical ontology of sound and its sensual phenomenology, the latter appear to be driven by the transcendental spilling over of timbral phenomenology into non-sensual realms that are sometimes evaluated in almost mystical terms. Both schools of thought have yielded important insights, as the previous chapters illustrate, but neither has proved conclusive, mainly because the paradoxical nature of timbre does not allow one-sided approaches. As a result, timbral researchers are trapped in the perceived gap between both, and resulting timbral theories are always incomplete. Advancing from a less exclusive perspective, I have argued that perhaps there are things to be said for both sides of each of these debates: rather than a clear 'either-or', timbre could be regarded as 'and-and'. This has led me to a long list of accumulated timbral paradoxes which, when taken together, sketch the timbral event in its complexity:

1. Timbre is an objective quantity *and* a subjective quality (Chapter 1).
2. The material origin and the much-less-material interpretation of timbre are entwined (Chapter 1).
3. Timbre is an ecological multiplicity *and* an unrepeatable singularity (Chapter 1).

4. The timbral event *does and does not* function as an index (Chapter 2).
5. The timbral event *does and does not* function as an icon (Chapter 2).
6. Timbre is able to evoke aporia or function as an *objet petit a* (Chapter 2).
7. Timbre offers a simultaneously sublime *and* tangible aesthetic experience (Chapter 3).
8. Timbre can be understood in terms of idealism *and* materialism (Chapter 3).

At the root of this list is what I will call paradox 0: the fact that timbre is both material *and* immaterial, or, in Lydia Goehr's terms, the fact of timbre's 'doubleness' (2004: 5). Paradox 0 is hard to classify in terms of quantification or qualia and impossible to think of in terms of materialist or idealist philosophies alone. The binarism that pervades timbral research as a result of this predicament not only cuts things loose which are inseparably entwined – however necessary that cut may be for the clarity and focus of our research projects – it also prevents a complete view of the topic that we think we are questioning. Timbre is not just *both* an (unstable) object *and* an (ungraspable) Thing, but moreover it inhabits the gap between those opposites. The health of Joan Sutherland's vocal chords and her ability to sing through chronic infections are not the only reasons that her voice enchants listeners: they are nothing more and nothing less than the corporeal alpha to a sublime omega. The secret of 'La Stupenda' is the paradox of timbre: the singular encounter of heterogeneous musical agencies at a prepared and yet entirely coincidental moment in time leading to unpredictably emergent but always affective sounds. Such an event is hard to analyse as a whole, and each separate component of it is powerful enough to grab one's full interest – but however gripping a synecdoche is, it remains inherently incomplete. The existing field of timbral reflection, thus, is comparable to a centrifugal force field that is polarized as well as held in orbit by the very theme it tries to understand.

In its paradoxical inclusivity of seemingly opposed characteristics, its inhabiting of several realms at once, timbre is representative of a great deal of ongoing debate in music philosophy. Timbre is not the only aspect of music that is characterized by a haunting simultaneity of material and immaterial characteristics, and of realist and idealist evaluations: the same goes for pitch and duration, melody and harmony, rhythm, dynamics and articulation. The only difference between these musical parameters and timbre is that there is no appropriate discourse around the latter. Lacking the disciplining structures of discursive embedding, tone colour's im/material vitality and materialist/idealist elusiveness are more highlighted than, say, melody's. But any separate building block of music, as well as the convergence of forces that is 'music itself', is endlessly paradoxical and frustratingly unknowable. Many current musicological debates – from issues around the ontology of the musical work versus that of musical performance, to the debate around musical meaning versus music's meaninglessness, to the question of the physicality versus the ephemerality of musical experience – are in one way or another determined by the polarization of opinions regarding im/materiality and realism/idealism. Musicology has not reached consensus on the question of whether music should be considered material or immaterial, and whether it wants to think of music in realist or idealist terms (for versions of these music epistemological debates cf. Cimini 2012; Dodd 2007; Goehr 2004: 6–47; Hamilton 2007: 95–118; Nancy 2007: 20–31; Wilson 2018: 8–11). Overcoming timbral binarism demands an engagement with a major unsolved problem in music epistemology.

If the two approaches to timbre coincide, how can they be linked? Is it possible to construe a theory of timbre that encompasses both these traditionally diametrically opposed strands of analysis and philosophy? To think the 'immaterialist materialism' of timbre that Lyotard has called for (1991: 45)? Chapter 3 introduced a fusion between transcendental idealism and transcendental realism that allowed for fluidity and movement between numinous ineffability and firm materiality. This chapter proposes to go a step further. In order to direct the intellectual vectors deeper into the timbral field, I must do more than just acknowledge the fact of paradox 0, of timbre's doubleness: following Goehr's incentive, I have to ride the timbral paradox itself (Goehr 2004: 28–9, 37–8, 135–6, 201–7). To do that, I will begin with what links both sides of the timbral coin: the vibrating connection between timbre as material sound source and timbre as immaterial percept.

Meta-acoustic vibration

A balance of ontological and phenomenological approaches to sound is achieved in Michel Chion's *Sound: An Acoulogical Treatise* (2016). As Chion's theory of acoulogy is the basis for the timbral theory that I propose here, the following section offers a detailed discussion of the book in order to flesh out its precise benefits for the understanding of timbre.

Chion's argument is based on the observation that sound is ontologically a material 'verberation', a physical sound wave that emanates from the vibration of sounding bodies and that touches the ear as well as other parts of the human body (ibid.: 16). Verberation has a slippery relationship with perception, which can be defined as the physical 'sensation' of vibration (ibid.: 21). Sound's objective and subjective intensities are not perceived consistently by the human body: rather than an objective observation of sound waves, the human ear is limited to offering auditory medians at best, auditory illusions at worst, and for most of the time auditory distortions (cf. Chapter 1). Psychoacoustics, Chion therefore declares, is 'a bizarre unit ... a bastard, dubious tool of quantification' (2016: 23).

Chion contends that both sound perception and sonic phenomenology are misguided by causal approaches to listening, which limit the sensation of sound to simplistic questions such as 'what is that' and 'where did that come from' (ibid.: 115–20). Such causalism is irrelevant in view of the spatially and temporally disrupted and disrupting qualities of most sonic events. Sound distorts the perception of space, time and vision in numerous ways: sonic distortions occur, for instance, in the Doppler effect, in echo, in visu-audition and its reverse audio-vision (cf. Chion 1994; Chion 2016: 152–65; on spatial and temporal distortion in sound perception see Parker 2009: 41–58). Chion further theorizes the inherent mnemonic and affective instability of any form of listening evidenced in sound's, but especially music's, capacity to stretch, speed up, warp or freeze time (2016: 29–41; cf. Kramer 1988). The spatially, temporally, visually and subjectively distorting aspects of sonic perception have been enhanced by schizophonia, which removes sound from its origin and annihilates the possibility of causality (Schafer 1994: 90–1; cf. Chapter 2).

With sound's relation to origin dismantled, listening and analytical practices based on causality are rendered hopelessly irrelevant. For these reasons Chion fiercely rejects the 'sonic naturalism' that imposes the dominance of such ambivalent phenomena as sonic causalism and sonic narrativity (2016: 119). As his arguments for this rejection are pertinent, also, to the debate around timbral identity and signification discussed in Chapter 2, they are worth quoting in full:

> I call the dogma that is implicit in most current discourses and in today's technical, cultural, social, and other practices *sonic naturalism*. The name fits because, according to this dogma, sound – and usually the question does not even come up – is considered as a sort of given that maintains a relationship of identity with the milieu from which it originates that implies isomorphism: the transfer onto the sound of the conditions in which it was produced; the perpetuation in the sound itself of the virtues or properties of the place where the sound was recorded, and so forth. This is most notable in the myth of the

narrative spontaneity of sound, where sound is taken as recounting of itself its cause or causes, as transposing or reflecting the environment from which it issues, and where there is supposed to exist a natural or authentic acoustic state – a state in relation to which recorded sound (which tends to be called 'fixed' in this regard) would be a more or less doctored or deformed trace.

(Ibid.: 119)

Chion argues against the causalist conviction that sound is an index pointing (only) to its physical origin. Chapter 2 traced the ways in which timbral perception exceeds the limits of indexicality and iconicity, and thereby causality and narrativity; Chion, who analyses not just timbre but sound in general, argues that music should always strive for such excess. He urges composers not to reveal their sonic sources 'in order to liberate listening *for imaginary sources*' (ibid.: 120, italics in original). Antony and the Johnsons's recording 'Deeper than Love', which was discussed in Chapter 2 as an example of timbral excess, does precisely that – tangible yet ineffable, Anohni's timbre transgresses, obscures, undoes.

Chion's proposal goes further than Pierre Schaeffer's acousmatics and R. Murray Schafer's schizophonia. Although he recognizes the importance of acousmatics in its isolation of a sound from its origin, he disagrees with Schaeffer that this isolated sound is an *objet sonore*, which was theorized in Chapter 3 in idealist terms as the timbral Thing-in-itself. Schaeffer considers timbre as a material identity entirely defined by origin. This restricted definition of timbre is of course 'fundamentally a causalist notion', and for this reason Chion wishes to 'shatter' the concept of timbre as a whole (2016: 174). Such a 'dissolution of the notion of timbre' that Chion had already suggested in 2011, however, would have to be described as an unfortunate case of throwing the baby out with the bathwater (Chion 2011).

Because sound is both cause and effect, because it is an event developing over time and through space, because it affects listeners, and because it 'stubbornly' refers us to something other than itself, Chion argues, sound is both an object and a non-object (2016: 201, 169–211). Not only can sound be analysed in two contradictory ways, it also impossibly unites these two distinct ontologies within its contradictory being – the sonic event '*is* this contradiction' (ibid.: 210). Again, the relevance of Chion's thinking for an inclusive timbre theory is striking. Jean-François Lyotard, in fact, describes timbre in exactly this line as 'immaterial matter' which is 'an-objectable' (1991: 140).

As the 'non-object' dimension of the sonic event is not material, the immaterial aspects of sound require closer study, and in order to do that Chion's acoulogy moves from ontology to phenomenology. He coins the notion of the 'auditum', the perceived sonic object (2016: 192–3). The concept of auditum focuses on the phenomenology of musicking by linking together the various modes of perceiving sound:

> The *auditum* is sound as perceived and cannot possibly be confused either with the real source (or the causal complex that constitutes its source) or with the vibratory phenomena studied by the discipline called 'acoustics'. Unlike Schaeffer's sound object, *the auditum is subject to all modes of listening* – reduced, causal, figurative, semantic, which make up different, at once linked and independent, levels of apprehension – knowing that it is helpful to distinguish among these modes of listening that take aim at the *auditum* and for which it is the foundation.
>
> (Ibid.: 193)

The difference between verberation and auditum is comparable to the two differing timbral manifestations that Cornelia Fales has observed in timbral perception: the sonic object in the physical world and the subjectively perceived concept (Fales 2002). While Fales focuses her analyses on psychoacoustic and ethnomusicological contexts, Chion studies the sound philosophical implications of the verberation-auditum divide. Chion recognizes that while verberation is demonstrably material, auditum, as 'something heard', is much less clearly so (2016: 192), and his book is ultimately an attempt to overcome the dogma of causal listening by integrating these two aspects theoretically. He does this by revisiting the theory of listening. The book ends with a reflection on an 'active' – Carolyn Abbate would say 'drastic' – form of listening (ibid.: 241–2). The greater significance of this surprisingly modest conclusion emerges when seen in the light of Chion's primary objective, which was to outline 'the science of what one hears considered from every angle' (ibid.: 210). Acoulogy is relational: it is the study of the manifold ways in which sound relates itself to listeners, of the equally abundant ways in which listeners relate themselves to sound, of the relations that emerge between any sound and any listener as well as those that come into existence between a particular sound and a specific listener. As such it offers an alternative within the context of sound theory to Christopher Small's relational theory of 'musicking' (1998).

The reconsiderations of sound and its perception that motivate Chion's acoulogical journey – from psychoacoustics to sonic objects to active listening – have important music philosophical implications. First, Chion argues that verberation and auditum are connected by way of sensation: the perception of sound equals being touched by sound. Auditum, in this logic, is in no way separated from verberation: they are fundamentally conjoined as two manifestations on what I will call a *vibrational continuum*. A similar point has been made by Amy Cimini, who criticizes Merleau-Ponty's dualist conception of sound as either embodied or somehow mystically disembodied. She argues that sound, as vibration, refuses to respect 'material or conceptual distinctions between subject and object, human and non-human, interior and exterior' (2012: 360). Sound-as-vibration, instead, should be thought of as a continuum in which such binaries only exist as the – material or conceptual – extremities of an internally continuous scale. Second, this practical observation of the vibrational nature of sound and its perception has analytical repercussions. If the sonic event and sonic experience are necessarily connected through vibration, their theorization requires a combined ontology and phenomenology: the notion of a verberation-auditum continuum connects two strands of sonic theory that often remain separated. Third, Chion insists that sound, precisely because it unites the sonic event with its perception, is both an object and a non-object: sound in itself, he states, *is* that contradiction (2016: 210). The paradox of the non/object, finally, connects the reflective forms of materialism and idealism. Acoulogy thus builds a music philosophical suspension bridge spanning two divides at once, each consisting of a practical observation and its implication for analysis and philosophy:

1a. The vibrational continuum between sound and perception;
1b. the vibrational continuum between sonic ontology and sonic phenomenology.

2a. The acoulogical concurrence of sonic object and sonic non-object;
2b. the acoulogical concurrence of sonic materialism and sonic idealism.

Because it connects strands of music philosophy whose enduring division sustains long-running musicological debates, Chion's acoulogy reaches into the heart of music epistemology: it intervenes precisely at the points of tension pertaining to materiality/immateriality and materialism/idealism that haunt musicological reflection. This epistemological nexus is inhabited and rendered audible by timbre. As acoulogy is based on the contradictions inherent to sound it is supremely suited to the analysis of timbre:

1a. Timbre is a sound as well as the perception of that sound;
1b. timbral analysis requires both ontology and phenomenology.

2a. Timbre is a material object as well as a sublime non-object;
2b. timbral analysis requires both materialism and idealism.

An acoulogical intervention in timbre theory could clarify timbral paradoxes and reveal connections between the opposing positions in timbral research. Acoulogy is based on the vibrating connection between verberation and auditum, so the next thing to explore is the vibrational continuum of timbre.

Hermann Helmholtz's *On the Sensations of Tone* (1885) was the first major empirical work on sound perception to recognize the problem that hearing occurs both on a physical and on a mental level, by the 'corporeal ear' as well as the 'mental ear' (Steege 2012: 58–79). Benjamin Steege refers to this simultaneity of perception as the ear's 'doubleness' (ibid.: 79, 83), and indeed the doubleness in Helmholtz's phenomenology refers to the same epistemological problem of sound perception as the doubleness in Goehr's music philosophy (ibid.: 79, 83). Helmholtz was fully aware of the philosophical implications of his work, and his attempts to connect the material aspects of sound perception with mental interpretation must be read as attempts to connect the materialism of his empirical experiments with Kantian idealism. The ideological fusion implied in Helmholtz's work was looked upon with great suspicion by his contemporaries, who were concerned that 'the very epistemological impasse into which the Kantian critique had long ago intervened was making an unfortunate return' (ibid.: 126). Helmholtz did ultimately maintain the distance between both versions of the ear as well as that between the materialist and the idealist philosophies that they represented, keeping the notion of sound in-itself as a noumenal Thing intact, and focusing mainly on the physical aspects of aural perception (ibid.: 95).

Influenced by Helmholtz, various twentieth-century phenomenologists have theorized the vibrational basis of musical perception. Maurice Merleau-Ponty's *Phenomenology of Perception* argued for a primacy of sensory perception that challenged Cartesian mind-body dualism (2002: 30–59, 429–75). The early twenty-first century has sparked a renewed interest in this approach. There has been a surge in vibration-based publications in sound studies over the last decade, all based on Helmholtz's notion of 'sympathetic resonance' or 'sympathetic vibration' which posited that hearing sound is physically sensing sound (2016: 36–49; e.g. Connor 2000, Goodman 2010). Because the ontological causes for sound are physical, in this reasoning, the phenomenology of sound must be considered first and foremost from a corporeal perspective. Clemens Risi states that voice, for this reason, is precisely a sympathetic vibration: 'I understand voice, then, to be the product of a relationship between a producer and a perceiver: a co-presence or, more, a *co-vibration*' (2016: 154; the term 'covibration' is also used by Chion, 2016: 185, 204–6). This carnal movement in sonic phenomenology has led to fruitful explorations of the quantitative aspects of sound and to important insights regarding the vibrational dimension of subjectivity (e.g. Cavarero 2005; Dohoney 2015), but has left the qualitative elements of sonic experience behind, thus offering incomplete and sometimes incorrect analyses (cf. Schrimshaw 2013: 36).

A remarkable theorization of the vibrational ontology of sound and music appeared in Nina Sun Eidsheim's book *Sensing Sound* (2015). Eidsheim considers music to be a 'practice of vibration' whose perception runs through multisensory channels (ibid.: 7–8; cf. Chion 2016: 206; Trower 2012). She extends Steven Connor's notion of the synaesthetic 'intersensoriality' of sonic perception to the perceived vibration itself. Sound's vibration, Eidsheim states, is 'intermaterial' (2015: 161): it permeates acoustic spaces, human bodies and materials of various types, from wood to metal to water and clothing. For this reason, she argues, the practice of musicking is 'always relationally and materially contingent' (ibid.: 155). Her analyses focus specifically on the corporeal performativity of singing and listening to singing, which leads to important re-interpretations of a wide range of vocal musical practices such as contemporary sonic art and singing pedagogy. Like the carnal phenomenologies discussed in Chapter 2, Eidsheim's tactile approach tends to disregard the immaterial aspects of musicking. She explicitly rejects any form of musical immateriality, polemically referring to immaterial approaches to music as 'metaphysical' (ibid.: 15).

In the middle of a fiercely materialist line of argument, however, Eidsheim makes a statement that may extend the ramifications of her claims beyond the field of corporeal identity. She asserts that if music is a vibration which is transferred from body to body and from material to material, then this sympathetic vibration, which she considers an energy, does not have an *a priori* ending:

> If singing and listening are the actions that give rise to sound – in the vibration that surges through the singer, and in the material that envelops the singer and listener – does this sound, this vibration, have a beginning or end? It does not. The vibration is expressed as transmission or as transduction, and depending on how we define a node within that continuous field, we may define its beginning and end. But the vibration or energy in itself does not imply or express a bounded object with a beginning or ending point ... The most extreme definition of music possible, then, is vibrational energy, which is an always already unfolding relational process.
>
> (Ibid.: 180)

The reduction that Eidsheim presents here is based on the equation of five elements:

music = sound = vibration = energy = longevity

Based on this equation she argues that music must be regarded as an ongoing energy vibrating from singer to material to listener to other materials and so on. As it is Eidsheim's aim to study the material nature of every element in this chain, *Sensing Sound* then traces the embodied relations engendered by the material vibrations of music. Eidsheim's reduction is built on the verifiable fact that sound = vibration, but its extensions on both sides (music = sound on one end and vibration = energy on the other) as well as its materialist overall claim are in need of further discussion. With some corrections, however, this statement could well be the basis for an analysis of the links between the five components.

Energy is a function of matter: it is the capacity to cause or do something. Energy is not matter itself, and not an object but a property of objects that can be transferred to other objects: the various types of energy include kinetic, thermal, chemical, nuclear, radiant and potential energy (Benenson et al. 2002). According to Newton's law of the conservation of energy, energy can neither be created nor destroyed, but only transformed. This law is demonstrated by a so-called 'Newton's cradle' pendulum of metal balls. A metal sphere on one side swings through the air, passes its energy through the middle spheres, and makes the sphere on the other side swing outward as if by its own accord. This, in turn, sets in motion a self-sustaining motion of kinetic energy. The idea of 'endless energy' experiences recurrent surges in popularity not just in the shape of desk toys but also in spiritualist discourses, which often lead to such mystical fictions as 'everything is energy' in various parareligious contexts. Just as not everything is matter, however, not everything is energy: moreover, not everything is either matter or energy. Rather than being mutually exclusive as the immaterial and material side of the same thing, energy and matter are two of the many different aspects of particles which are related to each other only through the special relativity of space and time (ibid.). Vibration and energy are far from interchangeable, and the notion of 'vibrational energy' that informs Eidsheim's book has no basis in empirical fact. As a mechanical wave form, vibration is a type of matter movement. It relates to energy in a number of ways: mechanical waves are *caused* by kinetic energy, these waves can *transport* various kinds of energy, and they can *transfer* the energy they carry from one context to another. The beginning and end of mechanical waves is determined by the resistance of the material in which they vibrate: only in a vacuum will they be able to continue without end.

The same principles and laws apply to sonic vibration and energy. Sound exists in mechanical waves of matter movement. Like any other mechanical wave form, sound waves have beginnings and endings: sound vibration starts with a release of power such as a heel on the pavement or a strum on a guitar, and gradually stops through the resistance of the materials that it meets – whether these materials are wood, stone, water, air, or the human ear (Parker 2009: 16–27). Sound waves transport sound energy, which is defined in the same way as other types of energy: it is not matter but a property of matter (ibid.: 24). From a scientific perspective, Chion is right when he argues that sound is simultaneously an object and a non-object (2016: 169–211). As mechanical energy, sound energy consists of the sum of kinetic and potential energy present. Like other forms of energy, sound energy is measured in joules. The sound intensity level (SIL) is the rate of sound energy transmission per unit volume measured in decibels: it is an objective quantity associated with a wave (Howard and Angus 2009: 21–6; Parker 2009: 24–7). Loudness, on the other hand, is the perceptual response to sound intensity: it is a subjective quality associated with a wave (Elert 1998–2017). Sound intensity levels and loudness are influenced by the amplitude of sound waves: if a sound wave's crests are larger, the rate of energy transmission will be greater and the sound will be perceived as being louder. The vibrating waves of sound are conduits for the sound energy passing through the human ear into human neurology. As an example, imagine a popping balloon. The kinetic energy of the explosion starts sound waves, and these sound waves carry the kinetic energy of the explosion, which has now been transferred into sound energy, to the cochlea in the human ear. Once the sound energy is transported to the cochlea, the hairs in the organ of Corti translate it into the electrical energy that governs human neuro-activity (cf. Chapter 1).

It is at this junction that the distinction between music and sound becomes apparent. All music is sound and moves in vibrations that carry sound energy; music, as a form of sound, enters the ear where its sound energy is translated to electric energy; but once in the human brain, the neuro-electricity of musical sound follows distinctly different pathways than that transmitted by other types of sound waves. There is a wealth of neurological research to support this thesis: listening to music activates not just the auditory cortex, but also involves, among others, the motor, language and visual cortices (cf. Chapter 1). As a result of this wide spread of musically induced neuro-activity, listening to music activates the muscle memory of static patients, increases the blood flow and white blood cell count, and, most spectacularly, enables patients with advanced Alzheimer's to reactivate forgotten memories, knowledge, emotions and identities (Levitin 2006: 165–88). I would therefore suggest that the distinction between music and sound is determined by the neural pathways generated by each form of sound energy. The sound energy of music allows the neurotransmitters in the human brain to function like amplifiers foregrounding such specific neural functions as emotion and memory. In the same way that guitar amplifiers work, the neurotransmitters in each individual's brain will highlight specific frequencies, specific harmonies and specific timbres in order to 'amplify' personal affects and memories. A similar metaphor was used by Helmholtz's mentor Johannes Müller who had developed the idea of the brain as a 'multi-stringed instrument' resonating with '*Sinnesenergien*', sensory energies (Steege 2012: 65–7). The non-cognitive co-vibrations – connotations – amplified by the neuro-system cannot in and of themselves be understood as meaning, but they are performative translations of the sound energy unleashed by music. It is clear that there can be no objective definition for music as distinguished from sound: only the outcomes of the individual neuropathways in each human brain will determine whether something is experienced as sound or as music. Neuroscience, as discussed in Chapter 1, is not (yet) able to capture and document such highly individual and divergent responses: but as sound and music behave so differently once they have entered the ear and the neuro-system, they cannot be equated with one another.

On the basis of these observations, music can be defined as a particular collection of sounds with particular energetic properties. Musical energy is a form of sound energy: every sonic component involved in music occurs in other sounds too, but the particular convergence of pitch, rhythm, harmony and timbre in what an individual recognizes as music has markedly different neural affordances. Like sound energy, musical energy is transported by the vibration of sound waves. Transported by this vibrational movement, the neuro-electronic manifestation of musical energy activates specific affective and mnemonic parts of the brain. Like any other form of energy, musical energy does not have a beginning or an end: a musical version of the Newton's cradle would illustrate the conservation of *musical* energy. In this Newton's cradle, musical energy moves from one vibrating entity to the other: from instrument to recording technology, from the concert hall to the listener's ear, from ear to brain, from cognition to emotion, and into the kinetic expression of an involuntarily tapping foot (cf. Levitin 2006: 59, 168–72). Like any other form of energy, musical energy is not matter but a property of matter, and it is transported by sound waves from the physical to the mental and back. It is evident from this that a focus on resonating bodies alone – as it prevails in sound studies and carnal phenomenologies of music – has the same relevance as a focus on the weight of metal balls in the analysis of a Newton's cradle. The material transmitters of energy are important, but they are certainly not the only part of the phenomenon: without the energy that moves those metal balls, the phenomenon ceases to exist. When we analyse only musicking material, we lose sight of the energy that fuels the event of musicking, and music ceases to exist.

The vibrational continuum now acquires more detail. Its vibration is not merely physical nor only immaterial, but the two are inextricably connected in what could be thought of as a *meta-acoustic motion*. What 'surges' through the singer and listener in Eidsheim's quote above is musical energy as it resounds in auditum: but contrary to her statements, this energy and the auditum that it affects are not, or not only, material. What she calls a 'continuous field' is the meta-acoustic continuum of sonic vibration that transports this energy. The notion of musical energy could offer a crucial additional ingredient not just to Chion's acoulogy and the sensorium of carnal phenomenologists but to the epistemological paradoxes surrounding sound, music and timbre that this book addresses. Overcoming musicological binaries through the laws of physics that underlie musicking, it *energizes* the acoulogical bridges between material and immaterial, materialist and idealist philosophies of music.

Vital materiality

Before I analyse timbre's vibrational and energetic specifics, I would like to refine my understanding of musical energy through the lens of Jane Bennett's vital materialism. As with Chion's acoulogy, a detailed introduction to this school of thought is required in order to explore its implications for musicology and timbre theory. Bennett's seminal work *Vibrant Matter: A Political Ecology of Things* (2010) formulates a 'new materialist' theory based on a vitalism that encompasses humans as well as non-humans. The book explores agency across the boundaries of such distinctions. Bennett describes this agency as 'vibrant matter', the vitality inherent to all materiality. The renegotiation of vitalist traditions as well as actor-network sociology enables her to achieve three important goals. First, her book proposes an ontology of vibrant matter. Second, as a result of this new materialist ontology, Bennett is able to overcome onto-theological binaries of life vs. matter, human vs. animal, and organic vs. inorganic. Finally, she employs these insights in radical political and ecological analyses (ibid.: x).

Bennett begins her exploration of vibrant matter with a fresh take on Bruno Latour's actor-network theory (ANT). Like Latour, she is interested in the agency of non-humans as well as that of humans. She attributes agency to non-human entities in what she calls 'thing-power', the power possessed by non-humans to (physically) affect other beings. The concept of thing-power is based on Baruch Spinoza's notion of '*conatus*': the vitality inherent to each thing and each body, the 'active impulsion' to persist (ibid.: 2). This vitality is absolute and necessarily exterior to human perception, knowledge and epistemology.

> I will try, impossibly, to name the moment of independence (from subjectivity) possessed by things, a moment that must be there, since things do in fact affect other bodies, enhancing or weakening their power. I will shift from the language of epistemology to that of ontology, from a focus on an elusive recalcitrance hovering between immanence and transcendence (the absolute) to an active, earthy, not-quite-human capaciousness (vibrant matter).
>
> (Ibid.: 3)

The ontology that she describes is that of things-with-agency, of things that should no longer be described as static or dead but as filled with a vibratory energy that exposes the irrelevance of such binary opposites as life vs. matter. She replaces this binary with a continuum of vibrating vitality which 'persists before and after any arrangements in space: the peculiar "motility" of an intensity' (ibid.: 57). This motility, the 'nomadism of matter' (ibid.: 59) can most literally be found at an atomic level: it characterizes the growth of organic matter as well as the many forms taken by inorganic materials such as metal.

As well as on Spinozan monism, Bennett's articulation of this vitality leans heavily on Gilles Deleuze and Félix Guattari's nomadology. Their description of the 'matter-movement, matter-energy, matter-flow' that is the vitality of matter is neither strictly material nor completely immaterial (Deleuze and Guattari 1987: 407). Instead they side with Husserl's reading of the profound and all-encompassing immanence of vital matter:

> [It] has two characteristics: on the one hand, it is inseparable from passages to the limit as changes of state, from processes of deformation or transformation that operate in a space-time itself anexact and that act in the manner of events (ablation, adjunction, projection …); on the other hand, it is inseparable from

expressive or intensive qualities, which can be higher or lower in degree, and are produced in the manner of variable affects (resistance, hardness, weight, colour …). There is thus an ambulant coupling, *events-affects* …

(Ibid.: 407–8)

These two characteristics of matter-energy, Deleuze and Guattari argue, do not demonstrate the separation of a concept and a Thing-in-itself, as in Husserl's Kantian philosophy, but rather the way in which the two are linked. Matter-energy confirms the inseparability of thoughts and things, and thus offers a new perspective on idealism. Energetic materiality carries 'singularities or *haecceities*' and can affect or be affected, both physically and spiritually (ibid.: 408). Deleuze and Guattari consider matter-energy to be a mediator or 'vague identity' crossing the gap between concept and reality (ibid.: 408).[1] By introducing this mediator, their theory of matter-energy explicitly rejects transcendental idealism in favour of a radical immanence.

Deleuze and Guattari's 'vague identity' is diametrically opposed to Theodor Adorno's theory concerning the same gap between subject and object. Rather than by the Hegelian 'vague identity' of a negotiating presence, Adorno argues that this gap is characterized by an absolutely absent 'non-identity', with which he 'disenchants' the idealist concept (2004: 11–12, 180–3). While thus distancing himself from idealism and arguing against the dualism at its root, his *Negative Dialectics* keeps strict separations in place: subject and object, materialism and idealism, transcendentalism and immanence, the sensible and the spiritual, matter and life, cannot be reconciled (ibid.: 183–207; cf. Bennett 2010: 13–17). The metaphysical desire for transcendence caused by such gaps, discussed in Chapter 3, invites a Romantic aestheticism of distanced reflection, which Adorno rejects: 'The transcendent is, and it is not … The theological conception of the paradox, that last, starved-out bastion, is past rescuing' (2004: 375; cf. 368–73). Bennett argues, however, that Adorno's non-identity keeps the 'messianic promise' of the Thing in place (2010: 16). Despite the obvious disjunctions between Adorno's and her own, immanent philosophy of vital energy, Bennett engages in a dialogue with him in order to elicit their shared urge: 'to cultivate a more careful attentiveness to the out-side' (ibid.: 17). Bennett's outside is not that of idealism: while idealism considers the outside-of-comprehension in still,

---

[1] I use the term mediator instead of Deleuze and Guattari's 'intermediary' in order to accommodate Latour's argument that intermediaries transmit, while mediators have their own independent agency (2005: 37–42).

indirect aporia, Bennett's vital materialist outside represents the non-human outside-of-subjectivity that cannot be still, and is as immediate as the (human or non-human) inside. In a manner different to Adorno's strictly objective version of dialectical materialism, Bennett's materiality is immanent and interactive, elusive and changeable. It is

> a materiality that is *itself* heterogeneous, itself a differential of intensities, itself *a* life. In this strange, *vital* materialism, there is no point of pure stillness, no indivisible atom that is not itself aquiver with virtual force.
>
> (Ibid.: 57, italics in original)

Based on the mediating flow of matter-energy proposed by Deleuze and Guattari, Bennett's immanent thing-power is able to overcome the life/matter and materialism/idealism binaries of transcendent philosophies, including Adorno's (cf. Wilson 2018: 3–6). By bridging that divide, thing-power extends Latour's theory of human and non-human agency to human and non-human vitality. By attributing agency to a life-in-matter independent from human intervention, moreover, it also liberates the concept of energy from utilitarian interpretation.

Vital materialism analyses the relations between material presences in the world, from food, water and electricity to humans, animals and art. The circulation of thing-power fuels continuous encounters and interactions between these heterogeneous entities. Thing-power is energy, and energy does not dissipate in transferral: it is transported, transformed and transmuted from body to body. Thing-power is relational, and Bennett considers these relations as moments of 'bodies-in-encounter' that engender affect (2015: 95–6). She describes the affective power of matter-energy as 'the capacity to affect (to make a difference upon other bodies) and to be affected (to be receptive to the affections of other bodies)' (ibid.). Bennett draws on the Spinozan definition of affect that has become the focus of affect theory since Brian Massumi's 1995 article 'The Autonomy of Affect'. Massumi defines affect as an 'involuntary intensity', such as the bodily response of goose bumps, that is filled with 'motion, vibratory motion, resonation', and argues for the integration of this intensity in cultural theory (1995: 86). Rather than an identifiable object, he contends in reference to Spinoza, affect is a potential or a property that 'emerges' in 'unexpected and inexplicable' events (ibid.: 87–8, 92, 105). This approach to affect has both been hugely influential and subject to a great deal of criticism. Ruth Leys has challenged affect theory's insistence on the corporeality of affect and its alleged forgoing of reason, consciousness and intentionality. She argues that in their effort to overturn the human/non-human divide, affect theorists reject cognitivism and revert to a strict mind/body dualism (2011: 468–71). Leys notes that the cognitive or intentionalist position does not limit cognition, intention or emotional embodiment to humans, and that therefore the dichotomy that seems to be at the basis of affect theories leads to an exclusive rather than an inclusive materialism (ibid.: 470–1). Bennett's exclusively corporeal definition of affect can indeed be adjusted without losing its relevance: affect's potential, the capacity to affect and be affected, may occur in encounters between any given constellation of human and non-human bodies *and minds*. Affect is not merely a single event but is itself also a driving force in the establishment of series of events. As the difference made in an encounter, affect can include a plethora of affordances occurring in as many contexts as there are circumstances. Affect defines diverse interrelations, material and less so: the interactions between food, the body and the mind are affective encounters; so are the partnership between the North Sea, rivers, the Dutch people and the landscape of the Netherlands; and affect defines the manifold ripples of social media as they vibrate between humans and non-humans.

Vibration is ongoing, and vital material is continually active and interactive. Bennett enlivens the Latourean assemblage of converging humans and non-humans with matter-energy, which can create and change, develop and disperse assemblages. Her notion of assemblage, like that of thing-power, finds its roots in Deleuze and Guattari's thinking. They describe an assemblage as 'every constellation of singularities and traits deducted from the flow [of matter-movement]', a continuously changing, organic motion of material energy (Deleuze and Guattari 1987: 406). Assemblages can be made up of any vital material, human or non-human, and their agency results from the chance encounter of their respective motilities. Assemblage agency, Bennett states, is 'distributive' (Bennett 2010: 23): it does not posit human subjects as the root cause of an event, but replaces the very notion of cause and effect by 'a swarm of vitalities at play' (ibid.: 31–2). Causality itself, freed from the totalitarian impulse of intentionality, becomes emergent: it is nonlinear, non-subject-centred and unpredictable (ibid.: 33). Any encounter between the world and 'a swarm of vibrant materials entering and leaving agentic assemblages' can have a range of effects (ibid.: 107). Vibrant thing-power runs to, through and from assemblages of things, leaving nothing untouched or unaffected. In the three examples mentioned above, vibrant materiality circulates in food, cutlery and human metabolism at supper; the vitality of water interacts with human energy and technological power in the Dutch assemblage landscape of rivers, ditches, windmills, dikes and sluices; thing-power distributes itself through software, algorithms, interfaces and social swarms on the Internet.

Bennett's philosophy has profound political implications. Inhabited and perpetually transformed by swarms of vibrant materials, the world is an assemblage of assemblages, a global ecosystem consisting of humans, non-humans, and their vitalities. As parts of these swarms, humans hold responsibility for their emergent effects, whether they play out in our private households, within our own bodies, in the social community of which we are a part, or in our contribution to climate change. The final chapters in Bennett's book examine questions of ecology and social justice through a vital materialist lens and make a plea for political reflection on the management of matter-energy. Vital materialism is ecology, and ecology is necessarily political.

Although Bennett does not write about music or sound, it is not difficult to discern the potential that vital materialism holds for music philosophy. As a number of recent publications demonstrate, Bennett's notions of vibrant matter, vitality and impersonal affect can readily be employed to provide new insights in music composition, performance, the work concept and musical material (e.g. Redhead 2020; Schuiling 2020; Wilson 2018). Aiming to complement these emerging musicological insights, the next paragraphs explore the ways in which the combined theories of vibration and vitality are able to substantially alter our understanding of musical and timbral epistemology.

Musical vibration and vitality

In many ways, vibration-orientated sonic theory repeats what are simple facts. Music has all the characteristics of 'new' materiality as it has been described by Diana Coole and Samantha Frost: in the same way that the matter theorized in new materialist theories is alive, music is 'an excess, force, vitality, relationality, or difference that renders matter active, self-creative, productive, unpredictable' (2010: 9; cf. Wilson 2018: 1–3). And music is 'vibrant matter' *par excellence*: at a basic sonic level, music, as sound, consists of the vibration of instruments, vocal organs, air, technology. At a multisensory level, musical vibrations are perceived through the vibration of the ear, the skin, the body. And at a neural level, sonic vibrations are translated into electric vibrations in the human brain. The recognition that vital materialism and musicology both revolve around a vibratory continuum is straightforward enough; but it also opens doors for much wider reconsiderations of the ways in which we think music.

If vital materialism is based on the assertion that vibration exists in assemblages of humans and non-humans, then a musical vital materialism would assert that musical vibration, similarly, passes through assemblages of instruments, air, water, technologies, bodies and any other material. Again, this is not so different from what musicology and sound studies are already doing. Eric F. Clarke's musical ecology is based upon the assemblages of humans and non-humans, and his notion of musical affordances comes very close to Latourean agency (cf. Chapter 1). Vibrational sound theorists like Eidsheim have argued that the 'intermateriality' of musical vibrations means that music is continuously in flux, ever-changing, never static (2015: 156). More than ecologies and carnal phenomenologies of music do, however, a vital materialism of music would stress the non-human agency (in Latourean terms) or thing-power (in Bennettean terms) that is active in such assemblages. Musical thing-power is pluriform: violins, vocal folds, microphones and mp3-players each have their own kind of musical agency, adding the brightness of a particular string, the ripple of a winter flu, the conductivity of copper or the synaesthesia of mobile listening to the vibrating assemblage (cf. Evens 2005: 14–24). Music is an ecosystem of ongoing vibrational relations between humans and non-humans: orchestras, bands, choirs, recording studios, home computers and PAs are the heterogeneous assemblages in which such relations take concrete shape (cf. Schuiling 2020). Vital materialism is able to identify the ways in which this ecosystem is infused with life.

In order to capture music's vital specificities, a musical version of vital materialism would have to refine the Latourean actor-network both in terms of the kind of actors involved in it and in terms of its interactive reach. Charlie Blake and I developed SMASL theory, a musical counterpoint to ANT that outlines the assemblage of actors in musical interaction (2015). The acronym SMASL stands for 'singer – microphone – amplifier – speakers – listener': these concrete actors represent musical possibilities that could be replaced by any actor involved in any musicking assemblage. SMASL actors can be human or non-human, musical or non-musical. A non-human reverb plate has as much musical thing-power as the human singer whose vocal track is run through this device; the non-musical computer that runs LFO software is as much involved in musicking as is the musical dubstep producer operating it. Purely musical actors like melody, harmony, rhythm, tempo, dynamics and timbre share with the other actors in the SMASL network the distributive agency that Bennett observes in assemblages: rather than thing-power, these actors possess what I would call music-power. Music-power, like thing-power, is the power to affect other beings, but as musical actors are not necessarily only objects (cf. Chion 2016: 169–211), their agency is not tied to things. Music-power can be found, for instance, as the energetic agency circulated in the interactions between various lines in Renaissance counterpoint: punctum contra punctum, each note possesses its own agency in relation to the other notes in its melody as well as the other melodies which it meets on its polyphonic journey. Counterpoint, from this perspective, can be heard as a distribution, redistribution and multiplication of musical energy.

Besides adding musical and non-musical actors and their agency to the humans and non-humans in ANT, a SMASL network differs from other actor-networks in that it includes the dimensions of the unseen and the unheard. As many of the actors in musical assemblages are marked by schizophonia, the network includes an acousmatic, spectral agency (here used as an acousmatic rather than sound-analytical term). As schizophonia pervades any recorded or electronically amplified music, the unseen dimension that it adds to the vibrational continuum, rather than being perceived as uncanny or ghostly, has become a naturalized part of musical interaction (Blake and Van Elferen 2015: 61–4). The agency of any musicking actor, moreover, also includes the inaudible dimension of hauntology. Because musical vibration includes neuro-electricity, the meta-acoustic space in which it resonates includes the vibrations of memory and emotion. In Derridean terms this scientific fact has to be understood as hauntology: involuntarily and unconsciously, but inevitably and inescapably, music evokes feelings and reminiscences which resonate hauntologically along with the audible vibrations of sound (ibid.: 64–6). Distributive agency in a musical assemblage, thus, is the thing-power and music-power possessed by human and/or non-human, musical and/or non-musical actors, and it distributes vibration through the meta-acoustic space of the entire vibrational continuum. This continuum includes spectral and hauntological dimensions, which extend its scope beyond the here and now of visibility and audibility.

Like ANT, vital materialism traces the social interaction that occurs between human and non-human actors. And like vibratory phenomenologies, vital materialism observes the fact that vibration pervades every part of the world. Combining these two observations, Bennett contends that every social interaction consists of the circulation of vibration between heterogeneous actors.

From there she goes on to identify the agency of the thing-power that animates vibrant matter and renders it 'aquiver with virtual force' (2010: 57): the vitality of matter-energy on which her philosophy hinges.

A musical vital materialism would involve a similar combination of perspectives. Considered from the perspective of ANT and its musical counterpart SMASL theory, musical interaction occurs through the distributive music-power of human, non-human, musical and non-musical actors. From the perspective of sound phenomenology, sonic vibration pervades every part of the vibrational continuum, from physical sound waves to the perception of music. Combining the two observations, we can assert that every musical interaction consists of the circulation of vibration from verberation to auditum by heterogeneous actors. To complete the trajectory towards a musical vital materialism, the next step is to identify the agency of musical matter-energy that animates singers, tape recorders, opera audiences and church organs alike: the next step is to identify the vitality of musical energy distributed by vibrating sound waves.

Earlier in this chapter I described the place of musical energy in the vibrational continuum through the laws of sound physics: sound waves transport and transfer musical energy from the sonic plane of verberation to the perceptive plane of auditum and the neural plane of brain activity. Embedded in vital materialism, these scientific facts have a transformative potential for the philosophy of music. A vital materialist reading of music enlivens the vibrational continuum with a vitality that, as an uninhibited force, is independent from human causation or intention. This vitality accounts for the propelling sway of music that surges through musical assemblages and that immerses listeners.[2] Bennett describes vitality as '*a* life' (2015: 54). Referring once again to Deleuze and Guattari, she stresses that a life, rather than an actual entity, is a virtual force or 'pure immanence' (Bennett 2010: 54). Musical vitality is precisely this: it is

---

[2] I refer to Heidegger here: music's sway, its 'emerging and abiding' is that of an autonomous, powerful Being (Heidegger 2000: xiii, 14–18). The sway and Being are coexistent and co-present in Heidegger's philosophy, and they are connected in *phusis*. Phusis is the key ontological quality of Being: it is 'what is, as such and as a whole' (ibid.: 17). Heidegger stresses that it includes both Being and becoming, and that it encompasses the physical and the 'ensouled' or that which is alive (ibid.: 16 17). *Phusis* is a force rather than an entity, a property rather than an object. It powers emergence and growth; earth, seas and heaven; plants and animals; humans, gods and history (ibid.: 15–16). This force arises and endures in an emerging and abiding sway. This sway in its presenting of life-force and in its violent *Walten* resembles the matter-energy, vitality or vital force of nature that Jane Bennett's philosophy traces.

the power immanent to any instrument, any musician, any rhythm, any timbre. It is not necessarily actualized, it does not necessarily make a sound: it is the potentiality of music that could become actual at any moment. Vibrating vitality, Bennett states, 'precedes, or subsists within, or is simply otherwise than, formed bodies', which in the case of music should be read as any actor in the musicking assemblage (ibid.: 55).

When this virtual force is actualized and released in vibrating matter, it can be experienced as beauty, but also as terror; it can be given meaning but is in and of itself meaningless (ibid.: 54). Bennett quotes Friedrich Nietzsche, who describes vitality in characteristically sweeping imagery as a terrifying energy:

> Do you know what Life is to me? A monster of energy ... that does not expend itself but only transforms itself ... [A] play of forces and waves of forces, at the same time one and many ... a sea of forces flowing and rushing together, eternally changing.
> (Nietzsche, *Will to Power*: entry 1067, quoted in Bennett 2010: 54)

These descriptions of vitality bear a clear kinship to the Burkean sublime (cf. Cox 2011: 150–2), and in musical terms are reminiscent of Vladimir Jankélévitch's lyrical descriptions of musical rapture. Jankélévitch considers music driven by an ineffable force that he calls 'Charm' and whose power 'bewitches' or 'hypnotizes' musicians and listeners alike (2003: 2, 9, 83). Charm represents those aspects of music that exceed quantification: Charm is the 'mystery' of being in the act of making music (ibid.: 83); it is the insufficiency of the brain's neuro-activity to capture beauty (ibid.: 52); musical Charm is the immersive evanescence of music's meaningless ineffability (ibid.: 52–3); and it is the 'infinite aporia' of the listening experience (ibid.: 96). It is able to harbour all these powers and potential roles because it is not per se actualized: rather, and here Jankélévitch reveals his indebtedness to Bergson, it should be considered as 'an infinite number of virtualities' that allows each melody to unfold at any given time (ibid.: 69; cf. Lochhead 2012: 231–2). As an immanent power rather than an actual object, time holds no power over musical Charm, which is always on the verge of emerging and arrests the listener or musician in the indefinite immediacy of an exclusively musical time-space (Jankélévitch 2003: 103, 122–3; cf. Gallope 2012: 240). Precisely these observations led Carolyn Abbate to her celebration of Jankélévitch's idea that music should be considered drastic rather than gnostic (Jankélévitch 2003: 77; Abbate 2004). Intangible, ineffable, unknowable, evanescent: in and because of all its evasiveness, Jankélévitch states over and over again, Charm is what makes sound become music, and what makes music musical.

The sublime evaluations of music discussed in Chapter 3 now acquire a new dimension. The musically sublime — and specifically as it is theorized in Jankélévitch's Charm — a vital materialist of music might say, is the music philosophical concept that perhaps comes closest to Bennett's vitality. It is not equivalent to sound-as-object but is a property of sound, like energy is a property of matter; in parallel to the way in which matter-energy vitalizes material, Charm vitalizes sound. Like Bennett's vitality, musical Charm pervades all actors involved in an assemblage, from the piano and the score to the pianist's fingers and the listener's brain. Just like Bennett's '*a* life', musical Charm is virtual rather than actual, immanent rather than transcendent. It is always on the cusp of affirmative emergence, 'an always-already unfolding relational process' (Eidsheim 2015: 180). While this force unfolds and becomes actual it has enormous energetic powers. Bennett attributes crucial weight to the interactive strength of thing-power, the ways in which vital materials can affect one another. In a similarly emphatic way, Jankélévitch's theory of Charm relies on the playful interaction of the musicking event with its social, cultural and technological environment. The drastic performativity that both he and Abbate identify as the core agency of Charm is conceptually comparable to the affective capacity of vitality in Bennett's theory. The difference between Charm and vitality, then, has less to do with their theoretical situatedness than with the manner in which they are described. This becomes especially evident in the stylistic disjunction between the two texts: Bennett's logically reasoned philosophy does not naturally resonate with Jankélévitch's poetically stylized aporia — except when she claims that the affects and intensities that emerge through vitality are a form of 'enchantment', a term that is ubiquitous in Jankélévitch's writing too (Bennett 2010: xi–xii; cf. Chapter 5). When Bennett does wax lyrical she employs citations, and in the striking similarity of, for instance, Nietzsche's description of life-as-energy and Jankélévitch's extolling of Charm-as-music, the similarities between the ideas they describe become apparent.

With some modification, the notion of Charm can function as the basis for a musical vitality that includes all the aspects discussed so far: musical vitality is the distributed, drastic musical energy that vibrates meta-acoustically from the musician's fingertips to the listener's neuro-system. In its interactive, intermaterial vibrations, as Eidsheim states, 'no music is ever the same' (2015: 156); in its energetic transformations, as Jankélévitch says, 'physical sonority is already something mental' (2003: 76); and it is this form of musical vitality that informed the sublime evaluation of music in Romantic art philosophy. Rather than by the transcendentalism envisaged in Jankélévitch's and Lyotard's philosophies of Charm and *sentiment sonore* (cf. Chapter 3), however, this musical vitality, like the vitality inherent to Bennett's vibrant matter, is characterized by an immanence that renders the distinctions between object and Thing – or, in Adorno's terms, between object and subject – irrelevant: what Goehr calls music's 'aesthetic reaching' for the sublime has nothing to do with transcendentalism, but is a dimension of its immanence (2004: 27, 112, 123). Thereby, musical vitality's philosophical 'doubleness' overcomes the 'theological conception of the paradox' that was dismissed by Adorno (ibid.: 28–9; Adorno 2004: 375). The same paradox is inherent to musical and timbral epistemology: its description as 'paradox 0' above marks the fact that although we base all our opposing timbral theories on its paradoxical appearance, it should not necessarily be considered a paradox at all.

Musical energy, as it represents music's 'moment of non-identity' (Goehr 2004: 125) is able to infuse music's doubleness with '*a* life' (Bennett 2010: 57). Thus it disarms the 'perennial thorn' that Adorno found pricking 'in the side of rigidified philosophy' (Goehr 2004: 42). In Nancy's words,

> [A]ll the arts had projected into musical interiority and expressivity the need for an energy detached from the moorings that till then had help fixed in place the connected registers of cosmological structure (of harmonic order) and of representational technique (of objective reference).
>
> 2007: (52–3)

As musical vitality is distributed through the vibrational continuum, a musical vital materialism emerges that erases paradox 0 and the binary timbral thinking that it gave ground to. This musical vital materialism, which replaces binarism with pluralism and multidimensionality, has every potential to revolutionize music epistemology.

Musical vital materialism

Bennett asserts that vital materialism dissipates onto-theological binaries such as that of life/matter, human/animal, will/determination and organic/inorganic (2010: x). Such oppositions can be replaced by the notion of 'animacy', which indicates the degrees of vitality conveyed by various types of matter, and which is 'neither simply physiological nor simply psychological but both' (2015: 98). Animacy is also a helpful tool to mitigate the binaries regarding musical im/materiality. Musical animacy enlivens the vibrational continuum between verberation and auditum. The mechanical waves of musical vibration transfer a specific type of sonic energy that can be theorized as musical vitality, and the distribution of this vitality includes the physical and the non-physical.

Musical vitality is distributed between all the actors in the musical assemblage indicated by the SMASL acronym (cf. Wong 2015: 6). Its energetic agency, its non-human animacy, is as relational as any other form of agency: like a spark of fire burning fuel and operating a car, it sparks life into the encounters between the various musical actors. Its energetic nature connects the corporeal to the non-corporeal and illustrates the redundancy of onto-theological dualism. Musical energy surges through any network of possible singers, microphones, amplifiers, speakers and listeners, bouncing between all these actors, making them musick, and activating various forms of interactive feedback. Such feedback includes neuro-activity, which is less tangibly material than, say, the interaction between a guitar and an amplifier, but is just as physically induced: the musicking brain functions like an amplifier operated by electrical energy transmission. The outcome of this transmission, however, can be theorized as hauntological remnants and premonitions, terms that may sound suspiciously metaphysical to the binary-minded. And they are arguably precisely that: because it vibrates through a meta-acoustic continuum of sound and perception, musical energy's performativity leads to metaphysical feedback (cf. Lyotard 1991: 199). Rather than as polemically charged life/matter or mind/body dualism, musical vital materialism should be understood as a dynamic, energetic relationality. The relationality of musicking, which has been central to performative musicologies since the turn of the century (Abbate 2004; Cook 2001 and 2013; Eidsheim 2015; Small 1998), is powered by music's metaphysical vital energy: musical vitality energizes the pianist as she enjoys playing those fast notes, it fuels the synergy between the members of a band as they jam, and it animates the electronic tape of an analogue keyboard as it is run through a space echo machine.

Musical relationality exists in interaction, and this interaction overcomes a second binary: that between object and subject. Bennett argues that assemblage agency is distributive, non-causal and non-subject-centred: the notions of cause and effect, subject and object, she contends, should be replaced by that of 'a swarm of vitalities at play' (2010: 23, 31–3). Bruno Latour, whose actor-network theory inspired Bennett's vital materialism, states that action in an actor-network is continuously distributed between actors, always overtaken or 'other-taken' by other actors (2005: 45–6). As the actors in any social situation can be human as well as non-human, moreover, he argues that the notion of inter-subjectivity should be replaced by that of 'inter-objectivity' (ibid.: 195). He cites Rimbaud's line that 'Je est un autre' (I is another) to stress the fact that even subjectivity, in this analysis, is socially, interactively and relationally construed: any subject position is demarcated and identified by its interaction with others, whether these others are human or non-human (ibid.: 45). In the musicking network, these observations seem even more pertinent than in other social situations. Without continuous distribution, movement and interaction, there simply would be no musicking. The step from inter-subjectivity to inter-objectivity is a small one in the light of the large number of non-human and non-musical actors in any SMASL network. The swarm of vitalities that is at play in a musicking assemblage is an audible example of the way in which distributed energy moves outside the boundaries of cause and effect, and this non-causality extends to musical subjectivity. As any form of musicking – whether composing, performing, listening or dancing – reconfigures subject position in relation to the musical event at hand, the musicking self has never been anything but emergent and performative. Jankélévitch opens his book with a description of music as an intruder that robs the listener of a self until she is nothing more than a vibrating string or a sounding pipe (2003: 1). In music, the human subject is but one of the numerous actors that share and distribute, alter and multiply musical energy; in music, more than in any other form of relational interaction, I is another.

The relationality of musical encounters is defined by affect. In the context of music, the mind/body dualism that Leys criticizes in affect theory (2011) seems not only unnecessary but also impossible to maintain: music's capacity to affect and be affected may occur in encounters between any given constellation of human and non-human bodies and minds. As subjectivity and causality do not necessarily play a role in vital materialist interaction, affect has to be thought as the non-causal and impersonal intensity of the encounter between heterogeneous materials (Bennett 2010: xi–xiii). Musical affect colours the diverse emergent relations in the musicking assemblage: the interactions between musicians, recording and playback technology in the studio; those between conductor, acoustics, score and orchestra in the concert hall; those between playback technology, a listener's ears and her memories (cf. Lubarsky 2015: 84). Marie

Thompson and Ian Biddle argue that musical affect includes the ways in which humans experience music emotionally and cognitively, but is not shaped by conscious knowing (2013: 6). Because of music's 'liquid materiality', they contend, musical affect theory has to be radical in its detachment from subjectivity and causality:

> Indeed, what affect theory demands, especially with regard to thinking affect in relation to music, is a dislodging of discourses about 'attachment', 'value' or 'belonging' from their Euclidean moorings such that we encounter the raw mutability of any such moorings.
>
> (Ibid.: 14)

Affect is an intensity but not a cause; affect affects subjectivity but is separate from it. If this is true for other forms of affect, it is especially poignant in a musical context with its already ambiguous relation to subjectivity and causality. Like the musical relations of which it is a part, musical affect is immanent and emergent, meta-acoustically transferred and metaphysically experienced. The intensity of affect, therefore, is both exterior and interior to subjectivity. In his exploration of musical affect, Will Schrimshaw sets out to excise affect from 'the *necessity* of subjective affirmation': he argues that affect shows its autonomy as it exceeds the limits of phenomenology (2013: 28, italics in original). In this excess, Schrimshaw recognizes a sonic materialism that is quantitative rather than qualitative, an ethics and an aesthetics of exteriority. The exteriority of musical affect finds its ultimate affirmation in non-cochlear sound art, which is a celebration of unheard sound (ibid.: 30–9; cf. Kim-Cohen 2009: 217). Non-cochlear sound is to sound theory what Quentin Meillassoux's speculative realism is to philosophy: as a counterpart to post-Kantian correlationism it reflects on beings that are outside of human perception as well as human thinking (Meillassoux 2008: 1–27).

While the speculative realism of non-cochlear sound art overcomes the 'dead end' of carnal phenomenology by turning radically towards the outside (Kim-Cohen 2009: xix), the epistemology of music is required to take into consideration both this exteriority *and* the interiority of musical perception. Both are part of musicking, as musical vitality travels between outside and inside, and musical affect occurs across the continuum (cf. Lubarsky 2015: 85). If it is both exterior and interior, then musical vitality, like Bennett's matter-energy, is a mediator between material reality and immaterial concept. Like matter-energy, musical vitality bridges the gap between object and Thing-in-itself, which can no longer be envisioned in the Adornean sense as an absent-absolute (cf. Bennett 2010: 14–17). Rather than maintaining the distance to the musical Thing-in-itself through sublime aporia, the musical vital materialist acknowledges music's evasiveness *and* its immediacy, the unembodied ephemerality *and* the tangible corporeality of the musicking experience. Just as it replaces the divide between ontology and phenomenology with a vibrational continuum, musical vital materialism replaces the divide between music philosophical materialism and idealism with a vital continuum.

The continuums of musical vibration and vitality are experientially enacted in musical aesthetics. By formulating a philosophy of vital material, Bennett aims to 'induce in human bodies an aesthetic-affective openness to material vitality' (2010: x). To achieve this openness we only have to listen, as any form of musicking is a powerful way of experiencing the circulation of material vitality. Following Jane Bennett and Jacques Rancière, my definition of aesthetics in this book departs from the idealist notion of detached reflection on an artistic object. Aesthetic experience is the voluntary and involuntary, conscious and unconscious, sensory and affective participation in the vital performative knot that is the aesthetic event (cf. Bennett 2010: 104–8; Rancière 2009: 1–15; cf. Chapter 5). An aesthetics of the vibrant and vital continuum presented by music could not be defined in any other way. Musicking is participating in the vibration of musical energy among humans, non-humans, musicals and non-musicals; it is the sensory and affective experience of musical energy. Musicking is an aesthetics of vibration.

> *It's an October afternoon with golden sunlight on the darkened leaves of the lime tree on the green by my house. As I write this I am listening, on my headphones, to a CD recording of Ensemble Alternance's performance of Raphaël Cendo's composition* Rokh *for bass flute, violin, cello and piano.*[3] *The piece is a saturated composition about destruction and resurrection, but I have not read the programme notes.*
>
> *I am overwhelmed by the music's intensity. All four instruments produce a wide range of sounds, timbres and gestures, but none of these correspond to anything I have ever heard before. The music bounces to and fro. In its unpredictable gestures it touches and moves a range of heterogeneous entities, and it makes them all sing.*

---

[3] A version of *Rokh* performed by the Barcelona Modern Ensemble can be found on https://www.youtube.com/watch?v=Qkhb4pCHmRE.

> *Music wiggles and bursts forth out of and into Cendo's thoughts and his affirmation; music envelops the flute's metal, the piano's strings and wood; music radiates from the violin and the cello's bow and bridge; music moves fingers; music follows the ebb and flow of breathing; music expands with melody and rhythm; music bends in vibrato, tremolo and glissando; music shines in percussion and bowing; music whispers in flageolets and diminuendo and scratches; music shrieks in fortissimo, trills, sforzando; music bounces off sound recording and engineering and through my excellent earphones, which allow me to perceive every detail of this work, into my ears.*
>
> *Music waves into and out of my baffled mind, my tingling skin, my overflowing heart; music awakens joy and fear, music feeds off the reminiscences that it annihilates; the music blinds and trembles; music multiplies life and destroys it in the same sway.*
>
> *All of reality is music. I hear, see, touch, breathe, think and hallucinate music. Music is Rokh, music is the ensemble, music is I: its energy envelops me, bounces off me, takes part in me as I take part in it. Music is motion, music is space, music is time. Music is outside me, inside me, and I never was.*
>
> *I. Never. Was.*
>
> *And then it stops. My ordinary senses rush back in. It's nice and sunny outside, and the lime tree looks beautiful at this time of year. I'm supposed to be writing...*

My pathos is as pathetic as any other attempt at analysing or describing this music. There is no point in reducing Cendo's *Rokh* to a score, to the composer's intention, to the intricacies of performance, or to its place in contemporary composing. Nor can this music be reduced to the musicians in the ensemble or to the acoustics of the studio in which the CD was recorded. Although both composition and performance are guided by saturation and articulation, which are at once some of the most highly materially informed and the most ephemeral performal aspects of timbral ecology (Cendo 2010; cf. Chapter 1), music, in my aesthetic experience, cannot be only located in materiality, instruments, articulation or phrasing. *Rokh* involves all the animate musical actors described here: the musicking assemblage including humans, non-humans, bodies, thought. Musical energy simultaneously fed, guided and emerged from our collective vibrations. The musicking experience encompasses all the intensities afforded by their circulation. Listening to *Rokh* demonstrates how Goehr's 'musicality', which she identifies as the 'heart and soul' of musicking, is led by musical vitality (2004: 129; cf. Chapter 3).

Music cannot be understood in terms of either work or performance, either matter or life: it is a continuum of vibrating vitality that affects and is affected. As sound waves circulate between instruments, technology, musicians and listeners, the matter-energy enlivening their inter-objective action is the peculiar form of vitality that transforms sound into music. Music is messy. Its agency is heterogeneous. It inhabits, shapes and exceeds motion and space and time: it is only this intensive moment and the next, this affirmation after that impossible affirmation. Music happens independently from subjectivity, independently from intention and from cause: it exists in an emergent, dynamic *now* made up only of intensities. It has nothing to do with me, but it does all sorts of things with me, is affective in me and through me. Music is *a* life.

And right at the heart of this musicking aesthetics is timbre.

Timbral vibration and vitality

Back, finally, to where it all started. My explorations of vibration and vitality in this chapter were prompted by the epistemological paradox of timbre. The timbral binarism outlined in the first three chapters of this book is symptomatic of the cluster of debates haunting music philosophy: musicological debate is divided into dichotomies between work and performance, materiality and immateriality, and with that into dichotomies between ontology and phenomenology, materialism and idealism. As the topic of timbre spans across each of these divides, it is not surprising that its theorization has devolved into similar dichotomies. The lack of a coherent musicology of timbre is not only caused by the complexities of the topic itself, it is also the result of the absence of a theoretical space for these specific complexities within current music philosophy. In order to outline a timbral theory, the creation of such a theoretical space was required first, and this led to a reconsideration of the ways in which we can understand music. Timbre is nothing more and nothing less than the trigger for the development of a musical vital materialism. Now that this theory has been outlined, how can vibration and vitality help us to understand the subject matter of tone colour?

Vibration

As argued in the first half of this chapter, the vibrational continuum between verberation and auditum can be described by the metaphor of 'double suspension bridges': the continuum of sonic vibration reaches across the ontology/phenomenology and the materialism/idealism divides in timbral binarism. As timbre is present in verberation as well as in auditum, it occupies the entirety of the vibrational continuum. From a materialist perspective, the difference between an oboe and a clarinet timbre is located in their material ontology: the shape of the instruments and their reeds; the embouchure and breath control of the woodwind players; and the shape, frequency and spectral envelope of the sound waves produced by each instrument. From an idealist perspective, the timbral difference between these two woodwind timbres is located in their perception, which is only partially material and barely quantifiable (cf. Chapter 1): the physiology of the listener's ears may perceive an oboe as acerbic or conversely as dark, and a clarinet as warm or conversely as hollow; the individual memories that their sonic hauntology awaken can be as varied as personalities and individual neuropathways are; and the cultural meanings attributed to either timbre have a very wide historical range, from pastoral bliss to phallic symbolism. It is incongruous to argue that either side of the vibrational slide offers a more valid assessment position than the other. The paradox that Cornelia Fales notes between timbre in verberation and timbre in auditum was reflected in Helmholtz's vibrational experiments, which led to the conclusion that both the corporeal and the mental ear were involved in the perception of timbre and it was unclear how they each related to one another (Fales 2002: 57–8, 91; Steege 2012: 133–41): these divergent manifestations and perceptions of timbre no longer pose a theoretical problem in view of the fact that the vibrational continuum connects and embeds both timbral contexts. Timbral ontology and phenomenology, materialism and idealism coexist: their paradoxical coexistence, as the previous chapters have argued, is in fact one of the key characteristics of timbre, and one of the most important reasons why timbre is so difficult to theorize.

A peculiarity about timbre's place in the vibrational continuum is that it appears to move very rapidly between the extreme ends of its meta-acoustic span: timbre can seem tangibly corporeal one moment but ungraspably ethereal the next – and, as Chapter 3 illustrates, often both at the same time. If sound, as Chion says, is both an object and a non-object (2016: 169–211), then timbre is the quintessence of that contradiction. As a sonic event, its ontology and perception are bound to temporality: this is why, in the fleeting moment of its occurrence, this object/non-object has the evaporating quality of a photo negative disappearing in light, and why its interpretation can move so swiftly from the firm materialism of its tangible presence to the ecstatic idealism inspired by its inevitable pastness. Lyotard hints at this curious doubleness in timbral aesthetics:

> Within the tiny space occupied by a note or a colour in the sound- or colour-continuum, which corresponds to the identity-card for the note or the colour, timbre or nuance introduce a sort of infinity, the indeterminacy of the harmonics within the frame determined by this identity.
>
> (1991: 140)

In its evasiveness, its eventness and its changeability, timbre is similar to the random assemblage of debris that Jane Bennett describes encountering one morning in a Baltimore street.

> [The items in the street] shimmied back and forth between debris and thing – between, on the one hand, stuff to ignore, except insofar as it betokened human activity ... and, on the other hand, stuff that commanded attention in its own right, as existents in excess of their association with human meanings, habits, or projects. In the second moment, stuff exhibited its thing-power: it issued a call, even if I did not quite understand what it was saying. At the very least, it provoked affects in me: I was repelled by the dead ... rat, and dismayed by the litter, but I also felt something else: a nameless awareness of the impossible singularity of *that* rat, *that* configuration of pollen, *that* otherwise utterly banal, mass-produced plastic water-bottle cap.
>
> (2010: 4)

Timbre is like one of the items in this debris. Let us return to the first movement of J.S. Bach's 'Actus Tragicus' (BWV 106, discussed in Chapter 2 above). Our affective encounter with its timbres lacks cause, direction or intention: we simply hear them as a part of this composition with its softly flowing melodies, its gentle counterpoint, its soothing harmonic slow-motion. But timbre also commands attention in its own right, as we are suddenly aware of being moved by the specific colours of the viola da gambas and the alto recorders. We may consider their verberation: the bow of the viols, the wood of the recorders, the musicians' mastery of their instruments, the acoustics of the space in which they play. We may enjoy the responses they evoke in auditum: the hushed, whispering sound of the viol, the mellow and warm sound of the *flauto dolce*, the quiet pleasantness of their combined sounds, the emotions and associations that these timbres stir. In their specificity, appearing and disappearing in the few passing minutes that this short movement lasts, we are namelessly aware of the 'impossible singularity' of *those* timbres. Even if we have prior knowledge of Bach's compositional and orchestrational choices then this gnostic knowledge is only one part of our drastic encounter with this musical agent.

Bennett's choice of words in describing debris offers a remarkably apt description of our musicking encounter with timbre. Phrases like 'commanding attention in its own right', 'affect', 'nameless awareness' and 'impossible singularity' are adequate descriptions of precisely those aspects of timbre that strike and surprise us, both aesthetically and intellectually: tone colour's autonomous agency, its unspeakable aporia and its paradoxically tangible ineffability. Lyotard discusses timbre in exactly the same way when he describes the indeterminacy of timbre's 'singularity', of '*this* constellation' of acoustic parameters (1991: 155).

The addition of Bennett's vital materialism to Chion's acoulogical architecture has helped us understand how the philosophical bridges of the vibrational continuum within the event of musicking are interactively animated. The connections that the continuum establishes are operated by the musical equivalents of human/non-human assemblages, agency and vitality. Timbre has a specific and powerful place in this musical vital materialism.

Vitality

The composers who formulated the timbral imperative spoke about tone colour in terms that are strikingly aligned with vital materialist philosophy. Arnold Schoenberg stated that *Klangfarbenmelodie* gives 'life from our life' to sound (1922: 507). Similarly, Karlheinz Stockhausen asserts that timbre represents the 'life of the sound' (2000: 97–9). Pierre Schaeffer, who dedicated almost all of his musicking life to timbre, uses even more vitalist terms in his *Traité*. He describes the musicality of sound as 'an energetic agent that gives [sound] life' (2017: 278). The ephemeral timbral quality of allure, he says, is especially important in this process: it 'suggests the dynamism of the agent and the kinaesthetic sense; it enables us to appreciate the vivacity and energy specific to the object' (ibid.: 443). If we cannot define timbre in any quantifiable manner, and if the qualia ascribed to tone colour are as numerous and variegated as listener subjectivities are, then 'the life of sound' may be the most appropriate way to describe it – by way of its vitalizing agency.

Timbre interacts with other entities in the SMASL assemblage of musicking: it is a non-human, musical actor interacting with humans (composers, musicians, listeners), non-humans (instruments, scores), musicals (melody, harmony, rhythm, dynamics) and non-musicals (acoustics, recording technology). The entity of tone colour however, is also a SMASL micro-assemblage in and of itself – a micro-ecology, as Chapter 1 argued. The alto recorder timbre in the 'Actus Tragicus', for instance, consists of the interaction between the wood type used to build the instrument, the block and hard edge of the mouth piece, the musician's breath flow, lips, tongue and fingers, her articulation and the acoustic environment in which the instrument is played. Both types of interaction have their own affordances: while the encounters between the actors in the timbral micro-assemblage (or micro-ecology) afford timbre, the encounters between timbre and other SMASL entities in the macro-assemblage (or macro-ecology) afford music.

'Different materialities, composed of different sets of protobodies', Bennett asserts, 'will express different powers' (2010: 31). It is in the specificity of its agency that timbre's place among other actors in musical assemblages becomes clear. As timbre is a musical actor that is a non-object, its distributive agency is defined as music-power rather than as thing-power. It shares this type of power with other musical actors such as melody, harmony, rhythm, tempo and dynamics: each of these musical non-objects has the capacity to affect other entities, but, as their musical protobodies differ, their music-power varies. The music-powers of different musical actors do overlap, but each will have specific agencies in particular areas of music. Rhythm and tempo, for instance, are both able to affect musical temporality in verberation and the perceived passing of time in auditum. Melody affects the flow of one musical moment to the next in verberation and can have a 'sing-along' effect in auditum. Harmony has a strong influence on rhythm and metre, as cadences and resolutions suggest a downbeat; these verberation aspects, consequently, affect auditum too in that cadences are predictable and the resolution of dissonance is a musical interplay with listener expectation. Timbre's music-power is much more ambivalent than that of the other musical actors. It is less equally distributed along the vibrational continuum than the other musical agencies: its most intense expression is located on either extremity of the continuum, with a much less clear vibrational connection between tangible verberation and ephemeral auditum than in the case of the other musical actors. Timbral music-power is very precise on the physical end of verberation: the sonic spectrum determined by its physical protobodies affects many aspects of music including pitch, tuning and harmony, the articulation and sustain of tones, and sometimes – in the case of a singer, say, who has a full head register but a weak belt, or a recorder block that is too humid to produce a bright tone – even the sheer possibility of performance. In the auditum part of the continuum, on the contrary, timbre's music-power is very strong but not at all so precise, evoking impressions of identity, colour and flavour that are as compelling as they are vague (cf. the 'timbral plane of immanence' in Asche's 'Doom' and Schmickler's 'Rekursi' discussed in Chapter 2). It is the ambivalence of its agency that marks timbre's special place among other musical actors. This ambivalence goes a long way to explain the paradoxes in timbral assessment. In the aesthetic experience of timbre, verberation and auditum are tied together by vibration: as the agency determining this vibrational aesthetic affords such varying results, the aesthetic experience spans a wide performative range and may appear to be paradoxical in critical assessment.

Timbral agency in verberation can be studied in some degree of detail through the physics of sound. The mechanical waves of vibration flowing through musical assemblages are charged with musical energy. Musical energy was described earlier as a type of sonic energy consisting of the collective energetic agencies of the actors in a musical assemblage; one of the components of this musical energy is timbral energy with its multifaceted agency. The energetic properties of timbre have been described in empirical experiments that analyse the frequency spectrum of the singing voice. The so-called 'singer's formant' is a particularly interesting case. The third, fourth and fifth harmonic in the vocal spectrum of male professional singers can sometimes have a special 'ring', called *squillo* or *squillante* in vocal practice, which enables singers to be heard over large choirs or orchestra. This 'ring' occurs in the overtone spectrum between 2500 Hz and 4000 Hz, where sound waves, when achieving a certain amplitude, can carry an unusually high amount of energy (Feldman 2015: 96–107; Howard and Angus 2009: 224; Parker 2009: 67, 202; Sundberg 1987: 102–15). The physicality of this aspect of timbral agency is not only determined by its frequency spectrum but also by biological factors (Sundberg 1987: 115–29). The 'ring' of sound energy that is brought forward is a specific constellation of physical circumstances: it only appears in chest voice, at a certain pitch and at a certain volume. While chest voice can reach 4000 Hz in overtones, head voice produces overtones of up to 2000 Hz (which explains the difference in assessment of these timbres in auditum: head voice is often considered 'pure', chest voice as 'rich'). The female voice changes into head voice above the *passaggio*, which is located around F sharp5 on average, and is therefore unlikely to reach the frequencies that are necessary for *squillo*. Male singers, on the other hand, are often able to keep their larynx down and provide the required breath support to sustain chest voice up to a higher pitch, and thus produce the frequencies required for the 'ring' (Feldman 2015: 99). The timbral phenomenon of the singer's formant, therefore, can be explained from its physical circumstances in verberation.

But *squillo* also illustrates timbral agency in auditum, which is at least as powerful. The 'ring' of certain voices is precisely one of those vocal qualities that tends to elicit lyrical evaluations of sublime performances. Martha Feldman notices the prominent place of the 'ring' of castrati voices in historical performance reviews (Feldman 2015: 96–112). Despite the terrifying facts of castrati vocal embodiment, these reviews do not discuss the quantitative aspects of the voice, which appear to be less relevant to the way in which the singers' timbre is perceived. Instead, commentators including Arthur Schopenhauer described the 'angelic' qualities of castrato *squillo*, its 'supernatural beauty' and 'indescribable power' (Feldman 2015: 106–7). When timbral intensity affects us most, as the examples in Chapter 3 illustrate, we revert to the aporia of the sublime.

Another, even more elusive example of timbral agency in auditum is the way in which timbral energy can dominate other components of musical energy in slow movements with sustained or repeated notes. Consider, next to Callas's performance of Vincenzo Bellini's 'Casta Diva', Roberta Flack's performance of 'The First Time Ever I Saw Your Face' (1969) and Barbra Streisand's performance of 'Woman in Love' (1980). Each of these three very slow vocal performances are characterized by the singers' *legato*, the ability to sustain musical interest and movement throughout the repeated notes of a slow composition.

A standout moment in Bellini's 'Casta Diva' are two brief but intense bars on the word 'sembiante' in verse 1 which is repeated on 'pace' in verse 2 (Figure 4.1). In the first bar, the soprano solo soars on a syncopated A over a slowly moving alternation between a diminished seventh chord on F sharp minor and a dominant seventh chord on A major. In the second bar, the soprano tumbles down in punctuated rhythms from B flat to G which are doubled in the orchestra.[4]

---

[4] Callas's performance can be found on https://www.youtube.com/watch?v=TYl8GRJGnBY.

Figure 4.1 Vincenzo Bellini, *Norma* (1831), excerpt from 'Casta Diva'.

Callas's performance of the repeated A on 'sembiante'/'pace' is of particular interest here as she achieves an uninterrupted, compelling musical phrase within what is only one repeated note. The libretto has even less variation than the musical setting, with stretched 'aaaaa-s' occurring both times. The accents in the score, which occur as dynamic and timbral intensifications in her performance, become focal points within the ongoing flow of musical energy rather than renewed iterations of the note.

Roberta Flack's 1972 'The First Time Ever I Saw Your Face' contains a very similar vocal moment (Figure 4.2). On the words 'I thought the sun rose in your eyes / And the moon and the stars', the vocal line circles melodically around E and G while the harmony moves slowly from A minor through E minor to F on the first line, and from G to G7 in the second line.[5]

Flack's performance of this passage is of interest in similar ways to Callas's 'sembiante/pace' performance. Flack is able to sustain power throughout this section by creating a long melodic arch despite the lack of melodic variation.

---

[5] Flack's performance can be found on https://www.youtube.com/watch?v=d8_fLu2yrP4.

Figure 4.2 Roberta Flack, excerpt from 'The First Time Ever I Saw Your Face' (1972).

Flack directs her musical attention to two notes only, E (on 'thought the sun' and 'stars') and especially G ('rose in your eyes' and 'moon'), which results in a listening experience in which this latter note stands out as the musical centre around which both phrases revolve.

Barbra Streisand's 1980 'Woman in Love' is a slow song whose melody includes many repeated notes and a number of remarkable arches. On the lines 'It's a right I defend / Over and over again' the melody moves gradually down a minor third, from D via C to B, supported by a slow and uneventful harmonic movement from D via A minor to B (Figure 4.3).[6]

In a similar manner to Callas and Flack, Streisand's legato powerfully maintains musical interest over this slow arch in semibreves. Her performance of this passage stretches these key notes' motion in such a way that they appear to obliterate the filler notes around them.

In all three cases, an already restricted melodic and harmonic movement is further reduced through performance; similarly, an already slow tempo is rendered almost motionless in all three performances. Embedded in melodic

---

[6] Streisand's performance can be found on https://www.youtube.com/watch?v=hQLGCX8D-1Y.

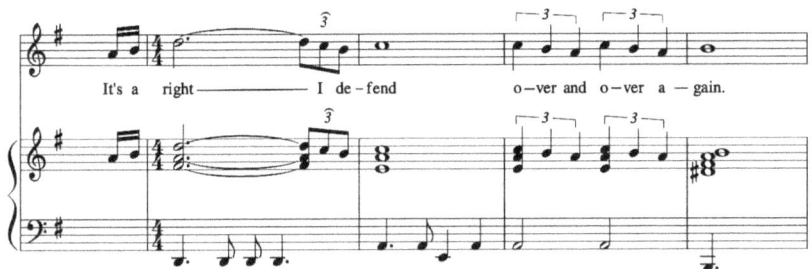

Figure 4.3 Barbra Streisand, excerpt from 'Woman in Love' (Barry and Robin Gibb 1980).

and rhythmic stillness, each of these three vocal performances is utterly mesmerizing. The only accurate way to describe the compelling power of Callas's, Flack's and Streisand's *legato* is that they all three succeed in sustaining musical vitality while they basically hold the same few notes. Without that prevailing energy the sustained notes would sound dull and lifeless. The result is quite magical. I am held in breathless captivation by something that does not move or change – something that is utterly still but that is *alive*. Musical vitality here is all but reduced to timbre only, to the energetic power present in tone colour. Melodic, harmonic and rhythmic vitality are halted in these performances, and the corporeal, verberational side of voice is forgone: the only agency that keeps the listener on her toes, her soul soaring, is the vitality circulating in timbral auditum.

Defining timbral vitality in this way presents a complex but not impossible challenge. Timbre's music-power affects various aspects of musical verberation and auditum, and the fact that it is specifically active on either extreme end of the vibrational continuum defines its remarkable, seemingly paradoxical power. The degree and type of animacy that a particular timbre has is changeable because the actors involved in the timbral micro-assemblage are changeable themselves. Similarly, the ways in which it affects other entities is variable because the actors involved in the SMASL macro-assemblage are variable, too. With timbre's concrete sound emerging in interaction with the contingencies of its physical production, and its perception developing in interaction with the contingencies of musicking, its music-power is not causal and not subjective, but rather distributive, virtual and immanent.

Dynamic relationality

The vital materialist approach understands music as a dynamic, energetic relationality that controverts life/matter dichotomies. Timbre, with its continuous motility between verberation and auditum, marks an important aspect of music's relationality. Timbre is a mediator between material reality and immaterial concept: as a dynamic force between object and Thing exerted by something that is neither an object nor a non-object, timbral vitality exceeds the boundaries of transcendent idealism. Any separation between a musical inside and outside, materialism or idealism is transgressed and eradicated by the meta-acoustic sound waves that transfer the musical energy of which timbral energy is a part.

The wild timbral variations in Cendo's *Rokh* are an illustration. Although any performance of this piece requires careful timbral preparation and rehearsal, *Rokh*'s tone colours do not represent a stable or predictable object. They are as changeable as the circumstances of their sonic realization, their sound entirely dependent on the chance meeting between a roughly bowed crescendoing glissando on cello and a sforzando flutter on bass flute. And although *Rokh* revolves around timbral energies and encounters emerging from 'the swarm of [in this case: timbral] vitalities at play' (Bennett 2010: 31–2), the affective intensities that they afford exceed understanding. There is no way to even imagine what these sounds say or mean, no real way to formulate even in metonymy what they do or how they make us feel. And if a sense of aporia is induced by *Rokh*, it is one that exceeds the Burkean sublime, replacing it, perhaps, by a Lovecraftian namelessness. By foregrounding the paradoxical *condition timbrale*, this composition renders audible the vibrating and vital negation that is immanent to timbre. There is no timbral object, no timbral Thing-in-itself: timbre is a coincidence, dependent on unpredictable contingencies both in verberation and in auditum.

When I listen to *Rokh*, 'Casta Diva', 'The First Time Ever I Saw Your Face', 'Woman in Love' or the 'Actus Tragicus', I engage with timbre. I may or may not be consciously aware of it, but I am sensorily, emotionally and cognitively moved by the strange vital energy that is specific to tone colour. Along with its vibrations across the continuum of music, my own physical and mental vibrations travel across the borders of life and matter.

Beyond timbral binarism: Towards a vibrant and vital aesthetics

'The continuity between mind and matter', Lyotard writes in his analysis of musical matter and time, 'appears as a particular case of the transformation of frequencies into other frequencies, and this is what the transformation of energy consists in' (1991: 43). Further exploring this energetic continuity in music, musical performance and musical perception, this chapter has outlined a theory of musical vital materialism.

It is interesting to revisit, briefly, the timbral concepts of *sentiment sonore* and *anima* which Lyotard bases on music's energetic continuity (cf. Chapter 3). He describes *sentiment sonore* or sound-feeling as the touch of music: 'the enigma of this touch is that it affects thought at the same time as the body' (1996: 41). What Lyotard says here, from the perspectives of vibration and vitality, is that music and timbre are active all along the vibrational continuum, and that their vitality can engender corporeal and mental intensities. The concept of *anima* or body/thought describes the ways in which music, and timbre specifically, has the same intensity when it touches the body as when it touches the mind. *Anima* is a 'substance soul with the faculty of being affected', and which indeed only exists *as* affected (Lyotard 1997: 242). From the perspective of vibration and vitality, what Lyotard is describing here is music-power's capacity to affect and be affected. The 'enigma' and aporia that he continued to find in musical experience throughout his writing, thus, are significantly less mysterious when his fundamentally idealist point of view is replaced by a vital materialist one.

A vital materialist musicology is able to supersede the timbral binarism sketched at the beginning of this chapter, suggesting instead that timbre's vibrational continuity should be matched by theoretical continua. Understanding the immanence of the timbral event, in other words, can only be achieved through a theoretical model that is similarly immanent, and so the existing transcendent models need to be replaced. The continuum of timbre's vibrations is enlivened by timbral vitality, the ambivalent music-power exerted by tone colour that affects all entities in the musical assemblage. Timbre's contribution to musical energy is powerful and seemingly ambivalent. Its 'impossible singularity' (cf. Bennett 2010: 4) affords such heterogeneous effects as material causalities and identities, the grain of the voice and its excess, affective intensities, hauntological lines of flight and sublime aporia. Timbre's vital sway is not that of a binarist knife, but that of the perpetual motion in a Newton's cradle.

A theory of timbre based on musical vital materialism addresses some of the problems at the nexus of musical epistemology. While my theoretical experiments here were prompted by the problems with which timbre presents musicology, the outcome of these experiments are by no means restricted to the musical or musicological area of tone colour. Timbre, as the great paradox haunting music epistemology, represents the nagging doubts caused by the unjoined dots and unfinished thoughts lurking in the dark corners of music philosophy. Trying to come to terms with timbre enables music philosophy to carve out new approaches for music's troubled epistemology – it invites us to revisit some of the dilapidated corners of music philosophy and fill in some of the heterogeneous gaps that we left there.

Musical vital materialism is a musicology that looks beyond the life/matter binary at a materiality that is 'as much force as entity, as much energy as matter, as much intensity as extension' (Bennett 2010: 20). Rather than either returning music philosophy to Romantic conceptions of absolute music or leading it into the 'cul-de-sac' of phenomenology and its exclusive corporeality (Kim-Cohen 2009: xix), this new materialist branch of musicology denounces musical mind/body dualism and, with that, can overcome the ontology/phenomenology and materialism/idealism divides dominating the field. It shares the vibrational approach to music outlined by carnal phenomenology but stretches beyond that through a focus on the agency of the vital material that enlivens the vibrational continuum. In music, outside and inside, body and mind, life and matter are inextricably entangled. The analysis of music as vibration and vitality leads to a reconsideration of musical aesthetics as the meta-acoustic and metaphysical participation in music.

Timbre has a special place in music's participatory aesthetics. The listener, as one entity in the musicking assemblage, participates in timbre's vibration and interacts with its vitality. Whether composing, playing, listening or dancing, her body and mind are touched by timbre. Engaging with timbre is participating in the dynamic motion between verberation and auditum: it is entering the gap between idealist binaries, into the alluring excess of meta-acoustic vibration. The final chapter of this book explores timbral aesthetics. What happens when we take the plunge into this gap? Where do timbral vibration and vitality lure us?

5

Aesthetics of vibration

Vital aesthetics and enchanted materialism

Aesthetics has received a significant amount of philosophical interest in recent years. While the grand narratives of 'high art' were under deconstruction, the idea of beauty as well as the reflective modes born from Kantian idealism were considered bourgeois relics from a bygone era. More recently, however, theorists have returned to aesthetics and attempted to redefine the experience of art as engaged, politically charged and philosophically relevant. One of the key theorists in this new aesthetic turn is Jacques Rancière, who wishes to rehabilitate the 'glorious sensuous presence' of art (2009: 2). His aesthetics confronts head-on the challenges posed by poststructuralist theory and postmodernist art criticism by rebuking the understanding of aesthetics as distanced reflection. Instead, he considers art, art experience and art reflection as a conjunction of thoughts, practices and affects. This convergence defines what art is, what art involves and how it works. Rancière argues that a disentanglement of these objects and practices, as professed by both traditional aesthetics and its opponents, obscures our view of their inseparable interrelations:

> If 'aesthetics' is the name of a confusion, this 'confusion' is nevertheless one that permits us to identify what pertains to art, i.e. its objects, modes of experience and forms of thought – the very things we profess to be isolating by denouncing aesthetics. By undoing this knot so that we can better discern practices of art or aesthetic effects in their singularity, we are thus perhaps fated to be missing that very singularity.
>
> (Ibid.: 4)

Rather than arguing for or against the notion of aesthetics as passive reflection, Rancière proposes to extend our understanding of it. He argues that aesthetics involves both *aisthesis*, a way of being that is affected by art, and *poiesis*, a way of doing art (ibid.: 7). Aesthetics should encompass all aspects of the experience of art, from the sublime to the mundane, from the immediacy of perception to the meanderings of interpretation, and it should include and confront the philosophical problems arising from these simultaneities (ibid.: 14). Although Rancière does not want to maintain the separation between the sensuous perception of art and the intellectual reflection on art, neither does he wish to continue the confusion that has evolved from their conflation. His writing explores this entanglement in its very entanglement, its distributive power, and, in that distribution and in that power, its relation to the world around it. In this sense, aesthetics is a way of identifying art precisely through and in its existence in the world.

In its ecology, its relation to the world, art is not just contingent but necessarily radical. Its radicality, Rancière claims, is 'the singular power of presence, of appearing and inscription, the power that tears experience from ordinariness' (ibid.: 19). Despite this choice of words, however, this singularity and this power should not be understood in terms of the sublime, which would suggest a dialectic (positive or negative) between the interiority of subjectivity and the exteriority of an 'absolute Other' (ibid.: 22). Rather, Rancière prefers to think of art as a *dispositif*, a symbolic and material setting or space-time in which the various 'things of art', and this emphatically includes art's audience, all participate (ibid.: 23–4).

From these considerations a new definition of aesthetics emerges, an aesthetics that is as much about art's beauty as it is about its political power, and as much about the materiality of the artwork as it is about the materiality of art's work:

> This distribution and redistribution of places and identities, this apportioning and reapportioning of spaces and times, of the visible and the invisible, and of noise and speech constitutes what I call the distribution of the sensible.
> (Ibid.: 24–5; cf. Rancière 2004)

Rancière's aesthetics is of necessity political in its distribution, but what is being distributed is, by an equal degree of necessity, tied to a certain discursiveness. The two realms of art's discursiveness and its distribution may be at tension with one another when we focus our aesthetic attention exclusively on either one of them (Rancière 2009: 44). It is only when we investigate the discursive shape of a book, play, painting, dance or composition in conjunction with its active place in the world that we can come to grasp its aesthetic performativity. In the inclusive definition of a 'distribution of the sensible' that Rancière proposes, aesthetic theory appears to be exhumed from its postmodernist grave. To truly revive it, however, would require endowing it with a life, and such a reanimation can be achieved by a vital materialist framework.

The 'aesthetic openness' that Jane Bennett aims to evoke through vital materialism owes a great deal to Rancière's aesthetic theory (Bennett 2010: x). Both are distributive and interactive in their operational mechanics, and both are explicitly ecological and political in their outlook. Both philosophies reject the separation of art object and art Thing that characterized idealist aesthetics in favour of a participatory model of aesthetic exchange. But Bennett, arguing that the distribution of the sensible is not exclusive to humans, importantly adds the aesthetic agency of non-humans to Rancière's premise (Bennett 2010: 106). The political powers that Rancière identifies in artistic interventions, she contends, flow through human as well as non-human bodies. The vibrant swarm of their intensities circulates in and affects assemblages of heterogeneous entities, and can have unforeseeable effects: 'In what ways does the effect on sensibility of a video game exceed the intentions of its designers and users?' (ibid.: 107). While sharing the basic assumptions of Rancièrian aesthetics, Bennett expands its implications far beyond his anthropocentric scope.

Like Rancière's aesthetic theory, Bennett's 'aesthetic openness' moves the reflective position of aesthetic analysis from both the primacy of the sublime Thing in idealist aesthetics and the primacy of the object in Adorno's negative dialectics to a more fluid, immanent model in which art engages in an active, embodied interaction with the world. Bennett replaces these dialectic aesthetic theories with a highly politicized interaction with art (ibid.: 17, 2015). More strongly than in Rancière's theory, ecology in vital materialism is on the verge of replacing aesthetics: perhaps it is for that reason that Bennett does not engage extensively with the discursive shapes of art. This makes it difficult, sometimes, to imagine what a vital materialist aesthetic regime identifies beyond the political ecology of vibrant matter.

Some theorists have attempted to connect the aesthetics of art's discursive structures with that of art's distributive political performativity. Most notably, a special issue of *Evental Aesthetics* dedicated to vital materialism contains essays on literature, dance, musical performance, and an article by Bennett herself on art and culture (2015). In her editorial for this special issue, Mandy-Suzanne Wong contends that a vital materialist aesthetic practice consists of 'human-nonhuman assemblages impacting one another affectively, physically, and creatively' (2015: 5). Wong describes aesthetics as concerned with the enchantment occurring in artistic experience – the affective, physical and creative impact of one entity upon another – and with the material and immaterial contingencies of that enchantment. The term 'enchantment' itself derives from Bennett's earlier work *The Enchantment of Modern Life*, where she defines it as

> a state of wonder, and one of the distinctions of this state is the temporary suspension of chronological time and bodily movement. To be enchanted, then, is to participate in a momentarily immobilizing encounter; it is to be transfixed, spellbound … [It] requires active engagement with objects of sensuous experience; it is a state of interactive fascination, not fall-to-your-knees awe.
>
> (Bennett 2001: 5)

Bennett's theory of enchantment explores the 'ethical energetics' of affect, materiality, non/humans that enables enchantment (ibid.: 131–58); it identifies the 'extraordinary' instances that 'live amid the familiar and everyday' and that can induce such enchantment (ibid.: 4). The impact and enchantment that define aesthetic interaction are operated by the circulation of vitality among humans and non-humans (ibid.: 80–4, 156–8). Thing-power fuels interactions between a painter, her brush, the canvas, light, colour, the painter's or viewer's eyes and visual appreciation; in a similar way, as the previous chapter argued, music-power energizes the encounters between a musician, her instrument, the score, acoustics, timbre, musician's or listener's ears and auditory appreciation. The task of vital materialist aesthetic analysis is to identify thing-power and the ways in which it affects entities in such aesthetic assemblages (Wong 2015: 12). Bennett describes affect in the context of art as 'transfers of energy from one site to another' (2015: 97). These energy transferrals can lead to the emergence of what we call meaning, but a meaning that has no causal or intentional relation to subjectivity and is not the outcome of a phenomenological epoché. Bennett therefore advocates a renewal of our understanding of semiosis 'to include what happens through these transports of affections' (ibid.: 97).

The vital materialist approach to aesthetics, which Bennett also refers to as 'enchanted materialism' (2001: 14, 156–8), has not yet been explored in great detail, but it offers exciting prospects for further analyses of the ways in which our engagement with art is as participatory and politically charged as Rancière proposes, as enchanting as Bennett and Wong suggest, and as driven by the immanent forces of thing-power as any other type of human/non-human assemblage. The vibrating swarms of aesthetic vitality moving through the world do not only invoke multifarious affects and meanings, they also invite a form of analysis that can transform the ways in which we study aesthetic experience. This chapter explores the possible implications of such an approach to the aesthetics of musical vibration and vitality, with specific attention to the confusing knot that is timbre.

Aesthetics of musical vibration and vitality

The gap between the outside of verberation and the inside of auditum has historically been as profound a concern for musical aesthetics as it has been for music epistemology. Often explicitly debated and always implicitly present, the ostensible irreconcilability of music's corporeality and its ineffability form a rift through music aesthetics. This division corresponds broadly to the two aesthetic realms identified by Rancière (see below): musical idealism developed into aestheticism, while musical materialism is increasingly deployed in views of music aesthetics as political agent. The musical aesthetics based on the continuum of vibration and vitality which I aim to develop here, however, would have to encompass both the *aisthesis* and *poiesis* of musical experience.

In *The Orchestral Revolution*, Emily Dolan analyses the development of musical aesthetic philosophy as parallel to that of the symphonic orchestra in the later decades of the eighteenth century (2013). She demonstrates how the idealist aesthetics of musical beauty and form which lead to the notion of absolute music in the nineteenth century had its origins in the attention to instrumental sonorities in continental Europe of the Enlightenment. In its early stages, this aesthetic theory involved physical instruments as they brought forth different sounds as well as the effects that these different sounds had on musical perception. Dolan regards aesthetics in this period as mediation between the sensible and the rational:

> The aesthetic was that force which built steps between the throne of cognition and the diverse, messy, and vibrant world of sensation and feeling … It was a study of *mediation*, and dealt in equal measure with immediate sensation and abstract reason.
>
> (Ibid.: 71)

Dolan discusses Johann Gottfried Herder's writings on music, which, as Chapter 3 argued, emphasize that hearing music includes both physical and mental activity. Herder contended that 'sensation always already implied cognition', that the two are inseparably entwined (ibid.: 74–5). Despite Herder's efforts to integrate both components of musical experience, contemporary philosophy – guided mainly by Immanuel Kant's idealism – explicitly separated sense from sensibility, musical touch from musical reflection (cf. ibid.: 80–5). As the aesthetic philosophy of music entered the Romantic age, its ambivalent roots became, to borrow Rancière's terminology, ever more disentangled: musical aesthetics became increasingly fascinated by the perception of musical beauty and the sublimity it seemed to evoke, and over the course of the nineteenth century the physical sounds, vibrations and sensuous touch of music gradually became disregarded as they were considered inferior to the ungraspable Thing of music in-itself. This eventually led to the much-debated idea of 'absolute music' in Romantic philosophy (Dahlhaus 1989: 34, 88–96, 142–4; Dolan 2013: 88–91; Goehr 2004: 106–16; Hamilton 2007: 66–94).

It is in response to this foregrounding of music's ineffability that Eduard Hanslick begins his 1854 essay *On the Musically Beautiful* with the reproach that musical aesthetics should not be concerned with the 'thousandfold flickering impressions and feelings' that 'take possession of us' when we hear music but rather with the 'objective nature' of music (1986: 1). In order to solve this problem, he suggests a separation of the physical sensation of music from the emotions it evokes, and proposes a focused aesthetic attention to the former (cf. Hamilton 2007: 81–9). Hanslick's ruminations on sensation mark the onset of material aesthetics and, when Helmholtz's *On the Sensations of Tone* appeared in 1891, the carnal approach to the phenomenology of music completed the separation between the two aesthetic realms despite his initial attempts to bridge the gap (Steege 2012: 126). By the end of the nineteenth century, musical aesthetics was categorically divided between verberation and auditum (cf. Goehr 2004: 88–131). In this split, the term 'aesthetics' itself became increasingly attributed to distanced, disembodied reflection and occupied itself only with what Chion calls auditum. Musical aesthetics gradually became synonymous with formalism, art for art's sake, mysticism, or a 'gnostic' approach to music (Abbate 2004; Goehr 2004: 91–7; Hamilton 2007: 85–6). The opposite of such immaterialism, in the meantime, was the rise to prominence, especially in the last decades of the twentieth century, of verberational studies that stressed the political potential of music *qua* sound and of sound *qua* physics. Referring to themselves as emanating from 'sound studies' rather than from musicology, these readings of sonic verberation do not occupy themselves with music *qua* music, and can, with some effort, be considered a 'haptic aesthetic' albeit not necessarily a musical one (Colebrook and Bennett 2009: 75).

Andy Hamilton's aesthetics of music offers a possible way out of the binary thinking that pervades the field. Hamilton's theory is based on a 'twofold thesis' that includes both ends of the dichotomy (2007: 108–11). He argues that listening to music has acousmatic and non-acousmatic components: in musical experience, he contends, the ephemeral purity of tone is met by the physicality of its origin. Hamilton defines the acousmatic as based on Schaeffer's *objet sonore*, but he argues that 'listening without seeing' in general has become equivalent to aesthetic listening since Kantian idealism. Acousmatic music, in this reading, becomes an inapproachable Thing-in-itself that is detached from the world. The aesthetic based on what he calls 'the acousmatic thesis' considers music as sound that is heard for its own sake, detached from its source or the contingencies of its production (ibid.: 95–108). The twofold thesis he proposes, by contrast, accepts the possibility and indeed the importance of acousmatic listening, but emphasizes that musical aesthetics also includes another type of listening which is much more material. As his thinking is tied to the Schaefferian sound-object, he describes the latter dimension of listening as causal and intentional, directed at the identification of the sound source (ibid.: 109–10). Hamilton's twofold thesis is a landmark in musical aesthetic theory, as it includes both (a demystified version of) musical idealism and (a phenomenological and causal version of) musical materialism. The aesthetic, he states, is 'an everyday and unmysterious phenomenon', that is 'an exercise of the intellect' with a 'grounding in the human body and its movement' (ibid.: 6). His theory reunites the two sides of musical experience that have been separated since the late eighteenth century.

As the two components of Hamilton's aesthetics are connected in the continuum of musical vibration and vitality, it is now possible to formulate a musical aesthetics that is not just 'twofold' (the term itself reveals an enduring dualism or, less rigidly, a dialectic rather than a continuum between both sides) but as continuous as the fluid non/matter it analyses. Interestingly, the kernel of such an approach was already present in Herder's writings in the late eighteenth century. As observed above, Herder emphasized that the sonorous includes sensation and cognition: the following passage from his *Viertes Wäldchen* acquires a remarkable significance when read in the light of the vibration and vitality distributed in musical experience.

> Still fewer concern themselves as to how tone, as tone, affects us. Not the physicist, who knows it only as sound (*Schall*). He tracks it from the string through the air, from the air to the ear, through all the hearing channels of the

ear nerves; but still as sound. So how can he know how the nerves are affected by what is no longer sound, by what is only simple tone (*Ton*)? How this tone works upon the soul and moves it?

(Herder 2006: 93)

As outlined in Chapter 3, Herder makes a clear distinction between sound (*Schall*) and tone (*Ton*) throughout his work, and by the latter he means timbre. He wishes to trace music's, specifically timbre's, capacity to affect, to follow it in its transferral from physical sensation to mental reception. From the perspective of vibration and vitality, he considers the entire vibrational continuum to be the aesthetic domain of music, with timbre at its affective nexus, and he considers the affective intensity of music-power, which he calls 'accents of passion' ('Accente der Leidenschaft') or 'accents of sensibility' ('Accente der Empfindung') to be active all across that domain (ibid.: 113, 117, 161). Two and a half centuries later Jane Bennett refers to precisely this type of interactive, sensuous aesthetic as enchanted materialism. Although she does not discuss musical experience herself, the philosophical kinship between her and Herder's aesthetics promise too fruitful a cross-pollination to leave unexplored.

Music has a stronger capacity to affect and enchant than any other form of art, as Jankélévitch's repeated references to the 'bewitchment by a sonorous phantasm' in musical experience leading to an 'enchanted chronology' emphasized (2003: 2, 70; cf. Priest 2013: 59). A vibrant aesthetics can explore the physical as well as mental embeddedness of musical affect, giving both sides of the vibrational continuum an equal amount of weight. In order to theorize the transferral of musical power from the string to the 'nerves', or in Chion's terms from verberation to auditum, Herder reverts to Leibnizian monads, which, via Deleuze and Guattari's monadology, are also the basis of Bennett's theorization of matter-energy, thing-power and vitality (Herder 2006: 114; Bennett 2010: x–xi, 119–21; cf. Dolan 2013: 77). Monads are the smallest indivisible units of substance. They have their own agency, and this matter-energy drives the vitality that I theorized in Chapter 4 as musical thing-power or music-power. Herder speaks explicitly of this 'energy' and 'energetic power', which he argues is the element of music that affects the soul in a lasting manner: the energetic power of timbre, he states, is the 'immediate instrument affecting the soul' (2006: 160–1). In a monist conception of the world, distinctions between the human and the non-human as well as those between object and subject are replaced by an immanent continuum in which monads do their work. For this reason, Herder considers the listener not as a passive recipient of music, but as an instrument participating in its vibrations, as part of the vibratory playing field of musical monads. Since each listener is a different kind of instrument, with her own kind of musical resonance, he contends, it is impossible to objectify musical experience (ibid.: 114–17; cf. Dolan 2013: 85–7).

Herder's inclusive and distributive views on musical aesthetics were overtaken by idealism on one side and materialism on the other, but the vibrant musical aesthetics that I want to propose here returns to his ideas. Based on music's meta-acoustic vibrations and their capacity to circulate musical vitality across the meta-acoustic realm affected by musicking, vibrant aesthetics rehabilitates the singular knot of musical sensation and musical reflection that was central to Herder's philosophy. Vibrant musical aesthetics renders the separation of aesthetic idealism and materialism irrelevant, as it is built on the ambivalence that is inherent to music: as a form of 'mediation' between the tangible and the intangible (Dolan 2013: 71), it studies the vibrating distribution of musical vitality in heterogeneous musicking assemblages within the metaphysical simultaneity of music's material and immaterial components. This musical aesthetics replaces the logocentrism of Rancière's 'distribution of the sensible' by the audible and the inaudible in their mutual continuity; moreover, it adds musical agents, musical assemblages, musical vitality and music-power to Bennett's collection of vibrant and enchanted matter. It studies the specificities of music-power and the ways in which it affects the entities active in musical assemblages.

The aesthetics I advocate here revolves around a vital form of musical autonomy. This autonomy differs from that of Romantic absolute music, which is based on the idea that music is independent from other arts through the peculiar 'emancipation from external reference' that Hegel found in music and which rendered it a 'language above language' (Hamilton 2007: 84, 74–8). This is the autonomy of Hanslickian formalism which became the heart of the doctrine of absolute music (Goehr 2004: 96–7). The musical autonomy that we can derive from musical vital materialism also differs from the autonomy of the *sensorium* by which Rancière's aesthetic theory distinguishes itself from Kant's (cf. Moreno and Steingo 2012: 496–7). Rather, a vital musical autonomy can be defined through the musical energy that fuels the interaction between musicking entities, along the lines of what Goehr proposes as music's 'autonomous voice' driven by 'musicality': this autonomy is the vitality that Bennett would call music's 'active impulsion' to persist (Goehr 2004: 92, 118–31; Bennett 2010: 2; cf. Chapter 3). An aesthetics based upon the autonomy of music-power directs attention to what Dolan calls 'the diverse, messy, and vibrant world of sensation and feeling', to what Abbate calls the 'transfixing and bewildering' presence of the 'drastic' musical event, and to what Jankélévitch calls 'Charm' (Dolan 2013: 71; Abbate 2004: 512, 532; Jankélévitch 2003: 83; cf. Chapter 4). As this aesthetics is interested in all aspects, manifestations and emergent effects of musicking, it takes account of the perfection of Masaki Suzuki's CD recordings of J.S. Bach's cantatas as well as of the imperfect spontaneity of J.S. Bach's organ improvisations (cf. Goehr 2004: 132–6; Hamilton 2007: 192–217).

A musical aesthetics of vibration and vitality includes the pleasure of recognizing a flute timbre as it mingles with other sonorities in the opening bars to Debussy's *Prélude à l'Après-Midi d'un Faune*; it also recognizes the music-power of the flute's chromatic melody as it unfolds and the way it interacts with the hushed tone colour of the instrument. A vibrant musical aesthetics appreciates the inscription of musical and extra-musical identity to that flute timbre but simultaneously the joy that ensues as this identity gradually dissipates in the dreamlike world evoked by the composition. It acknowledges the aesthetic involvement of our body and mind, affording emergent senses, affects and thoughts: aesthetic engagement comes into being in the equal agency of all the entities involved that distribute and multiply musical vitality – the instruments, the acoustics of the concert hall, musicians, listeners, all at one, an ecology of active musicking. A vibrant musical aesthetics, moreover, also investigates the disappearance of ordinary time-space into a musical time-space that is non-existent but tangibly and yet ephemerally present; and it includes our own willing disappearance into the time and space of musical experience. Vibrant musical aesthetics listens to music as it lives, and to listeners as they are affected by its power. It is, *tout court*, an aesthetics of musicking.

Tone-pleasure: timbre's aesthetic singularity

As Herder notes, tone colour occupies a specific and crucial area in the aesthetic experience of music. With its intense physical and mental music-power, timbre is at the nexus of the vibrant musicking aesthetics outlined here. It is the first thing that strikes us – tangibly *strikes* us – in a listening experience, and its vital sway sets in motion the drastic flow of a musical immersion that is simultaneously as tangible as that first strike and as ephemeral as 'the realm of the monstrous and the immeasurable' (Hoffmann 1965: 41; cf. Chapter 3).

Timbre's music-power affects both musical verberation and musical auditum, often at the same time: as its affective intensity simultaneously occurs on both extreme ends of the vibrational continuum, this music-power can appear paradoxical. It is not surprising that Roger Scruton, whose musical aesthetics fiercely defends musical intentionality and knowability, dismisses timbre as irrelevant to the aesthetics of music (1997: 78). Scruton's decision to join Chion's needless bathwater-throwing is prompted by his resistance to the apparent paradoxes of timbre (Chion 2016: 174). He maintains that timbre is somehow simultaneously 'baffling' because we cannot describe its intensity, *and*, as a causal sound-object pointing to its own origin, has no place in the acousmatic (and thoroughly idealist) aesthetics that he advocates (1997: 2–3, 77–8).

In his *Works of Music: An Essay in Ontology*, Julian Dodd states that Scruton's acousmatic dismissal of timbre is a 'mistake' (2007: 2013). He argues that the collection of timbres in a given musical work W is part of the set of acoustic properties Σ that defines that work's ontology. For this reason, Dodd contends that tone colour rather than being irrelevant, is 'normative' for musical aesthetics (ibid.: 213). He qualifies this 'timbral sonicism' by arguing, importantly, that this does not throw musical aesthetics back to instrumentalism (which is the timbral essentialism discussed in Chapter 2) or composer intention: precisely because timbral sonicism is a form of individuation, matters pertaining to prescriptive scores, intended aesthetic content, or historical context do nothing to deny the ontological importance of the simple acoustic presence of a musical work (ibid.: 214–76). As an important by-product of his search for an ontology of the musical work, thus, Dodd has pinpointed the aesthetic singularity of timbre: it is the sonic individuality of *this* piano in *this* performance of Beethoven's *Hammerklavier* Sonata – whether this piano is a Steinway grand or a 'Perfect Timbral Synthesizer' – which defines *this* music-aesthetic experience (ibid.: 223–4).

Andy Hamilton, too, takes issue with Scruton's cursory rejection of timbre's aesthetic value. He defines timbre as causal, just like Scruton does: but he argues that precisely because it identifies the source of sound, this non-acousmatic sound quality undermines the acousmatic thesis on which Scruton's aesthetics is based (Hamilton 2007: 103–8). In a similar way, he contends, the acoustic spatiality and corporeal tangibility of sound, as well as the imperfections or virtuosity of performance are arguments against the acousmatic thesis (ibid.: 104–6). All of these physical, non-acousmatic aspects of sound are as crucial to musical experience, Hamilton stresses, as its acousmatic reflections in musical metaphors, meaning and imagination. Rather than dismissing an aspect of musical experience because it does not fit music-aesthetic theory, he proposes to amend music-aesthetic theory to his 'twofold thesis' in order to accommodate all aspects of that experience (ibid.: 108–11). The coexistence of the non-acousmatic and the acousmatic in musical experience is especially poignant in the experience of timbre. From the perspective of Hamilton's aesthetics, tone colour with its manifest simultaneity of material causality and immaterial interpretation, epitomizes the twofoldness of musical experience. This simultaneity, of course, is why Scruton needs to reject timbre as part of musical aesthetics, and it is exactly what proves him – and traditional idealist aesthetics – wrong.

Following the line of argument set out in this book, it becomes clear that Scruton is pointing to the apparent irreconcilability of the two halves of the timbral paradox here, and, rather than choosing to direct his focus towards either side of timbral binarism like other theorists have done, refuses to acknowledge the aesthetic significance of either part of the field. Dodd and Hamilton are correct to rebuke Scruton's dismissal of timbre as a physical, non-acousmatic phenomenon: timbre's music-power in verberation is an important part of the music-aesthetic puzzle and to ignore it is to leave out half of the aesthetic experience of tone colour. But so is leaving out the other half of timbre's music-power, its strong agency in auditum, which Scruton only describes as 'baffling' and which Dodd's ontology-based aesthetics does not address in any detail. Hamilton's twofold thesis does allow for a coexistence of timbral verberation and timbral auditum, but it still separates them from each other. In order to acknowledge both sides of the timbral paradox and moreover the conditions of their aesthetic performativity, the aesthetics of vibration and vitality proposed here is based on the timbral event as it occurs, rather than on the detached reflection on that event. If the aesthetics of musicking is an autonomous, drastic and multifariously affective interaction with the vital energy transferred in music's vibration, then timbre's apparently contradictory effects are no longer separated but connected occurrences on a timbral continuum. In a vibrant and vital aesthetic, timbre represents an aesthetic singularity: the unique concurrence of material and immaterial enchantment fuelled by tone colour's autonomous music-power, which invites sensuous experience and intellectual reflection simultaneously.

Timbre's aesthetic singularity can be illustrated through what Ashley Woodward has called 'Lyotard's doubt' (2016: 122, 132). Chapters 3 and 4 detailed Lyotard's concerns regarding the relations between presentation and unrepresentable, audible and inaudible, matter and idea in music. Lyotard's writing includes both ends of the paradox while keeping the paradox itself intact in a manner similar to Hamilton's twofold thesis. Woodward describes this aspect of Lyotard's thinking on music as post-phenomenological (ibid.: 121, 134): in reference to Kant's 'given', he succinctly summarizes Lyotard's problem as 'in music, the inaudible is what gives the given – the audible – but is not itself given' (ibid.: 130). For Lyotard, this problem is epitomized in timbre or *sentiment sonore*, the inaudible matter of music that 'clandestinely inhabits the audible material' (Lyotard 1997: 230). As discussed in Chapter 3, Lyotard attributes this paradox to a form of the sublime (cf. Woodward 2016: 124–7), but from the perspective of vibrant and vital aesthetics this alleged sublimity is located in timbre's continuous vital negotiation between verberation and auditum, which allows the material and the immaterial sides of music, the mundane and the ineffable, to interact and intervene in each other's structure. Timbre is not a clandestinely inaudible occupant of the audible, nor is it even all that paradoxical. The only reason that existing theories of timbre amount to an accumulation of paradoxes is that none of these theories consider both the material and the less material sides of timbre's agency. If they did, it would be clear that rather than a paradox, timbre presents a particularly striking example of the 'knot' of aesthetic experience that Rancière theorizes (2009: 4): its music-power brings together the sensuous perception of art and the intellectual reflection upon art in the singular convergence of the colour of a violin bowing and the sway of timbral imagination.

The aesthetic singularity of timbre's music-power explains why tone colour is at the nexus of the unsolved materialism/idealism debates haunting music aesthetics and music epistemology. Timbre's vital capacity to affect plays out most powerfully on either end of the vibrational continuum: that is to say, its aesthetic performativity is strongest at points of extreme physicality and in moments of extreme ephemerality. The confusion that ensues – I am impressed by the shape and strength of Roberta Flack's vocal tract and in awe of the singer's control over her instrument, but at the exact same time I am entirely forgetful of that vocal tract and of the singer, mindlessly spellbound into ecstatic enchantment by this timbre's ineffable Charm – this conflation of pluriform aesthetic experiences is the same confusion that Rancière identifies as the aesthetic singularity that is art (2009: 4): this timbral confusion *is itself* the distribution of the sensible. Participating in timbral aesthetics is the vital interaction with the very core of musical epistemology, with confusion at its epicentre.

The aesthetics of timbre revolves around gaps: those between difference and identity, meaninglessness and signification, lack and surplus, mundane production process and sublime performativity, object and Thing. In terms of music philosophy, therefore, timbral theory cannot but bridge the gaps between the ontology and phenomenology of music epistemology on the one hand and the materialism and idealism of music aesthetics on the other. The tensions explored in the first three chapters of this book can each be considered as 'gap areas' within the aesthetics of timbre; each of these tensions can be solved if they are considered not as problem zones between two areas of aesthetic experience or theorization but as the very zones where timbre is active, as aesthetic continua inhabited by the vitality of tone colour. The praxis of timbre (Chapter 1) shows that even in the endlessly physical processes of tone colour production, the goal is always one of idealist aesthetics: the production of timbre is an attempt to create a seamless connection between verberation and auditum. The assigning of musical identities to musical difference (Chapter 2) is born from a formalist aesthetics: if Nina Eidsheim considers timbre an 'aesthetic straightjacket' in classical singing pedagogy, she does nothing more and nothing less than point out the shortcomings of that one-sided approach to vocal tone colour which is neither reducible to disembodied ephemerality nor to the singing body alone (2015: 140ff.). The sublime assessment of timbral experience (cf. Chapter 3) that became the idealist focus of Romantic and modernist aesthetics, finally, is the consequence of a disproportionate focus on timbre's music-power in auditum. Timbre is *about* aesthetics, *about* the distribution of the sensible – from the making of a Stradivarius violin to its sublime sounding in a violin concerto to the identification and fetishization of the Stradivarius timbre in classical music fan culture.

My ideas are far from new. Johann Gottfried Herder had already reached the same conclusion in the late eighteenth century:

> [Because] the ear, as an ear, cannot sense (*empfinden*) proportions, it is clear that the basis of all music lies in the first moment of sensation (*Sensation*), in simple euphony (*Wohllaut*).
>
> (2006: 96)

A few pages on, Herder refines his description of the simple delight in such 'euphony' as 'tone-pleasure' (*Tonwollust*, ibid.: 113). 'Tone-pleasure': could timbral aesthetics be described more succinctly? Herder stresses here the crucial importance of timbre in musical experience: the simple fact that tone colour is the tangible *and* ephemeral delight of hearing sound. Sensation and reflection are not just two sides of the timbral coin: they are the same. *Empfindsamkeit* includes both sense and sensibility. Its historical situatedness between the baroque fold, Enlightenment reason and the Gothic shadows of sublimity enabled its main theorist Herder to find the hinging point that links together all aspects of musical experience. Tone-pleasure: timbre's aesthetic singularity folds auditum in upon verberation, curls and folds again, an entangled knot that is alive with unparalleled music-power.

Musical enchantment and effiction

Taking his cues from Rancière's aesthetics, Barry Shank puts forward a political aesthetics of musical listening based on sensory participation. Like Rancière does, Shank argues that aesthetics is a distribution of the sensible in which art, audience and the world all take part. Listening to music, he argues moreover, should be considered a *re*-distribution of the sensible as musical beauty has the 'potential to transform the world' in other ways than other forms of art (2014: 4–5). He asserts that musical beauty does not and cannot itself take a political stance, as music's meanings are always ambivalent and its interpretation is necessarily haunted by previous interpretations (ibid.: 71). But musical listening does affect listeners in profound ways, both in private experience and in its shaping of the public and communities. Marie Thompson and Ian Biddle have theorized music as a means of affective manifestation, as a facilitator of 'acoustic entry into affective fields' (2013: 16). Musical experience enables listeners to engage with the world through affect, but the trajectory that the aural imaginary takes is to a large extent unpredictable and contingent. Precisely because listeners' affective responses to music are necessarily both intense and unpredictable, the political agency of musical aesthetics cannot be underestimated. Music forces us to listen; and in listening, unexpected things will happen. In this way, Shank argues, music is able to change the world, albeit in unintended and unpredictable ways (2014: 244–61).

In view of the fact that music's non-human thing-power resounds in verberation as well as in auditum it seems reasonable to argue that the musical redistribution of the sensible is not necessarily dependent on listening. As Kim-Cohen's and Schrimshaw's pleas for non-cochlear sound art demonstrate, sound and music's agency does not start at the ear (Kim-Cohen 2009; Schrimshaw 2013). While Shank limits himself to music's aesthetic power in auditum, and non-cochlear sound is restricted to verberational agency, I would argue that the aesthetic agency of music should be considered as operational throughout the vibrational continuum. Consequently, the transformations afforded by its vitality affect the entire span of musical vibration also.

As timbral aesthetics are one aspect of the musical redistribution of the sensible, its transformative potential becomes clearer. Timbre's autonomous music-power circulates between the human, non-humans, musicals and non-musicals in a musicking assemblage. In that process, infinite aesthetic encounters occur between various musicking agents: when the timbre of a soprano voice meets that of another soprano voice in a choir, both individual tone colours may adjust themselves to create a collective voice; when the choir timbre meets recording technology it may be altered by microphones, equalizers or producers; when the recorded choir timbre meets the listening ear it may arouse involuntary physical responses such as a moistening of the eyes or a crawling of the skin; when it meets the neuro-system it may evoke unpredictable connotations ranging from childhood church memories to horror film viewing experiences. None of these affects are planned: even if some of them happen on a conscious level, that consciousness is irrelevant to the aesthetic fact of sensory distribution. What is relevant is only the aesthetic agency of this swarm of timbral energies, their capacity to affect and be affected. Timbral vitality affords an aesthetic process that is marked not by passive reception but by active transformation: Bruno Latour's aphorism 'there is no in-formation, only trans-formation' is at least as valid for music-power as it is for thing-power (2005: 149).

In the previous chapter I defined the vital materialism of music in general, and of timbre specifically, as a dynamic energetic relationality. The aesthetics based on that musical vital materialism is similarly dynamic, and it is this vital relationality, this life-in-music, that makes musical aesthetic experience so transformative. Vladimir Jankélévitch introduces his ideas about the 'drastic' aspects of musicking in exactly this context: it is because musicking is a participation in vibration and in Charm (vitality) that the performer is an 'active re-creator' and the listener a 'fictive re-creator' (2003: 77). What is created and recreated in the event of music, in the tangible ephemerality of timbre? How is the sensible distributed and redistributed in the circulation of melodic, harmonic, rhythmic or timbral music-power?

The relationality of music-aesthetic experience is so strong, its transferral of vital energy so compelling, that for the duration of listening the only reference point for our perception of time, space and subjectivity is the music we hear. Music redistributes the sensible through the Newton's cradle discussed in Chapter 4: the vital sway of musical energy vibrates meta-acoustically through air, through the cochlea, and through our neuro-system. In the brain, where musical energy activates astoundingly many areas, music distributes and redistributes, it creates and recreates. Jankélévitch's *Music and the Ineffable* seeks to address this process. The book opens with a passionate statement.

> Music acts upon human beings, on their nervous systems and their vital processes ... This power – which poems and colors possess occasionally and indirectly – is in the case of music particularly immediate, drastic, and indiscreet: 'it penetrates the center of the soul, Plato says, 'and gains possession of the soul in the most energetic fashion' ... The man inhabited and possessed by this intruder, the man robbed of a self, is no longer himself: he has become nothing more than a vibrating string, a sounding pipe.
>
> (2003: 1)

Using poetic language with the deictic function to 'prepare the reader's ears for precise sonic effects, and [to establish] a particular receptive sensibility', what Jankélévitch attempts to evoke here is a lively image of the ways in which music's vibrant and vital aesthetics engenders an absolute de-contextualization, and a re-contextualization in music alone (Rings 2012: 219–20). For the duration of listening, music is time, space and self. The fact that listeners so eagerly ascribe meanings and identifications to music – and that these meanings and identifications are simultaneously not universal and fiercely defended – tells us one thing only: music means nothing, it does not even 'exist in itself', but it does everything (Jankélévitch 2003: 78). Musical aesthetics is *our*-life-in-music. 'There is only listening', says Shank, 'only listening to the musical beauty of a world remaking itself, and clining towards the meanings that beauty suggests' (2014: 261). In this 'clining', reality shifts. It is reshaped, becomes enchanted with music-power. Bennett points out the etymological relevance of the verb 'to en-chant': to be enveloped in music is to engage in magic (2001: 6, 34, 153).

Enchantment, in Bennett's definition, entails 'a state of wonder, and one of the distinctions of this state is the temporary suspension of chronological time and bodily movement' (2001: 5). This state of wonder removes distinctions between fact and fiction. Its spell overturns the categories of real, unreal, illusion, awakeness and dream. Enchantment's spell is not necessarily cast by a metaphysical agency. Bennett stresses that it comes into being in the interaction with the sensory world, that is a world of 'enchanted materialism' inhabited by animate matter and matter-energy (ibid.: 9–12, 80–90). This formulation hints towards the vital materialism that she developed later. Musical experience, consisting as it does of the affective interaction with musical vitality, easily induces such a state of wonder, and its reshaping of the world and of subjectivity are a particularly powerful form of enchanted time and space. To understand the specificities of musical enchantment it is useful to compare the envelopment in musical listening, briefly, to the immersion in a work of literature, a film or a video game. Musical experience does not place us in another world like a book or a film does: listening is nothing like reading about someone falling into a rabbit hole and finding a Wonderland at the end of the tumble. Musicking is not in the third person but involves me and my adventures down the rabbit hole, in the time-space of music. These adventures are not scripted and screened, like those in video games: musicking does not build another world with which to interact. As it connects the outside and the inside of human perception in vibration, there is no difference between third-person and first-person audition. Music is more direct, more immediate, more embodied, and more engaged than other immersive media: 'it does not propose something but *does* something' (Voegelin 2014: 32). When I open my mouth and sing, or open my ears and listen, reality becomes musicked; and I, too, am en-chanted as I musick.

In his book *Phantom Limbs: On Musical Bodies*, Peter Szendy describes the musicking experience of piano playing as an 'organic thrust not only removed from the ego's command but also unlinked from the drive of an id' (2016: 11). In this thrust, which he characterizes as a body-to-body (*corps-à-corps*) experience, the self is simultaneously highly involved and utterly obfuscated, to such an extent that even the physical body – of the pianist, of the piano, of the music – becomes an infinite chimera (ibid.: 6–11). Szendy theorizes the dissolution of fact/fiction and real/unreal distinctions as 'effiction', the convergence of 'fiction and its power, its efficacy' (ibid.: 15). His book explores this effiction or 'fiction in effect(s)' as it occurs in the experience of musicking, more specifically the strange emergence of phantom limbs in keyboard playing (ibid.). In doing so, he arrives at the relation between the effective body of the musician and the 'areality' in which that musician finds herself (a word he borrows from Nancy, Szendy 2016: 133–7). Engaging in musicking, Szendy argues, presupposes an instrumentality not just of the keyboard or of music, but also of the musician's body, her mind and the world around her: the musician's body is spatialized, externalized, 'arealized' (ibid.: 135–6). With the advent of electricity as energizing power, this musical spatiality becomes a networked areality that is potentially all-encompassing (ibid.: 140–7).

The concepts of effiction and areality are very pertinent in the context of vital and vibrant musical aesthetics. The *corps-à-corps* materiality of keyboard playing and the effictive power that such musical interaction has over the musician, in Szendy's work, resonates with the affective power of 'bodies-in-encounter' and resulting enchantment in Bennett's aesthetics (Bennett 2015: 95–6). Szendy's effiction describes the affective capacities of musicking as they play out in the meta-acoustic circulation of musical energy through SMASL assemblages of humans and non-humans. Importantly, he stresses that this redistribution of the sensible connects outside and inside, as musical energy vibrates into and back out of the musicking body. The drastic aesthetic encounter that is musicking en-chants by way of an endless folding: as it unfolds in time and space, music folds into and out of the body, and enfolds the listener in effictive time-spaces. With the performer as 'active re-creator' and the listener as 'fictive re-creator' (Jankélévitch 2003: 77), thus, musical enchantment means that the distinction between fact and fiction is replaced by effiction, and the distinction between reality and unreality is replaced by areality.

Timbre's place in the folding event of musical aesthetics becomes ever clearer. Tone colour's agency, powerful as it is on either end of the vibrational continuum, is instrumental – in Szendy's sense of spatialization – in the vital connection between outside and inside of the musicking body. Timbre's tangible strike keeps reminding us that musical life, musical redistribution and recreation, are not dependent on listening: music enfolds and enchants both the material and the immaterial world. Tone colour's curiously ambivalent musical agency affects verberation and auditum at the same time, and therefore timbral music-power is perhaps the most prolific redistributor of the sensible in musicking. Timbral effiction is participatory, embodied and reciprocal: in musicking, we are affected by timbre and we affect it. Our bodies and minds participate in tone colour areality. The precise shape of that areality depends on the specificities of the musical assemblage at hand – the type of instrument we use to produce it, the acoustic setting in which we listen, the state of our ears, the playback equipment that we employ to listen to music – but whichever agents are involved in that assemblage, the timbral areality painted by its colours will always span from the material and corporeal all the way to the immaterial and imaginary.

A particularly striking example of the meta-acoustic music-power of tone colour aesthetics can be found in the timbral field of reverberation. In his study of echo and reverb, Peter Doyle explores the spatiality of music and the ways in which it is enhanced through recording technology (2005). Reverberation effects are powerful means to suggest virtual spatiality in sonic experience: 'dry' or 'wet' acoustics (metonymy increasingly proves its pertinence) are the reverberant markers of any sonic space from an anechoic chamber to a Gothic cathedral. Employing Deleuze and Guattari's ideas around the musical negotiation of territory, Doyle argues that echo and reverb effects are forms of musical de- and reterritorialization. In the production of popular music, these sound effects engender what he calls a 'hyper-spatiality' that emphasizes, strengthens and sometimes alters the already spatial nature of sonic experience (2005: 17). He analyses the ways in which popular music recording and production technology can create the suggestion of, for instance, the otherness of the cowboy West or the uncanniness of urban alleys simply by adding or diminishing the reverb on certain tape tracks. This kind of spatiality, although it is only schizophonically present in a recording or even just virtually alluded to in production, envelops the listener and includes her in the hyper-space of music. The territory of music, then, extends beyond playback technology and speakers into the lived space of the listener: musical space and musical materiality are in direct connection with the space and materiality of listening. These spaces together comprise the territory of musicking aesthetics: this territory must be considered both virtual and real at the same time. In Szendy's terminology, echo and reverb effects would have to be considered as a form of 'effiction', as active components of the areality in which the musicking body finds itself. The effictive agency of reverberation transports the entire musicking assemblage into the space of musical aesthetics: and because musicking enchants time *with* space, any of these time-spaces becomes an 'infinite ... *now*' (ibid.: 234). As reverberation is an aspect of tone colour, Doyle's important study could be expanded to include the spatiality and materiality of timbre. Listening to timbre is participating in the hyper-spatial areality that it generates.

Arnold Schoenberg imagined that tone colour melody would be able to bring us closer to 'the illusory stuff of our dreams' (Schoenberg 1922: 507). The aesthetics of timbre's affective and effictive power reveals that those dreams are not illusions, but part of the enchanted areality afforded by musical experience. The hills are alive with the spellbinding colours of music.

Abyssal aesthetics, timbral threshold

Schoenberg is not the only one who has associated musical experience with dreams, and who has commented on the ways in which music, like dreams, destabilizes what seemed fixed. 'Such wandering is always a bit dream-like and nocturnal: this is Becoming', says Jankélévitch of music's power over the experience of time, '[f]luid and without an itinerary: such is music' (2003: 93). Many other theorists besides Schoenberg and Jankélévitch have argued that both the actual sound music and its aesthetic experience, in their dreamlike affective capacity, have much less to do with being than with becoming.

The main philosophers in this field are Gilles Deleuze and Félix Guattari, who have argued that music is 'on the side of the nomadic' because its experience challenges spatial and temporal constellations (1986: 88). Through its strong affective capacities – its neuro-stimulation of memory, emotion, cognition and motion – musical experience affords lines of flight that the listener cannot but embark on. Deleuze and Guattari's nomadic evaluation of music explains how it can be so instrumental for immersive processes. Music is a form of absolute deterritorialization: existing only in sonic waves, it occupies time and space but exceeds any concrete form of identity or context, signification or meaning. These qualities render music vectral as well as spectral: music activates vectors into the time- and space-defying realms of memory, emotion and imagination. In this capacity, it is more immersive than any other medium. Deleuze and Guattari state that

> [t]he musician is in the best position to say: 'I hate the faculty of memory, I hate memories'. And that is because he or she affirms the power of becoming.
> (Ibid.: 296–7)

Parallel to the temporal and spatial structure of musical events as they unfold, the enfolding aesthetic experience of that event appears simultaneously to affirm, destroy and reinvent temporality and spatiality. Musicking deterritorializes space and time, renegotiating those ontological categories within the rhizomatic territory of musical becoming (ibid.: 265–305). The redistribution of the sensible in musicking involves not just hearing and being touched, but the sensual and non-sensual immersion in a single time-space, in Doyle's terms a hyperspatial *here* that is also an infinite *now*, and its multi-coloured, multi-layered transition to countless other heres and nows. 'In the risk of musical body-to-body contact', Szendy says, 'the future, always, *is dispatched, pending*' (2016: 161, italics in original).

Jonathan Kramer and Jean-Luc Nancy have both argued that the spatiotemporal agency of music does not only affect the experience of a musical event. They each explore the ways in which the immersion in musical time-space has an impact on our phenomenological perception of the time and space of the non-musical world also: in Szendy's terms, they explore the spatio-temporal effiction of reality into areality through listening. Kramer contends that musical time unfolds independently from clock time in a manner very similar to Bergsonian *durée*, arguing that musical time should be considered as completely separate from – and separating itself from – ordinary time: the time of music has the agency to 'create, alter, distort, or even destroy time itself, not simply our experience of it' (1988: 5). In a similar vein, Nancy contemplates the ways in which listening creates its own space and time in what he calls a 'living present' that is 'always imminent and always deferred, since it is not in any time' (2007: 19, 67): 'The sonorous present is the result of space-time: it spreads through space, or rather it opens up a space that is its own, the very spreading out of its resonance, its expansion and its reverberation' (ibid.: 13).

Next to those of time and space, the third set of vectors activated by music-power concerns listener subjectivity, which is equally destabilized, renegotiated, enchanted and recreated in musicking. Musicking is entering a line of flight with unpredictable destination, as Deleuze and Guattari keep stressing (1987: 299–309). Jeremy Gilbert and Ewan Pearson assess the ways in which dance, as the corporeal participation in such musical lines of flight, 'problematizes … the distinction between internal and external experience' (1999: 60). They argue that the physical and affective immersion in dance leads to 'the ecstatic dissolution of self on the dancefloor' in the pervasive *jouissance* of dance as becoming-music (ibid.: 107). Dancing is an explicitly and consciously embodied form of musicking interaction in which the dancing body is a somatic extension of the musicking brain. But the musical dissolution of self does not necessarily require a choreography or a dance floor. Listening alone is enough to connect outside-the-body with inside-the-body in vibration, to participate physically in the ever-unfolding time-space of music. Nancy phrases the listening transformation of time, space and self in a manner strikingly appropriate to the vibrational continuum and its ongoing connectivity between verberation and auditum:

> To listen is to enter that spatiality by which, *at the same time*, I am penetrated, for it opens up in me as well as toward me: it opens me inside me as well as outside, and it is through such a double, quadruple, or sextuple opening that a 'self' can take place. To be listening is to be *at the same time* outside and inside, to be open *from* without and *from* within, hence from one to the other and from one in the other ... [S]onorous presence is an essentially mobile 'at the same time', vibrating from the come-and-go between the source and the ear, through open space.
>
> (Nancy 2007: 14–16, italics in original)

The sonic quality that inhabits, epitomizes and activates this motion between inside and outside, Nancy says, is timbre, which is simultaneously 'the timbre of the echo of the subject' (ibid.: 39).

Musical aesthetics equals a continual becoming, a radical departure from the known here and now as well as from the known me. The specific matter-energy that is musical vitality directly touches, affects and transforms listeners: music is involved in who I am, in who I was, and in who I will be (cf. ibid.: 17–20). Like the songs and symphonies that shape it, musical subjectivity is marked by a contextless vibration and vitality, by an excess of identity and meaning. In the middle of the expenditure that is music, I can only refer its vibrating vitality to my own imagination, filling the absence that it transmits with the presence of whatever my reality or my dreams happen to consist of at this moment and in this place: the unconscious imaginary readily fills music's an identity and ab-context, its un-signification and non-meaning. The musical void assumes whatever spatial, temporal and subjective dimension my fantasy, desire or anxiety allows it to assume. None of these dimensions of musical experience will ever be static, but their relentless immanence is always necessarily tied to the material exteriority of the non-cochlear. Music's nomadic distribution of the sensible, after all, is always meta-acoustic: even the most boundless spatiotemporal journeys and even the wildest transsubjectivities afforded by musical aesthetics are as much a part of the physical world as they are ephemeral. Music enchants and transforms both realms in their vibrational connectedness.

The strange im/material areality of musical aesthetics has the irresistible allure of the other-worldly. In a line of arguing reminiscent of Rancière and Bennett as well as of Jankélévitch, Eldritch Priest has argued that musical experience engenders a 'confusion' caused by the absence of meaning in music. This confusion, he states, is part of the 'charm' of music that seduces listeners into the 'vital elsewhere/elsewhen of nonsensuous affects' (2013: 57). Bennett, too, speaks of the allure of the enchanted unknown: the 'acute sensory activity' of aesthetic experience enchants the subject into 'a state of interactive fascination' with a vibrating cosmos that affords both wonder and uncanniness (2001: 5). The cosmos of musical vibration and vitality is a void without temporal, spatial and subjective dimensions, an unterritory that may acquire any effictive form or shape in aesthetic interaction. Musicking transposes listeners to the edge of this abyss: they are pulled into its vast expanse by the meta-acoustic music-powers of melody, rhythm, harmony, dynamics and, most compellingly, tone colour. As timbre resides in the gaps between signification and meaninglessness, identity and difference, mundane physicality and ineffable sublimity, there is no music-power with more abyssal allure. Timbre, the musical agent that evokes the most perplexing aesthetic paradoxes and the most tangible aesthetic pull, unites the joy of vibration with the tremble of the unknown. Timbre is *itself* the threshold, the limit of the musically sublime that contains 'the void that we deem beyond it' (Brillenburgh Wurth 2009: 20). And that is precisely why it is the very core of musical aesthetics.

Into timbre: Lyotard unsettled

In an interview about his composition *Rokh* (cf. Chapter 4), Raphaël Cendo talks about art's necessity to exceed limits. Referring explicitly to Deleuze's philosophy, Cendo states that 'excess teaches us to live as much as to die' (Menet 2012). Excess opens up a void that is not charged with symbolic meaning, and unhampered by finite notions of time, space and subjectivity: it consists only of the devastating and, as Cendo states, 'bewitching', deterritorialization of bare musicking (ibid.). The musical collapse of the known universe, which Cendo renders audible and tangible through the timbral excess in *Rokh*, is the moment when the abyss of musical aesthetics opens itself before the listener.

Trembling in timbre, I plunge into the abyss that is musical aesthetics. Beyond the *limen* of excess lies my willing suspension in vibration and vitality, my giving way to boundless becoming in musical effiction. In *Rokh*'s impossibly saturated timbrescape, reality ceases to exist – *never existed* – and is replaced by an enchanted areality. My 'catastrophic position' (ibid.), poised on the edge of the abyss, on the verge of listening-becoming/becoming-listening, has all the allure of the sublime.

So we must reconsider timbre's relation to the sublime as it has been theorized by Jean-François Lyotard and criticized in Jacques Rancière's aesthetics. Both philosophers reject the notion of mimesis in art and aesthetics (2009: 7–8). Rather than denouncing immersion along with mimesis, as Rancière does in the sweeping anti-idealism of his argumentation, Lyotard, conversely, argues for a theoretical intensification of the former:

> Art does not imitate nature, it creates a world apart, *eine Zwischenwelt*, as Paul Klee will say; *eine Nebenwelt*, one might say in which the monstrous and the formless have their right because they can be sublime.
>
> (Lyotard 1991: 97)

The idea of such a *Nebenwelt*, a world next to the ordinary world engendered by the immersion in a work of art, has been explored extensively in relation to music, from the 'multiple universes' that Jankélévitch discerns in the musical event to Salomé Voegelin's 'musical possible worlds' (Jankélévitch 2003: 83; Voegelin 2014). These explorations of musical immersion often tend towards an unreservedly sublime assessment of music without taking into account the idealist implications of this line of arguing. However, these implications, as already outlined in Chapter 3, form a serious epistemological obstacle to the formulation of a non-binary aesthetics of music.

It is because of the binarism implied in the concept of the sublime that Rancière criticizes Lyotard's reliance on this concept in his aesthetic writings. Theorized from the idealism that inspired its prominence in Kant and Burke's aesthetics, the notion of the sublime renders the experience of art one of observation instead of participation, of exclusivity and exteriority instead of inclusivity and immanence (Rancière 2009: 20–2, 88–105). For this reason, Rancière considers Lyotard's sublime an 'enslavement' and a destruction both of politics and of aesthetics which can lead to totalitarian doom scenarios in which '[r]esistance becomes nothing other than the anamnesis of the "Thing", the indefinite re-inscription, in written lines, painted brushstrokes or musical timbres, of subjugation to the law of the Other' (ibid.: 104–5). Leaving Rancière's misunderstanding of timbre (as a somehow reduced *objet sonore*) aside, if we consider the distribution of vital energy in art to be vibratory, then the sublime is part of this vibrant aesthetics, part of the vibratory continuum. In such an assessment, the sublime is but one of the many aesthetic modes – aesthetic others, in plural and without capitals – with which we interact: the monstrous and the formless have their place in aesthetic experience, 'their right' as Lyotard says, next to the technological, the social and the political.

More importantly, Rancière is mistaken to assume Lyotard's aesthetics of the sublime to be based upon an idealist or indeed binarist philosophical framework. In fact the opposite is the case: key to Lyotard's thinking about the continuity, rather than rupture, or immanence rather than transcendence, of the aesthetic experience is what can only be read as a negation of binarism through vibration and vitality: 'The continuity between mind and matter thus appears as a particular case of the transformation of frequencies into other frequencies, and this is what the transformation of energy consists in' (Lyotard 1991: 43). Lyotard describes here a distribution of the sensible not unlike that in Rancière's aesthetics, but one that is operated by the same vital energy that Bennett foregrounds as the agency circulating in social, political and aesthetic assemblages. Like Bennett does, Lyotard grounds his thinking about mind, matter, time and energy in Leibnizian monadology and Bergsonian *élan vital* in order to move away from binary models such as Cartesian dualism (ibid.: 36–46). With this vibrating distribution of vital energy at its basis, it is easy to understand why the point to which his aesthetics keep returning is timbre: once again it becomes clear that tone colour presents musicology and philosophy alike with the single most stringent reason to think of aesthetics as vibrant and vital.

Based on energetic continuity rather than material/immaterial binaries, Lyotard's sublime cannot be framed through idealism. It most certainly could not have had timbre – which does not let itself be theorized in binary structures – as its main manifestation if it was conceived in this dichotomous way. Lyotard's version of the sublime can be understood as a possible affordance of energetic interaction. This specific affordance is simultaneously located, throughout his work, in the ineffable aporia of the timbral Thing (ibid.: 142), and in the palpable, often mundane and at times painful physicality of the *sentiment sonore* (ibid.: 176). The sublime occurs in the singularity of the aesthetic moment, which always affects both corporeal and mental responses. Lyotard theorizes the aesthetic moment as the halting of thought in the midst of an event as it occurs and halts time within its own eventness: the event, which he conceptualizes as Heidegger's *Ereignis*, is 'infinitely simple', and because of this it can only be approached through a privation of thinking. The famous 'arrive-t-il' represents the disarmament of thought in the occurrence of the sublime event: we simply ask, '*is it happening, is this it, is it possible?*' (ibid.: 90, italics in original). In this suspension, this no-thought, there is only the intensity of the moment, which does not warrant any prediction or premonition. Anything may happen next, or nothing may happen. The surrender to the eventness of the event, as we await the unknown, may arouse anxiety or pleasure, and herein lies its affinity – rather than equation – with classical sublime aporia. Lyotard theorizes this unthinking occurrence through Spinoza as an 'intensification of being' that eliminates the possibility not just of thought but of any context: 'The mark of the question is "now", *now* like the feeling that nothing might happen: the nothingness now' (ibid.: 92, italics in original).

The 'now' of Lyotard's *arrive-t-il* was discussed in Chapter 3 in relation to the ineffable timelessness in the musical drastic, which Jankélévitch calls 'a timeless Now' (2003: 95, 127). It is the same 'now' that Doyle identifies in reverb, and the same Husserlian epoché of 'now' that Kim-Cohen identifies in musical aesthetics (Doyle 2005: 234; Kim-Cohen 2009: 94). Karlheinz Stockhausen made this 'nothingness now', this ab-temporality of musical experience the key aim of his 'moment forms' (*Momentforme*). In moment forms, Stockhausen argues, only 'every now' is eternalized in a verticalization of linear time which reaches into 'an eternity that is reachable in every moment' (1963–1984, vol. 1: 199; cf. Stockhausen 1963–1984, vol. 3: 109; cf. Kramer 1978: 177–80). These eternalized presents are introduced in his work by timbre in what he calls 'a purely verticalized *Klangmoment*' (Stockhausen 2000: 66–7). Timbre's music-power, Stockhausen argues in a remarkable compositional counterpoint to Lyotard's *arrive-t-il*, affords only 'Now! Now! Now! Now! Now!' (ibid.: 67).

The phenomenology of the *arrive-t-il*, of the timelessness inherent to every musical experience, pre-empts Rancière's concerns about a passive enslavement to the sublime Lyotard's aesthetics. It negotiates the Burkean sublime by replacing passivity with 'passibility', which is 'the possibility of experiencing', the phenomenological openness to the aesthetic event both in corporeal and mental ways (Lyotard 1991: 110–18). Passibility is the virtual potentiality to interact marking any human or non-human in an aesthetic assemblage, whether in a live acoustic setting, the reverbed acoustics of recording, or Stockhausen's WDR studios; in this context it is important to remember that this aspect of aesthetic experience is discussed in Lyotard's least anthropocentric work, *The Inhuman*. When actualized, passibility affords 'an immediate community of feeling demanded across the singular aesthetic feeling' (ibid.: 117). Passibility is *anima*'s faculty to be touched (Lyotard 1997: 242), or as Bennett would say, a human or non-human's capacity to affect and be affected. In musical terms, passibility is the potential to be touched by music, whether in verberation or in auditum, whether by the passing of sound waves through bodies or by the passing of electrical impulses through the neuro-system. Trent Leipert argues that passibility, as affective openness, provides a manner of understanding music's communicability outside the restraints of language and articulation: in this reading, passibility is neither material nor transcendent, but marks a suspendedness between the two (2013: 431–6; Woodward 2016: 130–1). Passibility to the music-aesthetic event of timbre, in Lyotard's terms, is the possibility to experience all the tangible and the sublime affordances of tone colour in the unthinking nothingness of suspended time, place and subjectivity.

> So we must suggest that there is ... a mindless state of mind, which is required of mind not for matter to be perceived or conceived, given or grasped, but *so that there be* some something. And I use 'matter' to designate this *'that there is'*, this *quod*, because this presence in the absence of the active mind is and is never other than timbre, tone, nuance in one or other of the dispositions of sensibility, in one or other of the *sensoria*, in one or other of the possibilities through which mind is accessible to the material event, can be 'touched' by it: a singular, incomparable quality – unforgettable and immediately forgotten – of the grain of a skin or a piece of wood, the fragrance of an aroma, the savour of a secretion or a piece of flesh, as well as a timbre or a nuance.
>
> (Lyotard 1991: 140–1, italics in original)

Passible to timbre, to the ephemeral immediacy of sound-feeling's touch, we must be mindless. And yet it affects our mindless mind. The aesthetic event of timbre is different from other music-aesthetic events because of the acutely perceptible simultaneity of verberational and auditum intensities in its occurrence. This simultaneity epitomizes both the energetic continuity and the aporetic passibility informing Lyotard's sublime, which is why timbre is at the forefront of his aesthetics. Timbre, Lyotard says, is a 'tiny space occupied by a knot or a colour in the sound- or colour-continuum' (ibid.: 140). When we are passible to it we suspend the activities of the mind and are touched by 'a singular, incomparable quality – unforgettable and immediately forgotten' (ibid.: 141). The aesthetic question regarding timbre is necessarily an epistemological one: how can I know this singular aesthetic knot, this material/immaterial, sublime and mundane, this intensely paradoxical und unrepeatable *now* that nevertheless is temporally bounded, *this* impossible singularity of timbre? In other words, the aesthetic question regarding timbre is precisely '*arrive-t-il?*' The epistemology of this particular event can only be revealed through epistemic engagement: by making ourselves passible to the timbral event we interrogate. And this is what Lyotard does, time and time again.

The timbral event, for Lyotard, marks the 'power of a loss', the 'Unnameable' (ibid.: 156, 158). Chapters 2 and 3 showed that such assessments of timbre are not unusual, and that these have been theorized as the lack, the *objet petit a*, or the aporia of the timbral sublime. Those chapters also demonstrated that any of these ineffable evaluations can be falsified, or at the very least need to be complemented, by such material – and sometimes refreshingly prosaic – considerations as the presence of physical sound cause, corporeal identity and signifying conventions. 'I use "matter" to designate this "*quod*"', says Lyotard: the undeniable validity of timbral materialism and realism, at times, appears to undermine that of the timbral ineffable. But the musical aesthetics outlined in this and the previous chapter does allow for ineffability, albeit an ineffability that is not conceptualized through idealism. Lyotard's sublime assessments of timbre can be reread as the timbral culminations of a vibrant and vital aesthetics of music. In terms of vibration, his description of timbre as a singular knot in a sonic continuum, a *sentiment sonore* that may elicit the profoundest of temporal, spatial and subjective dislodgements, is an identification of timbre's music-power affecting two ends of the vibrational continuum at once. In terms of vitality, the unknown nothingness to which Lyotard argues we are passible when touched by timbre identifies the openness to unpredictable energetic interaction in musical aesthetics (cf. ibid.: 180). When read from the perspective of vibrant and vital aesthetics, even the more colourful passages in Lyotard's writing reveal themselves as quite precise and quite concrete:

> Losing oneself in a world of sound. Hearing breaks down the defences of the harmonic and melodic ear, and becomes aware of TIMBRE alone. And then we have the landscape of Beethoven's late quartets.
> …
> Whether or not you 'like' a landscape is unimportant. It does not ask you for your opinion. … A landscape leaves the mind DESOLATE.
> …
> A lonely traveller, a lonely walker. It is not only that conversation, even conversations with yourself, and the intrigue of desires and understanding have to be silenced. As in a temple, a TEMPLUM, a neutralized space-time where it is certain that something – but what? – might perhaps happen … Inner desolation.

...

A landscape is an excess of presence. My *savoir-vivre* is not enough. A glimpse of the inhuman, and/or of an unclean non-world.

...

Landscape simply seizes [time]. What we call description is no more than a literary procedure which puts mental activity on a par with its narrative stance, and difference is reduced to the *shifting* of temporal indicators [pronouns, verbal tenses, adverbs, etc.). An operationalist reduction of what is 'in reality' (?) an ontological abyss.

(Ibid.: 183–8, capitals and italics in original)

Disenchantment has no place in this desolation, in this ontological abyss. Musical aesthetics is losing oneself in a world of sound, it is openness to a world alive with swarms of musical energy. Musical aesthetics is a perception that is passible to sonic enchantment; musical aesthetics is a templum, a neutralized space-time, the nothingness of an unheard sublime. It is the musical shifting and suspension of time and place, identity and meaning, knowing and feeling in the effiction of an infinite, nameless *now*. The ontological abyss of musical aesthetics is not a Lovecraftian cosmos (although Lovecraft's numinous voices may evoke it) nor is it mystical rapture (although J.S. Bach's eschatological flutes may invite it). It is the musical redistribution of sensible as it circulates through both the realm of the physical and that of the ineffable. Timbre, as perhaps the most powerful agent in musical aesthetics, provides the tangible, and irresistibly meta-acoustic, pull which seduces listeners into this abyss. We may try to capture that pull or that abyss in icons, but that is mere literary procedure, an operationalist reduction of the experience of standing at the threshold of a void.

Passible to timbral aesthetics, I listen to a track called 'The Unsettled' by Iszoloscope, a Canadian group of DJs whose dark industrial soundscapes are popular with Goth audiences. On their website, the DJs stress that their work is inspired by an interest in *musique concrète*, cosmology and quantum mechanics (Iszoloscope): Iszoloscope's albums bear such illustrious titles as *The Audient Void* (Ant.Zen 2005) and *Au Seuil de Néant* (Ant.Zen 2003). The artists describe their own music explicitly in terms of abyssal aesthetics:

Since 1999, Iszoloscope has been pushing the abstract conceptualization of isolation and its induced altered states of consciousness into a powerful, ominous, and immersive world of dark sonic aesthetic that can be called its very own.

(Iszoloscope)

The main musical vehicle to achieve this 'dark' aesthetic in Iszoloscope's work is timbre. Tone colour, cloaked as it is in metonymic guises and capable of evoking the haze of the mysterious and ominous, is a ubiquitous form of expression in music in Goth, and Iszoloscope is no exception (Van Elferen 2018: 23–6). With grinding electronic drones, expansive reverb effects, samples of wailing human voices and sonic references both to analogue technology and digital cybernetics, they push the ineffable expressive qualities of timbre to its darkest limits.

'The Unsettled' appeared on the album Beyond Within (Ant.Zen 2010).[1]

Introduced by the tail end of a church bell resonance and a hissing white noise, the track opens with an acoustic exploration of a large empty space set in lighter and darker shades of electronic sounds painted by reverb effects. As these sounds pan out in ever-expanding ripples, and the phantom space of reverb grows and grows, new sounds are introduced to the far left and right. The cognitive part of my brain eagerly wishes to identify these as falling drops of water – but immediately tries to answer the impossible question of whether there is water, or gravity, or any form of sonic identity in this non-existent acousmatic cosmos.

Next, a set of two alternating electronic figures appear close by, their fast upward glissandos moving in panning crescendos and decrescendos. As the glissandos exert their music-power, the sense of expanding space established by reverb effects is enhanced by their Doppler-effictive stretching of the boundaries of pitch and melody.

Slowly all these brooding and evolving timbres converge into the depth of F1, timbrally hard-edged, and followed, at 0'30', by a 4-to-the-floor beat. Even though the beat forces itself into the foreground of perception, releasing its kinetic energy into involuntary corporeal motion and unconscious mental wandering, its booming and my stomping remain ever fed and ever guided by the darkened bass and zooming snares in the background.

With these parameters dominating the soundscape, 'The Unsettled' configures a deeply disturbing musical areality. It is interrupted every once in a while by musical events that further dislodge the already unstable senses of space and time in the track. At around a minute in, and again at around two minutes, the tempo suddenly slows down and sounds appear that resemble analogue crackles. Overlaid with minimal reverb, they seem to occur in close proxemics to the ear. Because of the contrast with the digital smoothness and the wet acoustic of the other timbres in the track, these new sounds, with their analogue roughness and dry acoustic, have a

---

[1] The track can be found on https://www.youtube.com/watch?v=6PP8m-b3xC4.

strange agency. The music-power of their timbre is the power of timbral difference: the occurrence of medially connoted sonorities with a markedly distinct reverb print seems to question the medium through which I perceive these sounds – is this happening, is this vinyl? – and, with that, the trustworthiness of my perception and interpretation of them.

In the second half of the track, a similar timbral destabilization happens, this time with biological rather than medial connotations. Three minutes in, heavily reverbed and far in the back of the soundbox, an approaching vocal sample sets in. Its timbre is heavily produced, cold and metallic, but is just human enough to evoke the Jentschian uncanny – is this happening, are these voices? – of something that seemed dead but suddenly appears to be alive. Panning to the front in crescendo, and then right and left in the back again, the sample lasts for over a minute, an inhumanly sustained high F on 'eeeee-yyy-aaaaaaah-oow-ooooooooohh'. As the vowels change, so does the spectral spectrum of their frequencies: sometimes they blend with a synth chord but mostly they just float, unpleasantly present in their far-near non-space, in their human-inhuman non-identity. At four minutes the voices are doubled and then briefly disappear after a G-F cadence-like motif: they reappear at five minutes in the same way they did the first time, creeping in from the far end and slowly moving forward in crescendo.

The entire track is an exploration of timbre and what it is capable of. Listening to 'The Unsettled', I can hear very clearly how timbral music-power in verberation affects other musical agents such as rhythm, tempo, harmony, dynamics; I also experience the ways in which timbre's music-power in auditum can suggest – and annihilate – a plethora of possible connotations, feelings and half-memories. More than anything, however, I am involuntarily, relentlessly, made part of a sonic cosmos effected by timbral vitality, an impossible areality with its own spatiality, temporality and phantom identities. The artists of Iszoloscope contend they are interested in '[s]culpting harmonic ripples through the fabric of time and space' (Iszoloscope), and that is exactly what this track does. Timbral energy circulates between human and non-human, musical and non-musical actors, moves from one micro-assemblage to the next, constantly deterritorializing and never quite reterritorializing: timbre continually becomes, it continually unfolds new spaces, times and subjectivities.

When we are passible to timbre we allow its music-power to pull us into musical aesthetics, into an abyss that is both alive and unknowable. Timbral aesthetics is an immersion in the void that Iszoloscope calls 'Beyond Within', and that Lyotard calls a *Nebenwelt*: a world next to our own in which 'the monstrous and the formless have their right because they can be sublime' (Lyotard 1991: 97).

Aesthetics of vibration

Listening to timbre is entering the gap imposed by the dichotomies of post-Kantian aesthetics. Its meta-acoustic vibration unequivocally proves those binaries misguided. Timbre is not either sound source or sublime ineffability: it is both, *sentiment sonore*. Timbral aesthetics does not present either carnal sensation or cerebral Thingness: it offers both, in *Tonwollust*. Timbral paradoxes are not contradictions, but they are the delightful friction evoked by the most affective and effective of music's vital agents: the ungraspable qualia of sonorous difference.

The accumulation of paradoxes with which the peculiar agency of tone colour infuses music is the uneasy nexus of musical a/reality. It invites an aesthetic experience that is a cacophony of shifts, a series of potential transformations as we embark on the vectors across the vibrational continuum. Among these transformations are the suspension of time, space and self in sublime *arrive-t-il*: but this aporia occurs simultaneously with the identification of physical sound source in the *objet sonore*, and with the inscription of meaning in timbral convention. And while we float in suspension, timbre lives independently of us, also, in its non-cochlear, not-capitalized, thingness.

The *Nebenwelt* of timbre is one of the most poignant manifestations of music's aesthetics of vibrant vitality. Its alluring excess invites listeners into a sonic abyss in which timbral vitality swarms between the extremes of sublime and the mundane. It is in this circulation, in this abyss, in the dark, that aesthetic experience emerges, revealing itself as *a* life in and of itself, a vibrant, colourful ecology. But that living ecology is 'impossibly singular' (Bennett 2010: 4), as the strange aesthetic knot in which it occurs suspends any temporality, spatiality and subjectivity: in musical aesthetic experience, real and a-real blur together in the effiction of a boundless here-and-not-here, now-and-not-now, me-and-not-me. And this living aesthetic, this enchanted life-in-matter, equals our willing suspension in vibration.

Threshold

A new sound

Imagine a Dutch town in the late nineteenth century. Merchant houses stand tall by unmoving canals. Evening sunlight gently brushes over bridges and trees. The town is quiet at this hour. Horse carriages have come to a halt for the night, footsteps echo through the empty streets. Distant voices are softened by the green spring air. In the silence, a whistle.

Een nieuwe lente en een nieuw geluid: Ik wil dat dit lied klinkt als het gefluit,	A new spring and a new sound: I want this song to be like the whistling
Dat ik vaak hoorde voor een zomernacht	That I often heard before a Summer's night
In een oud stadje, langs de watergracht – In huis was 't donker, maar de stille straat	In an old town, along the canal – In the house it was dark, but the quiet street
Vergaarde schemer, aan de lucht blonk laat Nog licht, er viel een gouden blanke schijn Over de gevels van mijn raamkozijn. Dan blies een jongen als een orgelpijp, De klanken schudden in de lucht zo rijp Als jonge kersen, wen een lentewind In 't bosje opgaat en zijn reis begint. Hij dwaald' over de bruggen, op den wal	Gathered dusk, and in the sky gleamed Late light, a golden pale shine fell Over the gables of my window pane. Then a boy whistled like an organ pipe, The sounds tumbled in the air as ripe As young cherries, when a spring breeze Ruffles the bush and begins its journey. He wandered over the bridges, on the quay
Van 't water, langzaam gaande, overal Als 'n jonge vogel fluitend, onbewust	Of the water, going slowly, everywhere Whistling like a young bird, unconscious
Van eigen blijheid om de avondrust.	Of his own rejoicing in the evening's peace.
En menig moe man, die zijn avondmaal	And many a tired man, taking his evening meal,
Nam, luisterde, als naar een oud verhaal, Glimlachend, en een hand die 't venster sloot, Talmde een pooze wijl de jongen floot. Gorter 1997: 27–8.	Listened, as to an old story, Smiling, and a hand closing the window Tarried a moment while the boy whistled.

Herman Gorter's 1889 epic poem *'Mei'* ('May') was a defining work in the movement of the 'Tachtigers', a group of Dutch impressionist poets who aimed to transform literature through an aesthetics of synaesthesia, texture and nuance. The atmospheric opening verse of *'Mei'* cited here introduced the 'new spring' of the Tachtigers to the Dutch reading public. The 'new sound' of the poem takes the shape of a timbre as humble as that of a boy whistling in the evening air. Our encounter with Gorter's literary aesthetic happens in synaesthesia: while reading we experience the strange touch of sound in silent imagination. This sensory crossover matches the impressionist impulse driving the Tachtigers: just as Debussy painted colours in his compositions, so Gorter paints sound in his poetry. The poet reaches for the same timbral momentum as the composer: their art is perched on the threshold between sound, touch and vision, on the *limen* between aesthetic experience and the coming into being of another reality that Szendy calls 'effiction' (2016: 15; cf. Chapter 5). There is no better metaphor to convey this aesthetic aim than timbre. Timbre's agency is as strong here – described in words, perceived second-hand, in imagined tone colours only – as it is in the sounding phenomenon of Debussy's music.

> *I read the poem. Listening, as to an old story. The effect of this timbre is immediate and visceral. I am transported back to the country of my youth. I hear the boy's whistle moving through the still town, its echoes bouncing off the stones and hovering suspended over the water. Time retreats as I too am suspended in the evening air by the canal, in unison with the sound in my mind's ear. I feel the sound's vibrations, my vibrations, as they brush the leaves of a lime tree. We are lush and green with May's timbre.*
>
> *Only now do I realize how different the Netherlands sound, how easy it is to specify an entirely* Dutch *acoustic. Suddenly I yearn – with delicious, physically aching, unresolvable* Sehnsucht *– for the clarity of canal acoustics. For quiet voices on an evening quay, for soft reverberations against stone walls still warm from the day's sun. For the tenderness of whistling softened by watery air and Spring green. To hear my father's voice.*
>
> *I am there, I can almost touch it, but it must remain forever out of reach. Timbre's threshold:* sentiment sonore sublime.

If Gorter's words were read out to us, our perception of the timbre he describes would be entwined with that of the reader's voice. If that reading would be accompanied by a string chamber orchestra, or a distant accordion, or a church bell tolling, our imagination of the boy's whistling would be significantly different in each case.

> *But that would be dreadful. I want that timbre to remain silent, to exist in my head only, residing in my imagination as the sole companion to my innermost desires. Unheard melodies are sweeter, yes, possibly, but unheard timbres are more monstrous and more immeasurable. The sound's spectral touch affects my skin and unsettles my soul. But my soul – if there is such a thing, who can tell – my soul is itself the cause of its sound and of the desire which I inflict upon this non-object.*
> *I think I want to be unsettled by timbre.*

And you? What do you want from timbre?

Metaphors of differing

'Timbre', Dennis Smalley writes, is 'one of those subjects where the more you read and the more you have hands-on compositional experience the more you know, but in the process you become less able to grasp its essence' (Smalley 1994: 35). Smalley's observation is recognizable to every scholar, practitioner and listener who has engaged with timbre. This peculiar property of sound and music can be studied from a range of different angles: but whether we approach it through acoustics or psychoacoustics, as difference or as identity, as manipulable studio practice or as ephemeral aesthetic phenomenon, it escapes our grasp more with every bit of valuable knowledge we gain. 'It' escapes our grasp, I wrote there, as if timbre is an identifiable, delineated thing: but tone colour is not an object-thing, nor even a noumenon-Thing. It is both at once, and these two manifestations are inseparably entwined with each other. Looking for the 'essence' of timbre, as Smalley notes, is fruitless.

The search for a definition of timbre based on an 'essence', as I've argued throughout this book, can have no unambiguous result. The most basic of timbral definitions, McAdams's timbre-as-difference (McAdams 2001; cf. Chapter 1), leaves us with gaps only. Trying to fill those gaps, we may turn to materialism. Timbre-as-sound (in Chion's acoulogy: timbre in verberation) is determined by the material circumstances surrounding the shaping of sound. Because there are so many circumstances that contribute to this process, timbre-as-sound can only be described as an ecology, a convergence of material factors on micro as well as macro levels. As a layered ecology, timbre is relational in all possible senses. It emerges through interactions in assemblages of musical and non-musical, human and non-human elements, and its concrete shape and sound depends on the constant motion of these sonic agents. Timbre emerges in the unpredictable dance between musical rhythm and musicking fingers, moves as swiftly as wind on a reed, manifests in as nuanced a fashion as a portamento. Nancy notes that 'timbre is an evolving process, and listening evolves along with it' (2007: 40). McAdams's negative definition states that timbre marks sonic difference; Lyotard notes that timbre both '*differs* and *defers*' in that it makes a difference and defers identification (1991: 140). We could modify McAdams's definition in that timbre also *activates* difference, both because its sonic properties continuously evolve and because listeners are engaged in that process of differing. Timbre, in this sense, makes listeners 'passible' to difference (Lyotard 1991: 110–18; cf. Chapter 5).

Timbre-as-perceived (in Chion's acoulogy: timbre in auditum) is at least as heterogeneous, polymorphous and changeable as timbre in verberation: in listening to timbre, 'difference' is not an observation but a participation, not – or not merely – a passive recognition of dissimilarity but an active partaking of differentiation. This is partly because of the variations between individual hearing physiologies and neuro-systems which transmit tone in individual ways to individual effects and affects. Psychoacoustics struggles with the multivalence of timbral perception and gets lost in attempts to universalize the metaphors that have become the main vehicle for its methodology. In perception, moreover, timbre appears to become ever more elusive and ever more immaterial (depending on how material your definition of the outcome of neuro-activity is: how material is imagination?). In that case the intuitive im/precision of metaphor is the only means we have to approximate timbre: intuition and approximation still offer a more active engagement with our subject matter than shoulder-shrugging relativism. And so we describe 'warm' and 'bending' timbres, or we soar in the sublime exaltation aroused by what Schoenberg calls 'the illusory stuff of our dreams'.

The apparent irreconcilability of these two diametrically opposed approaches to timbre was the starting point for this book. The first three chapters are a reflection of my search for a timbral theory that is able to incorporate both the material and the less material manifestations of timbre. In so doing, I found that every timbral approach currently in use ultimately results in an impasse. Lydia Goehr's concept of 'doubleness' is a useful and neutral tool to gain insight into the ways in which the arguments around timbre have been structured. The eight propositions listed at the beginning of Chapter 4 demonstrate that structure, and from there it is possible to formulate paradox 0, the unspoken episteme of timbre's im/materiality, which lies at the root of the problem.

But paradox is in the eye of the beholder. In the case of timbre, paradox is in the eye (or ear) of those looking for essence. If we move away from the idea that the im/material timbral episteme is a paradox at all and replace the search for essence with a non-binary approach to timbre, a new vista opens. Chapters 4 and 5 aim to re-explore the eight propositions based on such an approach. Moving away from the transcendentalism at the basis of paradoxical thinking and towards an immanent theory of sound, music and ultimately timbre, the two extreme poles of timbral manifestation and appreciation reveal themselves as intricately connected. It is demonstrably true that timbre is strongly present in the material realm (to the point of being as tangible as the pain in your fingertips from playing the violin); it is equally true that it is strongly present in the immaterial realm (to the point of leading to the oblivion of sublime aporia). But that does not mean that it must be understood exclusively as *either* one *or* the other. Theorized through the concepts of the vibrational continuum and musical vitality, timbre is not transcendent but immanent, not exclusive but inclusive, not an essential but an emergent quality. Timbre makes audible and tangible the process of the energetic circulation in musical assemblages: the perpetual energetic motion between verberation and auditum establishes a scientifically observable connection between timbre-as-sound and timbre-as-perceived. With this in mind, timbre's aesthetic moment reveals itself as determined by simultaneity rather than paradox. The *empfindsam* philosopher Herder coined the compound noun 'tone-pleasure' to describe the simultaneity of physical touch and mental delight in timbral aesthetics; following the same line of reasoning, the poststructuralist philosopher Lyotard used the compound '*sentiment sonore*' to indicate the immediacy of an aesthetic event that affects the body and the mind at once. It is interesting that these two thinkers, situated as they are on either side of Kantian aesthetic theory and its idealist distinctions between object and Thing, had such strikingly similar insights, and that timbre was so central to both of them. In the exquisite aesthetic singularity of tone-pleasure, timbral touch and timbral sublime converge.

The first paragraph of this epilogue is an attempt to capture timbral aesthetics through the metaphorical approximation that is language, both by Gorter and – in reflection on his attempt – by me. Gorter's choice to frame his aesthetic renewal of Dutch poetry through the synaesthetic detour of an imagined timbre is remarkably appropriate. Timbre's vital agency, after all, is powerfully able to evoke tone-pleasure, even when it takes the shape of a poetically dreamed-up timbre. And while its (heard or imagined) presence is just as evocative as metaphors, when we try to describe any timbre in words we necessarily revert to metaphor, too. Tone colour's relation to linguistic icons is as imprecise and misleading as it is enduring and compelling. Timbre is a sonic form of metaphor on at least three levels: it is best described by way of metaphor (from 'tone colour' to 'warm' voices to 'oboe'); it functions as a metaphor (whether for a new kind of poetry, for a cinematic cliché, or for a *Nebenwelt* that is altogether removed from the here and now); and arguably it often becomes a metaphor for sound *qua* sound, as Pierre Schaeffer found out to his peril (for when you try to find the sound itself behind the metaphor, that essence, you're bound to be disappointed). My reflection on Gorter above is a patchwork of concepts from this book – from acoustics and sonic identity to the monstrous and the sublime – that aims to create a metaphoric blend matching my timbral experience. Your metaphoric blend, of course, is similar to mine only insofar as we both struggle to capture in words the wordless touch-feeling that determines sonic differing (or: to find language for a non-linguistic form of *différance*). And, I suspect, insofar as we both relish that struggle.

Timbre's aesthetic allure is the frustrating elusiveness of a tangible musical touch that is only definable as active difference. The possibility to keep wanting something from it. The relentless compulsion to invent metaphors for the different colours, flavours or moods of tone-pleasure we desire. It was for these im/precise reasons that timbre was a focal point in Debussy's impressionist composing, and that it provided the metaphoric shape for Gorter's poetic 'new sound'.

Simultaneity now

The vital materialism and vibrational aesthetics suggested here as the basis for an inclusive theory of timbre invite many more questions. Some are relatively practical. How does the aesthetics of tone-pleasure relate to acoustic design, instrument building, voice pedagogy? (Tone-pleasure is at the heart of those timbral materialisms, but we do not yet have the vocabulary to include it in them.) Can we invent psychoacoustic experiments around the touch of the *sentiment sonore*? (It would be interesting to do that, perhaps with test reports in the shape of poems or short stories.) Other questions prompted by the timbral theory proposed here require more extensive work. Which place can timbral vitality take within musical analysis and how does it relate to the vitality of melody, harmony and rhythm? (We'd have to review the premises of both musical notation and music theory.) In which way could music epistemology accommodate the immanence of musical vibration and vitality traced here though timbre? (We'd have to review the dualism at the basis of most music epistemological debate.)

A particularly pertinent topic of further investigation would be the temporal dimensions of the timbral event. Many of the authors discussed in this book emphasize music's time-transformative capacity, which exceeds even Bergsonian *durée*. It has been described as a suspension of time, as the introduction of an alternative time, or as an enveloping and developing *now* that eradicates the notion of time altogether (cf. Chapters 3 and 5). Tone colour occupies a curious position in music's relation to time, temporality and chronology. Like any other sound, timbre exists *in* time, it develops *with* time in the spectral envelope, and it can be argued to exist *as* time. Like rhythm and harmony, timbre is able to organize musical time: Debussy, Mahler and Schoenberg employed this temporal aspect of timbre, and dance genres such as dubstep are based on timbrally produced rhythms. Like any other musical parameter, moreover, timbre evokes strong associations and memories which can disjoint chronological time through the hauntology of revenants and premonitions. Lastly, the finitude inherent to all music makes itself felt in timbre's fleeting moments: this finitude induces the excitement of anticipation, the brief pleasure of the timbral moment, and the nostalgia when that moment has passed. While such permutations of temporality and chronology are more or less common to every element of musical aesthetics – from melody and harmony to rhythm and dynamics – they seem to be intensified in timbre. The immediacy of the timbral encounter makes listeners an active part of the finite event of music, places them physically as well as mentally within the musical *now*. Doyle identifies this 'infinite now' in the timbral gesture of reverb (2005: 234); it is by honing in on timbre's 'eternalising' potential that Stockhausen could create *Klangmomente* conveying only a 'Now! Now! Now! Now! Now!' (2000: 67).

Lyotard discusses timbre's relation to musical time in his essay 'Obedience'. Edgar Varèse's impressionistic use of tone colour as a structuring device, he argues, leads to a dissolution of the teleology of harmonic development (1991: 172–3). Without the chronological structure inherent to harmony, musical temporality is no longer organized as a diachronic narrative: replacing harmony with timbre, Varèse replaces traditional diachrony with 'a temporality of sound-events, accepting anachrony or parachrony' (ibid.: 173). Such radical timbral alteration of the progression of time engenders a musical experience that is a 'being-now' (ibid.: 176).

The catalyst for that non-time, Lyotard asserts, is the simultaneity of mental and physical touch in timbral sound-feeling. He goes on to argue that the coinciding of scientific quantity and artistic quality in timbre – noted also by Herder and Boulez – overcomes the 'false conflict' which has existed between music as science and music as art since Kant (ibid.: 175). While Helmholtz's late nineteenth-century experiments clearly demonstrated that any listening encounter takes place both on physical and mental levels, he contends, Kantian aesthetics have created an artificial 'paradox' between sound and audition (ibid.: 175–6). The 'ungraspable instant' between the two, the singular moment of sound-feeling, is timbre: music structured by timbre, like Varèse's, is a *Tonkunst* that marvels in that singularity, in the immediate *now* of the sound-event (ibid.: 177). The simultaneity that marks timbral aesthetics, then, also guides its intense and disruptive relation with time. Our encounter with tone colour is necessarily both corporeal and effervescent, and rather than presenting a paradox, this simultaneity introduces the aesthetic experience of what Goehr calls 'doubleness': the infinite *now* of sound-feeling, of tone-pleasure.

At the end of 'Obedience', Lyotard states that he would have liked to have approached the problem of sound-feeling 'from its energetical angle', as the energy flowing in sonic vibrations through air, past eardrum and into nerve-input connects music as sound and music as art (ibid.: 180). The vital materialism of timbral aesthetics proposed in this book offers a possible 'energetical' attempt to surpass the false paradox created by Kantian idealism, and a tentative starting point for timbre's temporal dimensions. Timbre and time hide inside one another. Their co-emergence is the germination of a *now* that is at once a present, a past and a future. In sound-feeling, the anticipation, pleasure and nostalgia for the musical ineffable are as tangible as goose bumps – even in imagined timbres such as that of a boy whistling by an evening canal.

Life

From diachrony to anachrony, from temporality to hauntology, from reality to *Nebenwelt*: being-now in the timbral event is not a standstill but a germination. Passible to the 'life of sound' (Stockhausen 2000: 98), we marvel at the sensory and sublime intensity presented by timbre's ephemeral moment. There is 'surprise at the heart of timbre', Gritten notes, 'the sheer shock of sound's distracting arrival onto the auditory scene, its sonic take-over and timbral resonance in the human subject' (2017: 541, cf. Introduction). Timbral surprise is the *arrive-t-il* of encountering something that ought to be a paradox but is a vibrant simultaneity. The singularity of timbre occurs before it means – *quod* before *quid* – and its aporetic instant is thoughtless wonder: 'Is it happening?' (Lyotard 1991: 90). In the touch of tone-pleasure, sonic life converges with our life. Timbral aesthetics is the surprise of a vital *now*, the enchantment of its endless fertility. On the threshold of a life, timbre grows listening vitality.

Is it happening, is this it, is it possible?

References

Abbate, C. (1993), 'Opera; or, the Envoicing of Women', in R. A. Solie (ed.), *Musicology and Difference: Gender and Sexuality in Music Scholarship*, 225–258, Berkeley: University of California Press.

Abbate, C. (2004), 'Music – Drastic or Gnostic?', *Critical Inquiry* 30 (3): 505–536.

Adorno, T. (2004), *Negative Dialectics*, translated by E. B. Ashton, London/New York: Routledge.

Alluri, V., P. Toiviainen, I. P. Jääskeläinen, E.Glerean, M.Sams and E. Brattico (2012), 'Large-scale Brain Networks Emerge from Dynamic Processing of Musical Timbre, Key and Rhythm', *NeuroImage* 59: 3677–3689.

Anderson, J. (2000), 'A Provisional History of Spectral Music', *Contemporary Music Review* 19 (2): 7–22.

Barthes, R. (1977), 'The Grain of the Voice', in *Image Music Text: Essays Selected and Translated by Stephen Heath*, 179–189, London: Fontana Press.

Barthes, R. (1985), *The Responsibility of Forms: Critical Essays on Music, Art, and Representation*, Oxford: Blackwell.

Belton, P. (2016), 'How Our Voices Could Unlock the Connected World', 12 July 2016. Available online: http://www.bbc.co.uk/news/business-36762962 (accessed 27 March 2020).

Benenson, W., J. W. Harris, H. Stöcker and H. Lutz, eds, (2002), *Springer Handbook of Physics*, New York/London: Springer.

Bennett, J. (2001), *The Enchantment of Modern Life: Attachments, Crossings, and Ethics*, Princeton: Princeton University Press.

Bennett, J. (2010), *Vibrant Matter: A Political Ecology of Things*, Durham, NC/London: Duke University Press.

Bennett, J. (2015), 'Encounters with an Art-Thing', *Eventual Aesthetics* 3 (3): 91–110.

Bennett, S. (2012), 'Endless Analogue: Situating Vintage Technologies in the Contemporary Recording & Production Workplace', *Journal on the Art of Record Production* 7. Available online: https://www.arpjournal.com/asarpwp/endless-analogue-situating-vintage-technologies-in-the-contemporary-recording-production-workplace/(accessed 27 March 2020).

Berger, H. M. and C. Fales (2005), 'Heaviness in the Perception of Heavy Metal Guitar Timbres: The Match of Perceptual and Acoustic Features over Time', in T. Porcello and P. D. Greene (eds), *Wired for Sound: Engineering and Technologies in Sonic Cultures*, 181–197, Middletown, CT: Wesleyan University Press.

Berlioz, H. ([1844] 2002), *Grand Traité d'Instrumentation et d'Orchestration Modernes*, translated by Hugh Macdonald, Cambridge: Cambridge University Press.

Bertola, M. F. (2017), 'The Sound's Remains: Some Thoughts on Harrison Birtwistle's *Orpheus Elegies* (2004) or: Timbre from Kant to Hegel', *Contemporary Music Review* 36 (6): 590–613.

Blake, C. and I. van Elferen (2015), 'Sonic Media And Spectral Loops', in J. Edwards (ed.), *Technologies of the Gothic in Literature and Culture*, 60–70, New York: Routledge.

Blesser, B. and L.-R. Salter (2007), *Spaces Speak, Are You Listening? Experiencing Aural Architecture*, Cambridge, MA: The MIT Press.

Bonds, M. E. (2014), *Absolute Music: The History of an Idea*, Oxford: Oxford University Press.

Bonenfant, Y. (2010), 'Queer Listening to Queer Vocal Timbres', *Performance Research* 15 (3): 74–80.

Boulez, P. (1987), 'Timbre and Composition – Timbre and Language', *Contemporary Music Review* 2 (1): 161–171.

Bregman, A. S. (1990), *Auditory Scene Analysis: The Perceptual Organization of Sound*, Cambridge, MA: MIT Press.

Brillenburgh Wurth, K. (2009), *Musically Sublime: Indeterminacy, Infinity, Irresolvability*, New York: Fordham University Press.

Bronfen, E. and B. Straumann (2002), *Die Diva: Eine Geschichte der Bewunderung*, Munich: Schirmer-Mosel.

Burke, E. ([1759] 1990), *A Philosophical Enquiry into the Origin of our Ideas of the Sublime and the Beautiful*, 2nd edn, edited by Adam Phillips, Oxford: Oxford University Press.

Camilleri, L. (2010), 'Shaping Sounds, Shaping Spaces', *Popular Music* 29 (2): 199–211.

Cavarero, A. (2005), *For More than One Voice: Toward a History of Vocal Expression*, Stanford: Stanford University Press.

Cendo, R. (2010), 'An Excess of Gesture and Material: Saturation as a Compositional Model', *Dissonance: Swiss Music Journal for Music and Creation*. Available online: https://www.dissonance.ch/en/archive/main_articles/876/abstract/en (accessed 27 March 2020).

Chanda, M. L. and D. J. Levitin (2013), 'The Neurochemistry of Music', *Trends in Cognitive Science* 17 (4): 179–193.

Chion, M. (1994), *Audio-Vision: Sound on Screen*, New York: Columbia University Press.

Chion, M. (2011), 'Dissolution of the Notion of Timbre', *differences* 22 (2-3): 235–239.

Chion, M. (2016), *Sound: An Acoulogical Treatise*, Durham, NC: Duke University Press.

Cimini, A. (2012), 'Vibrating Colors and Silent Bodies: Music, Sound and Silence in Maurice Merleau-Ponty's Critique of Dualism', *Contemporary Music Review* 31 (5-6): 353–370.

Clarke, E. F. (2005), *Ways of Listening: An Ecological Approach to the Perception of Musical Meaning*, Oxford: Oxford University Press.

Colebrook, C. and D. Bennett (2009), 'The Sonorous, the Haptic, and the Intensive', *New Formations* 66: 6–80.
Connor, S. (2000), *Dumbstruck: A Cultural History of Ventriloquism*, Oxford: Oxford University Press.
Connor, S. (2004), 'Edison's Teeth: Touching Hearing', in V. Erlmann (ed.), *Hearing Cultures: Essays on Sound, Listening, and Modernity*, 153–172, Oxford/New York: Berg.
Cook, N. (2001), 'Between Process and Product: Music in/as Performance', *Music Theory Online* 7 (2).
Cook, N. (2013), *Beyond the Score: Music as Performance*, Oxford: Oxford University Press.
Coole, D. and S. Frost (2010), 'Introducing the New Materialisms', in D. Coole and S. Frost (eds), *New Materialisms: Ontology, Agency, and Politics*, 1–44, Durham, NC: Duke University Press.
Cox, C. (2011), 'Beyond Sonic Representation and Signification: Toward a Sonic Materialism', *Journal of Visual Culture* 10 (2): 145–161.
Dahlhaus, C. (1989), *Nineteenth-Century Music*, translated by J. Bradford Robinson, Berkeley: University of California Press.
Day, T. (2000), 'English Cathedral Choirs in the Twentieth Century', in J. Potter (ed.), *The Cambridge Companion to Singing*, 123–132, Cambridge: Cambridge University Press.
Deleuze, G. and F. Guattari (1986), *Nomadology: The War Machine*, New York: Semiotext(e).
Deleuze, G. and F. Guattari (1987), *A Thousand Plateaus: Capitalism and Schizophrenia*, translated by B. Massumi, Minneapolis: University of Minnesota Press.
Deutsch, D. (1974), 'An Auditory Illusion', *Nature* 251: 307–309.
Deutsch, D. (1998), 'Grouping Mechanisms in Music', in D. Deutsch (ed.), *The Psychology of Music*, 2nd edn, 299–348, Cambridge, MA: Academic Press.
Dodd, J. (2007), *Works of Music: An Essay in Ontology*, Oxford: Oxford University Press.
Dohoney, R. (2015), 'Echo's Echo: Subjectivity in Vibrational Ontology', *Women and Music: A Journal of Gender and Culture* 19: 142–150.
Dolan, E. (2013), *The Orchestral Revolution: Haydn and the Technologies of Timbre*, Cambridge: Cambridge University Press.
Dolar, M. (2006), *A Voice and Nothing More*, Cambridge, MA: MIT Press.
Doyle, P. (2005), *Echo and Reverb: Fabricating Space in Popular Music Recording, 1900–1960*, Middletown, CT: Wesleyan University Press.
Dunsby, J. (2009), 'Roland Barthes and the Grain of Panzéra's Voice', *Journal of the Royal Musical Association* 134 (1): 113–132.
Eidsheim, N. S. (2015), *Sensing Sound: Singing & Listening as Vibrational Practice*, Durham, NC: Duke University Press.

Elert, G. (1998–2017), 'Sound: Intensity', in *The Physics Hypertextbook*. Available online: http://physics.info/intensity/(accessed 27 March 2020).

Elferen, I. van (2009), *Mystical Love in the German Baroque: Theology, Poetry, Music*, Lanham, MD: Scarecrow.

Elferen, I. van (2012), *Gothic Music: The Sounds of the Uncanny*, Cardiff: University of Wales Press.

Elferen, I. van (2018), 'Dark Timbre: The Aesthetics of Tone Colour in Goth Music', *Popular Music* 37 (1): 22–39.

Erickson, D. (2009), *Ghosts, Metaphor, and History in Toni Morrison's* Beloved *and Gabriel Garcia Marquez's* One Hundred Years of Solitude, Basingstoke: Palgrave Macmillan.

Evens, A. (2005), *Sound Ideas: Music, Machines and Experience*, Minneapolis: University of Minnesota Press.

Fales, C. (2002), 'The Paradox of Timbre', *Ethnomusicology* 46 (1): 56–95.

Fales, C. (2005), 'Short-Circuiting Perceptual Systems', in P. D. Greene and T. Porcello (eds), *Wired for Sound: Engineering and Technologies in Sonic Cultures*, 156–180, Middletown, CT: Wesleyan.

Feldman, M. (2015), *The Castrato: Reflections on Natures and Kinds*, Berkeley: University of California Press.

Fink, R., Z. Wallmark and M. Latour (2018), 'Introduction – Chasing the Dragon: In Search of Tone in Popular Music', in R. Fink, M. Latour and Z. Wallmark (eds), *The Relentless Pursuit of Tone: Timbre in Popular Music*, 1–17, New York: Oxford University Press.

Fleury, M. (1996), *L'Impressionisme et la Musique*, Paris: Fayard.

Foucault, M. (2000), 'A Preface to Transgression', in J. D. Faubion (ed.), *Michel Foucault: Aesthetics. Essential Works of Foucault 1954–1984*, vol. 2, 69–87, London: Penguin.

Frith, S. (1996). *Performing Rites: Evaluating Popular Music*, Oxford: Oxford University Press.

Gallope, M. (2012), 'Jankélévitch's Fidelity to Inconsistency', *Journal of the American Musicological Society* 65 (1): 235–241.

Gibson, J. J. (1986), *The Ecological Approach to Visual Perception*, Boston: Houghton Mifflin.

Gilbert, J. (2004), 'Becoming-Music: The Rhizomatic Moment of Improvisation', in I. Buchanan and M. Swiboda (eds), *Deleuze and Music*, 118–139, Edinburgh: Edinburgh University Press.

Gilbert, J. and E. Pearson (1999), *Discographies: Dance, Music, Culture, and the Politics of Sound*, London: Routledge.

Giordano, B. and S. McAdams (2010), 'Sound Source Mechanics and Musical Timbre Perception: Evidence from Previous Studies', *Music Perception* 28 (2): 155–168.

Goehr, L. (2004), *The Quest for Voice: Music, Politics, and the Limits of Philosophy*, Oxford: Oxford University Press.

Goodman, S. (2010), *Sonic Warfare: Sound, Affect, and the Ecology of Fear*, Cambridge, MA: MIT Press.
Gorbman, C. (1987), *Unheard Melodies: Narrative Film Music*, Bloomington/Indianapolis: Indiana University Press.
Gorter, H. (1997), *Mei: Een Gedicht* [1889], edited by Enno Endt, Amsterdam: Ooievaar.
Gracyk, T. (1996), *Rhythm and Noise: An Aesthetics of Rock*, London: I.B.Tauris.
Grey, J. M. (1977), 'Multidimensional Perceptual Scaling of Musical Timbres', *Journal of the Acoustical Society of America* 61: 1270–1277.
Grisey, G. (2000), 'Did you say spectral?', translated by Joshua Fineberg, *Contemporary Music Review* 19 (3): 1–3.
Gritten, A. (2017), 'Depending on Timbre', *Contemporary Music Review* 36 (6): 530–543.
Gumbrecht, H. (2012), *Atmosphere, Mood, Stimmung*, Redwood City: Stanford University Press.
Gunn, J. (1999), 'Gothic Music and the Inevitability of Genre', *Popular Music and Society* 35 (1): 31–50.
Hailstone, J. C., R. Omar, S. M. D. Henley, C. Frost, M. G. Kenward and J. D. Warren (2009), 'It's not What you Play, it's How you Play it: Timbre Affects Perception of Emotion in Music', *Quarterly Journal of Experimental Psychology* 62: 2141–2155.
Hajda, J. M., R. A. Kendall, E. C. Carterette and M. L. Harshberger (1997), 'Methodological Issues in Timbre Research', in I. Deliège and J. M. Sloboda (eds), *Perception and Cognition of Music*, 253–306, Hove: Psychology Press.
Hamilton, A. (2007), *Aesthetics & Music*, London: Continuum.
Hanslick, E. ([1854, 1891 3rd edn] 1986), *On the Musically Beautiful*, translated by Geoffrey Payzant, Indianapolis: Hackett Publishing Company.
Heidegger, M. (2000), *Introduction to Metaphysics*, New Haven: Yale University Press.
Helmholtz, H. ([1885] 2016), *On the Sensations of Tone as a Physiological Basis for the Theory of Music*, New York: Dover Publications.
Herder, J. G. ([1878] 2006), *Herders Sämtliche Werke*, vol. 4, London: Elibron Classics.
Hoffmann, E. T. A. ([1813] 1965), 'Beethoven's Instrumental Music', in O. Strunk (ed.), *Source Readings in Music History: The Romantic Era*, 35–57, New York: Norton.
Holmes, P. (1989), *Debussy*, London: Omnibus Press.
Holmes, P. (2011), 'An Exploration of Musical Communication through Expressive Use of Timbre: The Performer's Perspective', *Psychology of Music* 40 (3): 301–323.
Hornbostel, E. M. von and C. Sachs (1914), 'Systematik der Musikinstrumente', *Zeitschrift für Ethnologie* 46: 553–590.
Howard, D. M. (2005), 'Discussant Response to "Does the acoustic waveform mirror the voice?"', *Logopedics, Phoniatrics, Vocology* 30 (3-4): 108–113.
Howard, D. M. and J. A. S. Angus (2009), *Acoustics and Psychoacoustics*, 4th edn, New York/London: Focal Press.
Howard, D. M. and A. M. Tyrrell (1997), 'Psychoacoustically Informed Spectrography and Timbre', *Organised Sound* 2 (2): 65–76.

Hunt-Hendrix, H. (2010), *Transcendental Black Metal: A Vision of Apocalyptic Humanism*. Available online: https://genius.com/albums/Hunter-hunt-hendrix/Transcendental-black-metal-a-vision-of-apocalyptic-humanism (accessed 27 March 2020).

Ihde, D. (2007), *Listening and Voice: Phenomenologies of Sound*, Albany: SUNY.

Jankélévitch, V. ([1983] 2003), *Music and the Ineffable*, translated by C. Abbate, Princeton: Princeton University Press.

Jensen, E. F. (2014), *Debussy*, Oxford: Oxford University Press.

Kane, B. (2014), *Sound Unseen: Acousmatic Sound in Theory and Practice*, Oxford: Oxford University Press.

Kim-Cohen, S. (2009), *In the Blink of an Ear: Toward a Non-Cochlear Sonic Art*, New York/London: Continuum.

Kittler, F. A. (1999), *Gramophone, Film, Typewriter*, translated by G. Winthrop-Young and M. Wutz, Stanford: Stanford University Press.

Kleiner, M. S. and A. Szepanski, eds, (2003), *Soundcultures: Über elektronische und digitale Musik*, Frankfurt am Main: Suhrkamp.

Kramer, J. D. (1978), 'Moment Form in Twentieth Century Music', *The Musical Quarterly*, 64 (2): 177–194.

Kramer, J. D. (1988), *The Time of Music: New Meanings, New Temporalities, New Listening Strategies*, New York: Schirmer.

Lacan, J. (1977), *The Four Fundamental Concepts of Psycho-Analysis*, edited by J.-A. Miller, translated by Alan Sheridan, London: Penguin.

Lacan, J. (2007), *The Other Side of Psychoanalysis. The Seminar of Jacques Lacan: Book XVII*, translated by Russell Grigg, New York/London: Norton.

Lasocki, D. (2001), 'Recorder: 1. Nomenclature', *Grove Music Online*. Available online: https://doi.org/10.1093/gmo/9781561592630.article.23022 (accessed 27 March 2020).

Latour, B. (2005), *Reassembling the Social: An Introduction to Actor-Network-Theory*, Oxford: Oxford University Press.

Leipert, T. (2013), 'Destination Unknown: Jean-François Lyotard and Orienting Musical Affect', *Contemporary Music Review* 31 (5–6): 425–438.

Lesure, F. and R. Nichols (1987), *Debussy: Letters*, London: Faber.

Levitin, D. J. (2006), *This is Your Brain on Music: The Science of a Human Obsession*, New York: Dutton.

Lewcock, R. and R. Pirn (2001), 'Room Acoustics', *Grove Music Online*. Available online: https://doi.org/10.1093/gmo/9781561592630.article.00134 (accessed 27 March 2020).

Leys, R. (2011), 'The Turn to Affect: A Critique', *Critical Inquiry* 37(3): 434–472.

Liimola, H. (2000), 'Some Notes on Choral Singing', in J. Potter (ed.), *The Cambridge Companion to Singing*, 149–157, Cambridge: Cambridge University Press.

Lochhead, J. (2012), 'Can We Say What We Hear? Jankélévitch and the Bergsonian Ineffable', *Journal of the American Musicological Society* 65 (1): 231–235.

Lubarsky, E. (2015), 'A Cameo of Frances Pelton-Jones: For her, for Jane Bennett, (and for us, too)', *Evental Aesthetics* 3 (3): 80–90.
Lyotard, J.-F. (1991), *The Inhuman*, Cambridge: Polity Press.
Lyotard, J.-F. (1996), 'Music and Postmodernity', *New Formations* 66 (2): 37–45.
Lyotard, J.-F. (1997), *Postmodern Fables*, translated by G. van den Abbeele, Minneapolis: University of Minnesota Press.
Major, N. (1987), *Joan Sutherland*, London: Queen Anne Press.
Massumi, B. (1995), 'The Autonomy of Affect', *Cultural Critique* 31: 83–109.
McAdams, S. (2001), 'Psychology of Music: II. Perception and Cognition: 3. Timbre', *Grove Music Online*. Available online: https://doi.org/10.1093/gmo/9781561592630.article.42574 (accessed 27 March 2020).
McAdams, S. and B. L. Giordano (2016), 'The Perception of Musical Timbre', in S. Hallam, I. Cross and M. Thaut (eds), *Oxford Handbook of Music Psychology*, 2nd edn, 113–124, Oxford: Oxford University Press.
McAdams, S. and M. Goodchild (2017), 'Musical Structure: Sound and Timbre', in R. Timmers (ed.), *The Routledge Companion to Music Cognition*, 129–139, New York: Routledge.
McClary, S. (2008), 'More Pomo Than Thou: The Status of Cultural Meanings in Music', *New Formations* 66: 28–36.
Meillassoux, Q. (2008), *After Finitude: An Essay on the Necessity of Contingency*, translated by R. Brassier, London: Continuum.
Menet, J.-L. (2012), 'Le Dessin Sous-Jacent: Entretien avec Raphaël Cendo'. CD liner notes for Raphaël Cendo, *Rokh*, Ensemble Alternance, Stradivarius.
Merleau-Ponty, M. (2002), *Phenomenology of Perception*, London/New York: Routledge.
Middleton, R. (2006), *Voicing the Popular: On the Subjects of Popular Music*, New York: Routledge.
Moore, A. F. (2012), *Song Means: Analysing and Interpreting Recorded Popular Song*, Farnham: Ashgate.
Moore, B. C. J. (2001), 'Hearing and Psychoacoustics', *Grove Music Online*. Available online: https://doi.org/10.1093/gmo/9781561592630.article.42531 (accessed 27 March 2020).
Moorefield, V. (2010), *The Producer as Composer: Shaping the Sounds of Popular Music*, Cambridge, MA: MIT Press.
Moreno, J. and G. Steingo (2012), 'Rancière's Equal Music', *Contemporary Music Review* 31 (5-6): 487–505.
Moylan, W. (2007), *Understanding and Crafting the Mix: The Art of Recording*, 2nd edn, Amsterdam: Focal Press.
Nancy, J.-L. (2007), *Listening*, New York: Fordham University Press.
Nattiez, J.-J. (1990), *Music and Discourse: Toward a Semiology of Music*, translated by C. Abbate, Princeton: Princeton University Press.

Parker, B. (2009), *Good Vibrations: The Physics of Music*, Baltimore: The Johns Hopkins University Press.

Paul, J. ([1795] 1965), 'Garden Concert by Stamitz', in O. Strunk (ed.) *Source Readings in Music History: The Romantic Era*, 24–34, New York: Norton.

Perevedentseva, M. (2018), 'Timbre as "Structuring Structure" in Underground Electronic Dance Music', unpublished conference presentation quoted with author's permission.

Pinch, T. and F. Trocco (2004), *Analog Days: The Invention and Impact of the Moog Synthesizer*, Cambridge, MA: Harvard University Press.

Plazak, J. and D. Huron (2011), 'The First Three Seconds: Listener Knowledge Gained from Brief Musical Excerpts', *Musicae Scientiae* 15 (1): 29–44.

Pratt, R. L. and P. E. Doak (1976), 'A Subjective Rating Scale for Timbre', *Journal of Sound and Vibration* 45 (3): 317–328.

Priest, E. (2013), 'Felt as Thought (or, Musical Abstraction and the Semblance of Affect)', in M. Thompson and I. Biddle (eds), *Sound Music Affect: Theorizing Sonic Experience*, 45–63, London: Bloomsbury.

Rancière, J. (2004), *The Politics of Aesthetics: The Distribution of the Sensible*, London/New York: Continuum.

Rancière, J. (2009) *Aesthetics and its Discontents*, Cambridge: Polity Press.

Redhead, L. (2020), 'Vibrant Echoes: A Material Semiotics of the Voice in Music by Iris Garrelfs and Marlo Eggplant', *Contemporary Music Review*.

Reigle, R. (2008), 'Spectral Musics Old and New', in R. Reigle and P. Whitehead (eds), *Spectral World Musics: Proceedings of the Istanbul Spectral Music Conference*, Istanbul: Pan.

Reiterer, S., M. Erb, W. Grodd and D. Wildgruber (2008), 'Cerebral Processing of Timbre and Loudness: fMRI Evidence for a Contribution of Broca's Area to Basic Auditory Discrimination', *Brain Imaging and Behavior* 2: 1–10.

Reynolds, S. (2012), *Retromania: Pop Culture's Addiction to its Own Past*, London: Faber & Faber.

Rings, S. (2012), 'Talking and Listening with Jankélévitch', *Journal of the American Musicological Society* 65 (1): 218–223.

Risi, C. (2016), 'Diva Poses by Anna Netrebko: On the Perception of the Extraordinary in the Twenty-First Century', in K. Henson (ed.), *Technology and the Diva: Sopranos, Opera, and Media from Romanticism to the Digital Age*, 150–158, Cambridge: Cambridge University Press.

Sachs, C. (1930), *Handbuch der Musikinstrumentenkunde*, 2nd edn, Leipzig: Breitkopf & Härtel.

Schaeffer, P. (1952), *À la Recherche d'une Musique Concrète*, Paris: Éditions du Seuil.

Schaeffer, P. (1966), *Traité des Objets Musicaux*, Paris: Éditions du Seuil.

Schaeffer, P. (2017), *Treatise on Musical Objects: An Essay across Disciplines*, translated by C. North and J. Dack, Berkeley: University of California Press.

Schafer, R. M. (1994), *The Soundscape: Our Sonic Environment and the Tuning of the World*, Rochester, NY: Destiny.

Schmidt Horning, S. (2012), 'The Sounds of Space: Studio as Instrument in the Era of High Fidelity', in S. Frith and S. Zagorski-Thomas (eds), *The Art of Record Production: An Introductory Reader for a New Academic Field*, 29–42, Farnham: Ashgate.

Schoenberg, A. (1922), *Harmonielehre. II. vermehrte und verbesserte Auflage*, Vienna: Universal-Edition.

Schrimshaw, W. (2013), 'Non-cochlear Sound: On Affect and Exteriority', in M. Thompson and I. Biddle (eds), *Sound Music Affect: Theorizing Sonic Experience*, 27–43, London: Bloomsbury.

Schuiling, F. (2020), '(Re)assembling Notations in the Performance of Early Music', *Contemporary Music Review*.

Scruton, R. (1997), *The Aesthetics of Music*, Oxford: Oxford University Press.

Seashore, C. E. (1936), 'The Psychology of Music', *Music Educators Journal* 23 (1): 24–26.

Seashore, C. E. (1967 [1938]), *Psychology of Music*, New York: Dover.

Sendin, G. (2017), 'Miracle in Cremona? The Science behind Stradivarius', *Neurokunst*, 22 March. Available online: http://www.neurokunst.com/2017/03/22/miracle-in-cremona-the-science-behind-stradivarius/(accessed 27 March 2020).

Sethares, W. A. (2005), *Tuning, Timbre, Spectrum, Scale*, 2nd edn, London: Springer.

Shadrack, J. H. (2017a), 'Denigrata Cervorum: Interpretative Performance Autoethnography and Female Black Metal Performance', Doctoral thesis, University of Northampton.

Shadrack, J. H. (2017b), 'From Enslavement to Obliteration: Extreme Metal's Problem with Women', in R. E. Jones and E. Davies (eds), *Under My Thumb: Songs that Hate Women and the Women Who Love Them*, 170–184, London: Repeater Books.

Shank, B. (2014), *The Political Force of Musical Beauty*, Durham, NC: Duke University Press.

Shaviro, S. (2006), 'A Voice and Nothing More'. Available online: http://www.shaviro.com/Blog/?p=489 (accessed 27 March 2020).

Sheinbaum, J. J. (2005), 'The Artifice of the "Natural": Mahler's Orchestration at Cadences1', *Journal of Musicological Research* 24 (2): 91–121.

Siedenburg, K., I. Fujinaga and S. McAdams (2016), 'A Comparison of Approaches to Timbre Descriptors in Music Information Retrieval and Music Psychology', *Journal of New Music Research* 45 (1): 27–41.

Siedenburg, K. and S. McAdams (2017), 'Four Distinctions for the Auditory "Wastebasket" of Timbre', *Frontiers in Psychology* 8, 4 October 2017, 1747. Available online: https://doi.org/10.3389/fpsyg.2017.01747 (accessed 27 March 2020).

Slawson, W. (1985), *Sound Color*, Berkeley: University of California Press.

Small, C. (1998), *Musicking: The Meanings of Performing and Listening*, Middletown, CT: Wesleyan University Press.

Smalley, D. (1986), 'Spectro-morphology and Structuring Processes', in S. Emmerson (ed.), *The Language of Electroacoustic Music*, 61–93, Basingstoke: Macmillan.

Smalley, D. (1994), 'Defining Timbre – Refining Timbre', *Contemporary Music Review* 10 (2): 35–48.

Smith, J. (2008), *Vocal Tracks: Performance and Sound Media*, Berkeley: University of California Press.

Smith, S. D. (2012), 'Awakening Dead Time: Adorno on Husserl, Benjamin, and the Temporality of Music', *Contemporary Music Review* 31 (5-6): 389–409.

Steege, B. (2012), *Helmholtz and the Modern Listener*, Cambridge: Cambridge University Press.

Steiger, R. (2002), *Gnadengegenwart: Johann Sebastian Bach im Kontext lutherischer Orthodoxie und Frömmigkeit*, Stuttgart-Bad Canstatt: fromann-holzboog.

Sterne, J. (2003), *The Audible Past: Cultural Origins of Sound Reproduction*, Durham, NC: Duke University Press.

Sterne, J. (2016), 'Afterword: Opera, Media, Technicity', in K. Henson (ed.), *Technology and the Diva: Sopranos, Opera, and Media from Romanticism to the Digital Age*, 159–164, Cambridge: Cambridge University Press.

Stockhausen, K. (1963–1984), *Texte zur Musik*, 4 volumes, Cologne: Verlag M. DuMont Schauberg.

Stockhausen, K. (2000), *Stockhausen on Music: Lectures & Interviews*, compiled by Robin Maconie, London/New York: Marion Boyars.

Stoel, B. C. and T. M. Borman (2008), 'A Comparison of Wood Density between Classical Cremonese and Modern Violins', *PLoS ONE* 3 (7): e2554. Available online: https://doi.org/10.1371/journal.pone.0002554 (accessed 27 March 2020).

Sundberg, J. (1987), *The Science of the Singing Voice*, DeKalb, Il: Northern Illinois University Press.

Szendy, P. (2016), *Phantom Limbs: On Musical Bodies*, New York: Fordham University Press.

Tagg, P. (2013), *Music's Meanings: A Modern Musicology for Non-Musos*, New York/Huddersfield: The Mass Media Music Scholars' Press.

Taylor, C. and M. Campbell (2001), 'Sound', *Grove Music Online*. Available online: https://doi.org/10.1093/gmo/9781561592630.article.26289 (accessed 27 March 2020).

Thompson, M. and I. Biddle (2013), 'Introduction: Somewhere between the Signifying and the Sublime', in M. Thompson and I. Biddle (eds) *Sound Music Affect: Theorizing Sonic Experience*, 1–24, London: Bloomsbury.

Trower, S. (2012), *Senses of Vibration: A History of the Pleasure and Pain of Sound*, New York/London: Continuum.

Tunbridge, L. (2014), 'Opera and Materiality', *Cambridge Opera Journal* 26 (3): 289–299.

Voegelin, S. (2014), *Sonic Possible Worlds: Hearing the Continuum of Sound*, New York/London: Bloomsbury.

Vogels, B. (2017), 'Performative Sounds: The Threatening Touch of Timbre', *Contemporary Music Review* 36 (6): 544–561.

Walser, R. (1993), *Running with the Devil: Power, Gender, and Madness in Heavy Metal Music*, Hanover, NH: University Press of New England.

Watkins, H. and M. Esse (2015), 'Down with Disembodiment; or Musicology and the Material Turn', *Women and Music* 19: 160–168.

Wilson, S. (2018), 'Notes on Adorno's "Musical Material" During the New Materialisms', *Music and Letters* 99 (2): 260–275. Available online: https://doi.org/10.1093/ml/gcy002 (accessed 27 March 2020).

Wong, M.-S. (2015), 'Introductory Editorial: Towards Vital Materialist Aesthetics', *Evental Aesthetics* 3 (3): 4–14.

Woodfield, I. and L. Robinson (2001), 'Viol', *Grove Music Online*. Available online: http://www.oxfordmusiconline.com/grovemusic/view/10.1093/gmo/9781561592630.001.0001/omo-9781561592630-e-0000029435 (accessed 27 March 2020).

Woodward, A. (2016), 'Lyotard on Postmodern Music', *Evental Aesthetics* 5 (1): 118–143.

Yarnall, S. (2017a), 'The "Real" Me: Practical Application of Research into the Perception of Vocal Timbre', *Contemporary Music Review* 36 (6): 562–579.

Yarnall, S. (2017b), 'Metaphors Matter'. Available online: http://SingingUnique.com (accessed 24 November 2017).

Zacharakis, A., K. Pastiadis and J. D. Reiss (2014), 'An Interlanguage Study of Musical Timbre Semantic Dimensions and Their Acoustic Correlates', *Music Perception: An Interdisciplinary Journal* 31 (4): 339–358.

Zagorski-Thomas, S. (2014), *The Musicology of Record Production*, Cambridge: Cambridge University Press.

Zak, A. J. III. (2001), *The Poetics of Rock: Cutting Tracks, Making Records*, Berkeley: University of California Press.

Zaza, C. and V. T. Farewell (1997), 'Musicians' Playing-related Musculoskeletal Disorders: An Examination of Risk Factors', *American Journal of Industrial Medicine* 32 (3): 292–300.

Websites

Actor Project: Analysis, Creation and Teaching of Orchestration (McGill University Montreal) https://orchard.actor-project.org (accessed 27 March 2020).

Aural Sonology, http://www.auralsonology.com (accessed 27 March 2020).

Graindelavoix, http://www.graindelavoix.org (accessed 27 March 2020).

Institut de la Recherche et Coordination Acoustique/Musique (IRCAM) http://recherche.ircam.fr/anasyn/schwarz/da/specenv/Spectral_Envelopes.html (accessed 27 March 2020).

Iszoloscope, https://www.facebook.com/pg/iszoloscope/about/?ref=page_internal (accessed 27 March 2020).
Steven Connor, http://www.stevenconnor.com/dumbstruck/(accessed 27 March 2020).
Strad3D, http://strad3d.org (accessed 27 March 2020).
VocaMe, http://www.vocame.de/en/(accessed 27 March 2020).
Voiceovers, http://www.voiceovers.co.uk (accessed 27 March 2020).

Discography

Antony and the Johnsons, *Antony and the Johnsons*. Durtro 2000.
Barbra Streisand, *The Essential Barbra Streisand*. Sony Music Entertainment 2002.
Iszoloscope, *Beyond Within*. Ant.Zen 2010.
Iszoloscope, *False Vacuum*. Ant.Zen 2016.
Raphaël Cendo, *ROKH*. Ensemble Alternance. Stradivarius 2012.
Roberta Flack, *Softly with These Songs: The Best of Roberta Flack*. Warner Music 1993.
Vincenzo Bellini, *Norma*. Callas Remastered. Warner Classics, 2014.
VocaMe, *Cathedrals*. Christophorus 2018.

Index

Abbate, Carolyn 10, 53, 76, 78, 120, 123, 126, 129–30, 138, 154, 155, 157, 180, 184
absolute music 12, 105, 119, 174, 179, 180, 183
acoulogy 13, 59–60, 135–45, 165, 211, 212
acousmatics 25, 30, 58, 66, 81–2, 91, 99, 112, 137, 152, 181, 185–6, 205
acoustics 2–4, 8, 11, 18, 26–34, 41, 45–9, 53, 55, 61, 65, 82, 92, 111, 113, 116, 120, 137–8, 141, 158, 161, 164–6, 178, 184–6, 189, 193, 194, 201, 205, 210, 214
Actor-Network-Theory (ANT) 146, 151–3, 157–8
'Actus Tragicus' (BWV 106) 70, 164–6, 172
abyss 88, 198–9, 204–7
adjectives 67–70, 74, 76
Adorno, Theodor 147, 156
ADSR envelope (note envelope) 20–1, 34–8, 43, 58, 117, 163, 215
aesthetic openness 79, 91, 160, 177, 201–4
aesthetic reaching 2, 95–7, 99, 106, 117, 126–7, 156
aesthetics 7, 9, 12, 14, 24, 47, 70, 79–80, 88–9, 94–7, 99, 101–17, 122–31, 147, 159–62, 164, 173–207
affect 1, 14, 73, 101, 115, 125, 130, 144, 147–50, 152, 158–62, 165–8, 171–3, 177–8, 181–3, 185, 189–90, 195, 198, 212
affective encounter 70, 149, 164
allure 14, 47, 91, 131, 165, 197–9, 214
alto voice 24, 47, 54, 60, 61, 70, 74, 82–3
ambiguity 13, 18, 25–6, 43, 48, 57, 79, 85, 91, 115, 127, 159, 211
analogue recording 121, 157, 205
Ancrage 72
anima (body/thought) 125–6, 128–9, 173, 201
animacy 156–7, 171

Antony and the Johnsons 82–4, 89, 137
aporia 13, 14, 15, 70, 79, 82, 86, 88, 100, 125–31, 133, 148, 154, 155, 160, 165, 168, 172–4, 200–1, 203, 207, 213
areality 192–9, 205–6
armonica/glass organ 42
arrive-t-il 200–7, 217
articulation 4, 6, 7, 19, 46, 47, 63, 73, 116, 134, 161, 166, 167, 202
Asche 56, 58, 87, 167
assemblage 6, 11, 14, 74, 149–58, 161, 164, 165–8, 171, 173–4, 177–8, 183, 190, 193–4, 200–1, 206, 212, 213
attentive/inattentive listening 44
auditum 13, 14, 138–40, 145, 153, 157, 163, 164, 166–8, 172, 174, 179, 180, 182, 185–9, 190, 193, 197, 202, 206, 212, 213
authenticity 95, 118, 137
autonomy 96, 101–2, 105, 113–4, 116, 119, 148, 153 n. 2, 159, 165, 183–6, 190

Bach, Johann Sebastian 2–3, 28, 70, 80, 110, 119, 164–5, 184, 204
Baroque 5, 24, 69–70, 115, 118, 129, 189
Barthes, Roland 3, 12, 52, 72, 76–80, 81–2, 85–7, 92, 94, 97, 126, 130
Batcave 74
bass voice 54, 61, 70
Beethoven, Ludwig van 100–1, 103, 104, 185, 203
Benedicamus from Codex Calinxtinus 17–8, 32–3, 45, 46
Bennett, Jane 13–4, 121, 145–50, 152–60, 164–6, 172, 173, 174, 177–8, 182, 183, 191–2, 193, 197, 198, 200, 201, 207

Bergson, Henri 126, 127, 154, 196, 200, 215
Berlioz, Hector 23, 28–9, 70, 103–4, 105, 107, 115, 118
Bertola, Mauro Fosco 124, 125, 129
binaries 10, 13–5, 59, 60, 84, 94, 96–7, 123, 127, 133–5, 139, 145, 146, 148, 156, 157, 162, 163, 173–4, 181, 186, 199, 200, 207, 213
Black Books 80–1, 87
Black Sabbath 51, 61, 71
blackvoice 61–2
Blake, Charlie 84, 151–2
Blesser, Barry and Linda-Ruth Salter 27, 28, 31, 33
Blige, Mary J 61
body 14, 24, 30, 52, 53, 59–60, 62–7, 77–80, 81–2, 84, 85, 91, 93–4, 115, 121–2, 125–6, 130, 136, 141, 146, 148–9, 150, 173–4, 181, 184, 188, 192–3, 194, 196, 213
Boulez, Pierre 12, 107, 114–7, 123, 124, 126, 216
Brel, Jacques 63, 66, 77–8
Brillenburg Wurth, Kiene 95, 98–100, 103, 198
Burke, Edmund 12, 97–106, 116, 125, 131, 154, 172, 199, 201

Callas, Maria 1–2, 9, 120, 131, 168–72
Carlos, Wendy 119
carnal phenomenology 9, 53, 86, 140, 141, 145, 151, 159, 174, 180
Cash, Johnny 61, 64
"Casta Diva" 1, 168–9, 172
castrato voice 91–2, 168
causality 5, 11, 58, 60, 79, 83, 87, 136–8, 149, 157–9, 171, 173, 178, 181–2, 185–6
Cendo, Raphaël 25, 45, 160–1, 172, 198
charm 128, 154–6, 184, 187, 190, 198
Chion, Michel 5, 13, 40, 45, 55, 58, 59–60, 67, 135–41, 143, 145, 152, 163, 165, 180, 182, 185, 211, 212
choir/choral singing 2, 4, 34, 46, 64–6, 69, 89, 151, 167, 190
chronology 127, 178, 182, 191, 215
church organ 2, 68, 102, 153, 184, 209

Cimini, Amy 135, 139
Clapton, Eric 5–7, 9, 11, 118
clarinet 19, 28, 60, 103–4, 163
Clarke, Eric F. 11, 38, 44–5, 46, 151
cochlea 4, 41, 143, 159, 189–90, 191, 197, 207
Cole, Nat King 53
compression 30, 31, 53, 73, 120
conatus 146
condition timbrale 172
Connor, Steven 30, 62–3, 81, 82, 140, 141
connotations 2–3, 51–2, 54, 57–9, 68, 70–2, 74, 113, 144, 190, 206
counterpoint/polyphony 17, 46, 152, 164
cover versions 61–2, 64, 65, 77, 78
co-vibration 140, 144
Cox, Christoph 10, 55, 75, 154

Dahlhaus, Carl 103, 104, 180
Daleks 56, 59
Damrau, Diana 1, 2, 12
Debussy, Claude 107–8, 184, 210, 214, 215
"Deeper than Love" 82–3, 89, 137
definition of timbre 17–49
Deleuze, Gilles and Felix Guattari 146–7, 148, 149, 153, 182, 194, 195–6
desire 12, 15, 17, 33, 63, 80–89, 91, 95, 96, 97, 99, 106, 147, 197, 203, 211, 214
difference 11, 17 – 49, 53, 54, 65, 69, 70, 74, 77, 80, 86, 89, 92, 102, 103, 104, 107, 108, 110, 124, 143–4, 163, 166, 179, 183, 188, 198, 204, 206, 207, 210, 211–4
digital music 56–7, 60, 119, 205
disembodiment 81, 91, 139, 180, 188
disenchantment 12, 119–21, 147, 204
distortion 20, 25, 30, 55, 56, 73, 88, 119, 136, 196
distribution of the sensible 14, 176–7, 183, 187, 188, 189–90, 193, 195, 197, 200, 204
Dodd, Julian 10, 135, 185, 186
Dolan, Emily 8, 9, 22–4, 26, 35, 54, 57, 101, 102, 103, 130, 131, 179, 180, 182, 183–4
Dolar, Mladen 12, 64, 85–9, 91, 94, 99, 106, 130
Doppler effect 136, 205

doubleness 13, 94–5, 105, 106, 122–3, 124, 126, 127, 129, 130–1, 134, 140, 156, 164, 212, 216
Doyle, Peter 25, 27, 31, 194, 196, 201, 215
drastic musicology 10, 76, 80, 84, 89, 123, 126, 129–31, 138, 154, 155, 165, 184, 186, 190, 193, 201
dreams 12, 48, 104, 109–10, 114, 184, 192, 194, 195, 197, 212, 214
dualism 94, 95, 126–30, 139, 140, 147, 149, 157, 158, 174, 181, 200, 215
dubstep 56, 119, 151, 215
durée 127–8, 196, 215
dynamics 17, 19–20, 20, 30, 41, 47, 134, 151, 166, 198, 206, 215

ear 11, 19, 20, 27, 34, 35, 40–3, 47, 60, 63, 65, 101, 112, 120, 126, 136, 140, 143, 144, 150, 163, 181–2, 188, 190, 197, 203
echo 27, 29, 30, 31, 80, 94, 110, 136, 157, 194, 197, 209
ecology 11, 44–9, 56, 114, 133, 145, 146, 150, 151, 161, 166, 176, 177, 184, 207, 211
effiction 189–95, 196, 198, 204, 205, 207, 210
Eidsheim, Nina Sun 53, 64, 69, 75, 120, 141–2, 145, 151, 155, 157, 188
electronic dance music 56
electronic music 12, 56–61, 86, 87, 113–6, 119–20, 152, 157, 205
elusiveness 43, 48, 49, 54, 67, 68, 73, 74, 80, 94, 98, 102, 105, 115, 130, 134, 148, 168, 212, 214
embodiment 66, 79, 80, 81, 84–6, 91, 114, 120, 121, 130, 139, 142, 149, 160, 168, 177, 192, 193, 196
enchantment 117–20, 127, 129, 155, 173, 177–8, 182, 183, 186, 187, 189–99, 204, 207, 217
energy 141 – 43
   kinetic energy 142, 143, 144, 205
   musical energy 144–5, 152–61, 167–9, 172, 173, 183, 191, 193, 204
   sonic/sound energy 14, 27, 40, 143–4, 157, 167
   timbral energy 14, 167–8, 172, 190, 206

enlightenment 23, 24, 95, 106, 179, 189
epistemology 4, 5, 9, 10, 11, 14, 15, 57, 60, 67, 79, 97–8, 123, 126, 135, 139–40, 146, 156, 159, 174, 179, 187–8, 199, 202, 215
epoché, phenomenological 58, 94, 112, 128, 130, 178, 201
equalization (EQ) 30, 31, 53, 120, 190
Erwartung 109
essentialism 12, 56, 59, 61–2, 64, 65, 72, 75, 78, 84, 185
ethnomusicology 3, 8, 9, 106, 138
Evens, Aden 25, 26, 28, 35, 46, 57, 151
event 5, 6, 9, 10, 35, 44, 48, 70, 80, 88–9, 92, 93, 112, 124, 128, 129–30, 131, 133–4, 137, 139, 145–9, 155, 158, 160, 164, 165, 173, 184, 186, 190, 193, 195, 196, 199, 200–3, 213, 215, 216
excess 3, 12, 14, 22, 32, 52, 57, 64, 66, 76–98, 125, 127–8, 131, 137, 150, 154, 159, 162, 164, 172, 174, 195, 197, 198, 204, 207, 215
extimacy 85–6, 89, 93
extra-musical 39, 61, 67–8, 74–5, 80, 95–6, 105, 184

Fales, Cornelia 1, 8, 9, 42, 43, 44, 54, 56, 73, 106, 138, 163
Feldman, Martha 65, 91, 121, 167, 168
Fender Stratocaster guitar 5, 7, 56, 118
fetishization 80, 91, 118, 188
film 2, 72, 190, 192
finitude 89, 127, 129, 215
Flack, Roberta 168, 169–71, 187
flute 2, 3, 23, 24, 28, 67, 68, 70, 82, 102, 103, 104, 108, 110, 124, 160, 161, 172, 184, 204
formalism 13, 61, 94–6, 105, 107, 120, 180, 183, 188
formant 20, 34, 36, 52, 68, 167–8
Fourier analysis 25, 28
French horn 22, 68, 110
frequency spectrum 11, 25, 31, 34–9, 41–3, 47, 48, 56, 92, 93, 114, 119, 163, 167

Gallope, Michael 126, 128, 129, 154
gender 72, 83-4, 168
genre 4, 73-4, 119
Gesang der Jünglinge 113-4
Gibson guitar 5, 51
Gluck, Christoph Willibald 23, 103
gnostic musicology 10, 126, 129-30, 154, 165, 180
Goehr, Lydia 13, 61, 62, 94-7, 100, 101, 102, 105, 106, 107, 123, 126, 127, 129, 134, 135, 140, 156, 161, 180, 183, 184, 212, 216
Gorter, Herman 209-10, 213, 214
Gothic 2, 3, 4, 17, 45, 57, 70, 72, 74, 87, 89, 189, 194, 204-5
grain of the voice 3, 12, 76-86, 89, 92, 94, 97, 116, 131, 173
Grieg, Edvard 68
Grisey, Gérard 45, 114, 123
Gritten, Anthony 6, 217

Hamilton, Andy 25, 105, 135, 180, 181, 183-7
Hanslick, Eduard 94, 96, 105, 180, 183
harmonics 20, 22, 27, 28, 31, 34-5, 42, 52, 68, 73, 109, 120, 164
harmony 1, 7, 14, 19, 41, 57, 82, 101, 102, 104, 115, 134, 144, 151, 166, 167, 169, 198, 206, 215
harpsichord 2, 19, 70, 72
hauntology 152, 157, 163, 173, 215, 216
Haydn, Joseph 8, 54, 130
Heidegger, Martin 127, 153 n. 2, 200
Helmholtz, Hermann 34, 35, 36, 140, 144, 163, 180, 216
Hendrix, Jimi 25, 56, 105, 118
Herder, Johann Gottfried 14, 101-2, 106-7, 109, 110, 112, 114, 116, 117, 124, 126, 129, 179, 181-3, 184, 188-9, 213, 216
Hoffmann, E.T.A. 100-1, 103, 184
Holiday, Billy 63, 64
Hornbostel-Sachs method 21, 22, 36, 104
Husserl, Edmund 111, 112, 146, 147, 201

icon 9, 11, 12, 51, 67-75, 78, 79, 80, 84, 87-8, 91, 92, 93, 94, 96, 98, 105, 111, 116, 120, 122, 130, 134, 137, 204, 214

idealism 9-13, 58-9, 92-7, 103, 105, 107, 110-48, 160-4, 172-88, 199-200, 203, 213, 216
identity 3, 11-2, 14, 25, 37, 51, 52-67, 69, 70-88, 102-18, 124, 126, 136, 137, 141, 144, 147, 156, 164, 167, 173, 184, 188, 197, 198, 203, 204, 206, 211, 214
Ihde, Don 53, 55, 65, 86
immanence 13, 57, 89, 127, 129, 146-8, 153-6, 159, 167, 171, 173, 177, 178, 182, 197, 199-200, 213, 215
immaterial 10, 11, 13-5, 57, 59-60, 79, 87, 92, 122-31, 134-5, 137, 139, 141-2, 145-6, 159, 162, 172, 178, 180, 183, 186-7, 193-4, 200, 202, 212, 213
Impressionism 54, 108, 210, 214
index 9, 11-2, 25, 51-67, 69, 71, 75, 77-80, 81, 83-4, 87, 88, 91, 93-4, 96, 98-99, 105, 115-8, 120, 122-4, 134, 137
ineffable 3, 4, 14, 76, 78-9, 80, 94, 97, 99, 105, 110, 116, 120-22, 123, 126-7, 129, 135, 137, 154, 165, 179-80, 187, 191, 198, 200-4, 207, 216
instrumentalism 185
intensity 83, 89, 143, 146, 148, 158-9, 160, 168, 173, 174, 182, 185, 201, 217
IRCAM 36, 114
Iszoloscope 204-7

Jankélévitch, Vladimir 13, 123, 126-30, 154-5, 158, 182, 184, 190, 191, 193, 105, 197, 199, 201
Jouissance 79-80, 81, 87, 97, 196

Kane, Brian 58, 59, 80, 81, 86, 112
Kant, Immanuel 94, 95, 97, 100, 101, 105, 113, 125, 129, 140, 147, 159, 175, 180, 181, 183, 187, 199, 207, 213, 216
King, B.B. 6, 80
Kircher, Athanasius 23
Kim-Cohen, Seth 59, 61, 75, 159, 174, 189, 190, 201
Kirkby, Emma 73
Kittler, Friedrich 55, 60
Klangfarbenmelodie/tone colour melody 54, 80, 109-11, 114, 116, 118, 165, 194
Kramer, Jonathan 136, 196, 201

Lacan, Jacques 55, 57, 85–7
lack 12, 14, 65, 80–7, 89, 91, 96, 99, 188, 203
language 3, 7, 8, 22, 23, 39, 43, 53, 55, 67–80, 84, 85–6, 92, 95, 98, 99, 103, 116, 117, 126, 128, 130, 143, 183, 191, 202, 213, 214
larynx 34, 52, 168
Latour, Bruno 146–9, 151, 157, 190
legato 17, 27, 28, 32, 46, 168, 170–1
Leipert, Trent 202
Léonin and Pérotin 17, 28
Leys, Ruth 148–9, 158
LFO software 119, 151
Lieder ohne Worte 100
life 110, 113, 121, 146–8, 151, 153–7, 161, 162, 165–6, 172, 174, 177, 190–1, 193, 207, 216–7
Ligeti, György 25, 46, 80
limit/limen 96, 100, 125, 131, 146, 198, 210
LinnDrum machine 53
liquid materiality 159
literature 82, 192, 210
Lochhead, Judy 127, 128–9, 154
loudness 18–26, 31, 32, 41, 43, 98, 102, 143
Lovecraft, H. P. 172, 204
Lyotard, Jean-François 13–4, 57, 123–30, 135, 137, 156, 157, 164, 165, 173, 186–7, 199–207, 212, 213, 215–6, 217

Massumi, Brian 148
materialism 9–11, 13–4, 53, 54, 58–9, 61, 64, 72, 75, 78, 96, 112, 114, 118, 120, 122, 131, 133–4, 139–41, 145, 147–9, 159, 160, 162–4, 172, 174, 179, 181, 183, 187–8, 203, 211
materiality 3, 9, 10, 11, 13–4, 17–67, 77–9, 85, 92–3, 96, 117–24, 126, 130, 135, 139, 145, 147–50, 157, 161, 162, 174, 176, 178, 193, 194, 213
matter 57, 64, 77, 124–6, 130, 137, 142–3, 145–8, 150, 155, 156–7, 162, 172, 173, 174, 181, 183, 187, 192, 200, 202, 207
matter-energy 146–50, 153, 155, 159, 162, 182, 192

McAdams, Stephen 5, 18–9, 21, 25, 38, 42, 46, 53, 211–2
Meillassoux, Quentin 159
melody 1, 7, 14, 19, 29, 41, 57, 66, 82, 95, 104, 110, 115, 134, 151, 152, 154, 161, 166, 170, 184, 198, 205, 215
memory 59, 79, 115, 121, 144, 152, 158, 163, 190, 195, 206, 215
Merleau-Ponty, Maurice 139, 140
meta-acoustic 13, 135, 145, 152, 157, 159, 163, 174, 183, 193–4, 197, 198, 204, 207
metaphor 5, 7–8, 9, 12, 18, 22, 23, 26, 33, 35, 40, 44, 48–9, 51–2, 54, 67–75, 76, 78–9, 83–4, 87, 88, 91, 93, 96, 103, 104, 106, 108, 144, 186, 201, 211–4
metaphysics 13, 94, 96–8, 103, 105, 127–8, 130, 133, 141, 147, 157, 159, 174, 183, 192
microphone 29, 30, 53, 120, 151, 157, 190
monads 182–3
monstrous 33, 103, 184, 199–200, 207, 211, 214
Moog synthesizer 25, 118–9
Moore, Allan 25, 29–30, 45
Moore, Gary 80
Moorefield, Virgil 29, 31
Moylan, William 29–30, 31–2, 48
multidimensionality 37–40, 116
musicality 78, 84, 95–6, 161, 165, 183
musical work, philosophy of 10, 61, 135, 185
musicking 2, 53, 64, 76–8, 84, 94, 95, 120, 129–30, 138, 131, 145, 151–2, 154, 155, 157–62, 165, 166, 171, 174, 183–4, 186, 190, 192–6, 198, 212
musicology 3, 8–10, 18, 45, 53, 59, 76–7, 92, 94, 120, 129, 135, 139, 145, 150–1, 157, 162, 173–4, 180, 200
music-power 96, 152–3, 166–7, 171, 173, 182–91, 193–4, 198, 203, 205–6
musique concrète 57, 111, 119, 204
mysticism 128–9, 133, 139, 180, 204

Nancy, Jean-Luc 3, 76, 92–5, 97, 99, 103, 135, 156, 193, 196–7, 212
Nattiez, Jean-Jacques 53, 59, 76, 112
Nebenwelt 199, 207, 214, 216

negative dialectics 147–8, 177
neurophysics 3, 11, 18, 42–5, 48, 68, 118, 143–4, 152, 154, 155, 157, 163, 190–1, 195, 202, 212
Newton's cradle 142, 144–5, 174, 191
'New Musicology' 10
new materialism 146, 150, 174
Nietzsche, Friedrich 154, 155
nomadism 47, 146, 195, 197
non-cochlear sound 159, 189–90, 197, 207
non-human 14, 53, 59, 87, 139, 145–53, 158, 160–1, 165, 166, 177–8, 182, 189, 190, 193, 201–2, 206, 212
non-identity 124, 147, 156, 206
non-object 70, 94, 137, 139, 143, 163–4, 166, 172, 211
nostalgia 91, 121–2, 215–6
notation 7, 19, 215
noumenon 12, 94, 100, 104–5, 110, 112, 117–8, 122–3, 125–31, 140, 211
now 89, 127–30, 152, 162, 194, 196–7, 201–2, 204, 207, 214–7

objet petit a 12, 52, 55, 85–9, 91, 94, 99, 106, 130, 134, 203
objet sonore/sound object 6, 54–61, 66, 75, 81–2, 91–2, 97, 111–2, 115–6, 128, 137–8, 181, 185, 199, 207
oboe 2–3, 7, 52, 53, 68, 80, 104, 105, 163, 214
obscurity 97–9, 101, 105–6, 116–7, 123, 124, 130–1
onomatopoeia 68
ontology 4–5, 10, 54, 55, 58–60, 67, 75, 79, 88, 92–4, 128, 133, 135, 137–41, 145–6, 153 n. 2, 160, 162–4, 174, 185–6, 188, 195, 204
onto-theology 146, 156, 157
opera 12, 27, 56, 63, 70, 108, 120–1, 153
orchestra 2, 24, 29, 53, 54, 118, 158, 167, 168, 179, 210
orchestration 2, 3, 7, 8, 11, 12, 19, 22–3, 25, 28, 41, 46, 54, 101–4, 107, 108, 110, 115, 118, 165
organ of Corti 41–2, 143
organology 3, 11, 18, 21–6, 38, 42, 48, 57, 118

passibility 201–6, 212
paradox 8–15, 18, 43, 48, 55, 57–8, 60, 66–7, 75, 79, 85–9, 93, 95–7, 99–100, 105, 106, 113, 116, 121–6, 130–1, 133–5, 139–40, 145, 147, 156, 162, 163, 165, 167, 171, 172, 174, 185–7, 198, 202, 207, 213, 216, 217
paradox 0 13, 133–5, 156, 213
Parton, Dolly 47
Paul, Jean 100, 110
Peirce, Charles S. 51, 53, 67
performance 2, 7, 10, 12, 23, 26, 28–30, 32, 45, 46–7, 61–6, 73, 76–8, 80, 88, 91, 95, 105, 108, 118, 120–1, 129, 135, 150, 160–2, 167–72, 173, 177, 185
performativity 2, 10, 39–40, 46–7, 48, 53, 59–61, 64, 66, 70, 75, 78, 84, 129–30, 141, 144, 155, 157–8, 160, 167, 176–7, 186–8
pharynx 32, 34, 52, 63
phenomenology 4–6, 9–10, 53, 58–60, 67, 82, 86–7, 92–4, 111–2, 117, 128, 133, 135–6, 138–41, 145, 151–3, 159–60, 162–3, 174, 178, 180–1, 187, 188, 196, 201
physics of sound 8, 11, 18–21, 46, 92, 142–45, 153, 167–68, 180
pitch 2, 5, 18–21, 22, 24, 26, 30, 31, 32, 34, 37, 41, 42, 56, 63, 65, 83, 98, 102, 104, 109, 113, 134, 144, 167–8, 205
playing-related musculoskeletal disorders (PRMDs) 120–1
plus de corps 64, 85, 130
plus de c(h)oeur 66, 189, 130
Popp, Michael 32
post-phenomenology 187
Praetorius, Michael 22
Prince 53
projection 81–2, 84, 87, 146, 156
programme music 67, 98
psychoacoustics 3, 8, 11, 19–20, 33–40, 42, 43, 44–5, 48–9, 68, 112, 118, 136, 138, 211, 212, 214

qualia 46, 48, 68, 78, 131, 133–4, 165, 207
quantification 3, 11, 18–21, 33, 35, 37–8, 40, 44, 46, 48, 68, 93, 94–5, 97, 102, 131, 134, 136, 154, 163, 165

Quantz, Johann Joachim 23, 28
Queen of the Night aria 1, 11
quid/ quiddity 126, 217
quod/quiddity 126, 202–3, 217

Rancière, Jacques 14, 160, 175–80, 183, 187, 189, 197, 199–201
real, Lacanian concept of 55, 57
'Real Me' in vocal pedagogy 52, 62–3
realism 123, 126, 129–30, 133–5, 159, 203
recorder 70, 164, 166, 167
reduced listening 58–60, 93, 138
relationality 138, 141, 148, 150, 155, 157–8, 172, 190–1, 211
Retromania 121–2
reverb/reverberation 2, 25, 27–31, 32, 53, 56, 73, 74, 83, 120, 151, 194, 196, 201, 205–6, 210, 215
Ricercar a 6 110–1
ring (*squillo*) 167–8
Rokh 160–1, 172, 198
Romanticism 12, 42, 94–122, 128, 131, 147, 158, 174, 180, 183, 188
Rousseau, Jean-Jacques 22, 23, 24, 26, 98, 102
rhythm 1, 7, 14, 19, 28, 42, 56, 57, 73, 95, 104, 107, 112, 115, 119, 134, 144, 151, 154, 161, 166, 168, 171, 190, 198, 206, 212, 215

Sachs, Curt 21–3, 42, 48, 57
saxophone 48–9
Schaeffer, Pierre 12, 26, 36, 47, 55–9, 75, 77, 79, 82, 91, 92–3, 97, 107, 111–3, 116–9, 123, 126, 128, 131, 137–8, 165, 181, 214
Schickler, Markus 56, 58, 167
schizophonia 55, 57, 60, 81, 136, 137, 152, 194
Schoenberg, Arnold 12, 54, 107–18, 126, 165, 194–5, 212, 215
Schopenhauer, Arthur 94–6, 105, 168
Schrimshaw, Will 141, 159, 189–90
Scruton, Roger 5, 185–6
Sehnsucht 97–106, 131, 210
semiotics 51, 53, 71, 72, 75, 77, 79, 101
sensation 81, 125, 128, 130, 136, 138, 140, 179–83, 188–9, 207

sensibility/*Empfindung* 125, 177, 180, 182, 189, 191, 202
sensory 92, 101, 109, 110, 130, 140, 141, 150, 160, 189, 190, 192, 198, 202, 216
sentiment sonore/ sound-feeling 125, 128–31, 156, 173, 187, 200, 203, 207, 210, 213, 214
Shadrack, Jasmine Hazel 51, 66
Shank, Barry 189–91
Shaviro, Steven 88–9
signification 3, 12, 51, 71–88, 93, 99–100, 104, 116, 123–7, 130, 136, 188, 195, 197–8
signifiance 77, 79
singularity 44, 46–8, 52, 57, 64, 66, 70, 72, 75, 124–5, 131, 133, 134, 147, 149, 164–5, 173, 175, 176, 183, 184–9, 200–3, 207, 213, 216, 217
Sinnesenergien 144
Simone, Nina 77–8
simultaneity 31, 48, 96, 102, 118–9, 126, 128, 134, 140, 176, 183, 186, 202, 213–7
singing 2, 32, 34, 45, 52, 61–6, 77–8, 83–4, 85, 87, 114, 120–1, 141, 167–8, 188
Slowhand 6, 118
Small, Christopher 76, 157
Smalley, Dennis 37, 38, 55, 75, 211
SMASL 151–3, 157–8, 166, 171, 193
sonic naturalism 136
soprano voice 2, 4, 11–2, 17, 19, 24, 32, 46, 47, 62, 65, 70, 73, 87, 89, 114, 168, 190
soul 2, 64, 70, 84, 85, 94, 96, 101, 106, 125, 129, 153 n. 2, 162, 171, 173, 182, 191, 211
soundbox 29–31, 83, 206
sound in-itself 58, 94, 112–3, 140
sound source 9, 11, 19, 21–7, 36–8, 42, 45–8, 51–3, 56, 61–2, 69, 71–2, 78, 82, 92, 130, 135, 181, 207
sound technology 13–4, 24–30, 36, 44, 54–7, 60, 92, 112–3, 117–24, 144, 158, 162, 166, 190, 194, 200, 205
sound waves 4, 13–4, 27–8, 41–1, 56, 62, 94, 120, 135–6, 143–5, 153, 162, 163, 167, 172, 202

spatiality 29, 114, 130, 136, 185, 193–8, 203, 206–7
Spector, Phil 29
spectral analysis 34–7
spectral music 36, 114, 118
Spinoza, Baruch 146, 148, 201
spiritual 64, 110, 113, 142, 147
Steege, Benjamin 110, 140, 144, 163, 180
Steinway piano 46, 185
Sterne, Jonathan 25, 120–1
Stockhausen, Karlheinz 12, 25, 26, 107, 113–9, 165, 201, 215, 216
Stradivarius violin 118, 120, 122, 188
Streisand, Barbra 168, 170–1
studio production 29–31, 45, 48, 56
subject 6, 43, 44, 64, 79, 86, 94, 127, 139, 147–8, 156–8, 182, 197–8, 217
subjectivity 33, 38, 40, 41, 43–4, 48, 61–2, 64, 66, 78, 85–7, 89, 92–3, 99, 127, 141, 146, 148, 158–9, 162, 165, 176, 178, 191–2, 196–8, 202, 206–7
sublime 3, 4, 9, 12–4, 17, 23, 33, 49, 79, 91–131, 134, 139, 154–6, 160, 168, 172, 174, 176–7, 180, 187–9, 198–207, 210, 212, 213, 214, 217
Sundberg, Johan 34, 65, 167
surplus 3, 64, 66, 80, 85–9, 94–5, 188
surprise 6–7, 64, 165, 217
Sutherland, Joan 63, 120, 134
swarm 119, 149–50, 157–8, 172, 177–8, 190, 204, 207
sway 84, 153, 161, 174, 184, 187, 191
symbol 51, 55, 70, 74, 118, 198
symbolic, Lacanian concept 55, 73, 84
Symphonie Fantastique 70, 104
sympathetic vibration 140–1
synesthesia 7, 18, 23, 37, 68, 71, 108, 141, 151, 210, 213
synthesizer 25, 38, 57, 114, 119, 123, 185, 206
Szendy, Peter 192–4, 196, 210

temporality 28–9, 35, 36, 66, 89, 92, 114–5, 127, 130, 136, 164, 166, 195–8, 201–4, 206, 207, 215–6
"The First Time Ever I Saw Your Face" 168–70, 172
"The Unsettled" 204–6

Thing (in-itself) 12, 59, 86–7, 94–5, 103–4, 112, 115, 117, 125–31, 134, 137, 140, 147–8, 156, 159–60, 172, 177, 180–1, 188, 199, 200, 207, 211, 213
thing-power 146, 148–55, 164, 166, 178, 182, 189–90
Thompson, Marie and Ian Biddle 159, 189
threshold 100, 198, 204, 210, 217
timbral imperative 12, 110–22, 124, 126, 165
timbral sonicism 185
timbral staging 30
time 4, 19, 21, 28, 30–1, 32–3, 35, 48, 89, 92, 107, 114, 127–8, 131, 136–7, 142, 146, 154, 161, 162, 166, 173, 176, 178, 184, 191–207, 200–7, 210, 215–6
Ton 8, 101, 102, 182
Tonkunst 124, 126, 216
tone-pleasure/*Tonwollust* 14, 184, 188–9, 213–4, 216, 217
touch 2, 13, 54, 81, 93, 123–5, 131, 136, 139, 160–1, 173–4, 180, 196, 197, 201–3, 210–1, 213, 214, 216, 217
Traité des Objets Musicaux (Schaeffer) 58–9, 111–2, 128, 165
transcendence 120–1, 131, 146
transcendentalism 13, 94–7, 100, 105, 107, 111–3, 122–3, 125–30, 133, 135, 147–8, 155–6, 172–3, 200, 202, 213
trombone 19, 70–1, 81, 110, 118
Tunbridge, Laura 120, 121
twofold thesis 181, 186–7

U2 61
uncanny 2, 4, 83, 91, 152, 206
unnameable 105, 106, 125, 128, 203
unpredictable 6–7, 11–3, 47–8, 61, 134, 149, 150, 160, 172, 189–90, 196, 203, 212

Varèse, Edgard 25, 80, 123, 215–6
ventriloquism 81–2
verberation 13, 14, 135–40, 153, 157, 163–4, 166–8, 171–2, 174, 179, 180, 182, 185–9, 193, 197, 202, 206, 211, 212, 213

vibrant matter 13–4, 145–6, 149–50, 153, 156, 177
vibration 27, 41, 135–74, 179, 181–2, 184, 186, 190, 192, 196–8, 200, 203, 207, 215
vibrational continuum 13–4, 139–40, 145, 152–3, 156–7, 160, 163, 165–6, 171, 173–4, 182, 185, 187, 190, 193, 197, 203, 207, 213
vibrato 36, 46, 119, 161
video games 72, 73, 177, 192
viola 118
viola da gamba 59, 70, 164
violin 19, 26, 28, 34, 46, 47, 72, 80, 82–3, 102, 103, 110, 115, 118, 120, 122, 151, 160–1, 187, 188, 213
virtual 29–31, 33, 44, 48, 92, 148, 153–5, 171, 194, 201
Visconti, Tony 73
vitalism 145, 165
vitality 14, 134, 145–50, 153–62, 165, 171–4, 178–9, 181–4, 186, 188, 190, 192, 197–8, 200, 203, 206–7, 213, 215, 217
vital materialism 13–4, 96, 145–62, 165, 172–8, 183, 190, 192, 214, 216
vocal chords 9, 73, 134, 151
vocal pedagogy 8, 9, 36, 62, 64, 69

VocaMe 17, 32, 46, 47, 49
Voegelin, Salomé 192, 199
voice 1, 2, 4, 7, 12, 17, 19, 24–5, 27, 29–36, 46, 47, 52–6, 59–89, 91, 95, 96, 101–2, 130, 134, 140, 167–8, 171, 173, 183, 190, 204–6, 209–10, 214
voice banks 71, 75
voiceprint 52
void 66, 80, 84–5, 88–9, 100, 197–8, 204, 206
Vox, Bono 61

Walser, Robert 51, 73–4
wave form 20, 28, 34, 36, 52, 119, 142, 143
Webern, Anton 110–1, 116
Werktreue 61, 95
Wilson, Samuel 135, 148, 150
wobble 119
"Woman in Love" 168, 170–2
Wong, Mandy-Suzanne 157, 177–8
wonder 6, 7, 178, 191–2, 217
Woodward, Ashley 126, 186–7, 202

Xenakis, Iannis 25, 80

Yarnall, Susan 36, 52, 62–3, 69

Zagorski-Thomas, Simon 27, 30

www.ingramcontent.com/pod-product-compliance
Lightning Source LLC
Chambersburg PA
CBHW072145290426
44111CB00012B/1982